FAITH *and* FORCE

FAITH *and* FORCE

A Christian Debate about War

DAVID L. CLOUGH
and
BRIAN STILTNER

GEORGETOWN UNIVERSITY PRESS
Washington, D.C.

Credit:

"Dulce et Decorum Est" by Wilfred Owen, from *The Collected Poems of Wilfred Owen*, © 1963 by Chatto & Windus, Ltd. Reprinted by permission of New Directions Publishing Corp.

As of January 1, 2007, 13-digit ISBN numbers have replaced the 10-digit system.
13-digit Paperback: 978-1-58901-165-6
10-digit Paperback:1-58901-165-1

Georgetown University Press, Washington, D.C.

Library of Congress Cataloging-in-Publication Data

Clough, David, 1968–
    Faith and force : a Christian debate about war / David L. Clough and Brian Stiltner.
        p.   cm.
    Includes bibliographical references and index.
    ISBN-13: 978-1-58901-165-6 (alk. paper)
    ISBN-10: 1-58901-165-1 (alk. paper)
    1. War—Religious aspects—Christianity.   2. Pacifism—Religious aspects—Christianity.   3. Just war doctrine.   I. Stiltner, Brian, 1966–   II. Title.

    BT736.2.C575   2007
    241'.6242—dc22

                                                              2006031181

14 13 12 11 10 09 08 07   9 8 7 6 5 4 3 2
First printing

Printed in the United States of America

To Grace, Anna, Matthew, Brendan, and Rebecca

In the hope that you may grow up and play your part
in creating a more peaceful world

CONTENTS

CONCLUSION

TABLES

PREFACE

This book began in an argument between friends who were surprised to find themselves on opposite sides of the debate about whether the United States and the United Kingdom should invade Iraq in 2003. Situated on opposite sides of the Atlantic, in different churches, and on different sides of the just war/pacifist fence, we exchanged long emails that rehearsed on a small scale the national and international debates that were taking place around us. We discovered the common ground we shared as well as some predictable and some surprising points of difference. We watched together as our nations embarked on another war against Iraq in our name, and we mourned together the loss of Iraqi, American, and British lives.

When the initial hostilities ended, our conversation continued, and we felt the urgency of contributing to a wider Christian debate about if and when war can be justified. We began to wonder whether the dialogue we had shared might be a good way to present the ethical issues at stake in Christian thinking about war in the context of the beginning of a new century and millennium. Ethics is essentially a dialogic task, in which truths are discovered and tested in debate and discussion, yet most ethics texts settle either for a calm overview or a strong case for one side or the other. We planned a book that would instead retain the spirit of the argument in which it originated while also providing enough background to make the debate intelligible to those who have not previously reflected on these issues. Indeed, one of the book's distinguishing and—we hope—most informative features is a debate section between the authors at the end of each main chapter. We wrote these debates back and forth in real time, and we have resisted polishing them too much so as to retain their conversational character.

The writing of this book has been assisted by feedback from students at Sacred Heart University, Connecticut, and St. John's College, Durham, England. We are grateful for their engagement and insights. We are indebted to those who have read chapter drafts and provided feedback, especially General Sir Hugh Beach, Eric Gregory, Todd Speidell, and the anonymous readers for Georgetown University Press. Colleagues who engaged in conversation with us and shared helpful ideas include Amy Laura Hall, Karen Peterson-Iyer,

William Danaher, Steven Michels, Warren Smith, Nigel Biggar, and participants at a student–faculty seminar at Princeton University, as well as many colleagues at our respective universities and in the Society of Christian Ethics
(U.S.) and the Society for the Study of Christian Ethics (U.K.). We appreciate
the student research assistants who assisted us at different stages of the project: Rosie Bonhomme, Joyanna SanMarco, and Caitlin Robles. The responsibility for the remaining errors and omissions, of course, is entirely our own.
Brian Stiltner gratefully acknowledges support from his university in the form
of a sabbatical leave and an Arts and Sciences research course-release. We are
tremendously appreciative of the support and understanding showed by our
spouses, Lucy Clough and Ann Stiltner, throughout the long writing process,
and for the same from our children, to whom we dedicate the book.

As we complete this book almost four years after President George Bush
declared victory, there are some signs of hope in the development of new
political institutions, but many soldiers and civilians continue to be killed in
Iraq week by week in ongoing battles and terrorist attacks. Both the United
States and the United Kingdom are on high alert, fearing further terrorist attacks on their own territories. This context of our reflections is a reminder
that the costs of decisions to go to war both in the short and the long term
are very high indeed. Yet we both recognize that there will continue to be circumstances presented to the international community where the costs of inaction are also high: where a threat to a nation or ethnic group is significant
and growing and where resolute action in the short term may prevent a large-
scale humanitarian catastrophe. This is the moral seriousness of the issues
we have discussed throughout this book.

In response to demanding decisions such as these, we believe that the
Church needs to continue to seek greater understanding of the thinking of
its tradition in relation to warfare and how this inheritance bears on the particular questions raised by war at the beginning of the twenty-first century.
We hope that the discussion we have presented will be a useful resource for
this task. Most of all we hope and pray for a renewed understanding of the
role of the Church at all levels in building peace, so that, despite their differences and in myriad ways, Christians can be one in living out their vocation
as peacemakers.

The Debate over War in a Christian Context

There is a war on. In fact there are many wars on. Some started recently; some started a long time ago. Some are close to home; some are far away. Some are civil wars; some are international wars; some are a messy combination of the two. Some are fought in the name of self-defense, some in the name of autonomy, religion, ethnic identity, or political allegiance. Despite the hopes of many, war is still a common way for nations, as well as ethnic, political, and religious groups, to address disputes with one another at the beginning of the twenty-first century. Even countries not at war are spending a significant proportion of their wealth on preparing for the possibility of war in the future. Citizens of these countries have an ongoing obligation to reflect on the morality of the wars that are being fought, or are being prepared for, in their name. When, if at all, is it right for a country to go to war? What rules should be observed during warfare? Should one serve in the armed forces? How much, if anything, is legitimate to spend on the military?

The beginning of the twenty-first century puts these long-standing questions in a very particular geopolitical context. The September 11, 2001, al Qaeda attack on the United States and the many global events precipitated by it lead to questions such as, What is the appropriate response to a terrorist attack? What are the appropriate criteria for national self-defense? What responsibility do nations have to obey the judgments of the United Nations?

This book addresses these questions in the context of the long tradition of Christian reflection on war. Unlike most books on this topic, however, it does not present one answer. Instead, it represents both sides of the long-standing argument Christians have had with one another, between those who think that war is sometimes a regrettable necessity and those who think

1

that the use of force is never right. For most of the history of the Church, most of its members have believed that war could sometimes be justified, but a significant minority has considered war to be always illegitimate. Throughout this book Brian Stiltner, an American Roman Catholic theologian, takes the former view, and David Clough, a British Methodist theologian, takes the latter. In each chapter we start by outlining some common ground and end by debating where Christians should stand. We hope that accompanying us in the course of the debate will help our readers to become clear about where they stand on this fundamental ethical issue.

What does it mean to debate war ethically? At the beginning of chapter 1 we will describe two approaches to ethical reasoning within Christian ethics. These and most other methods of reasoning about ethics aim to assist people to be thoughtful about fundamental questions of human meaning and to live in accord with the values indicated by their answers to those questions.

This very general statement can be developed in many different ways, but one basic agreement in Western traditions is that ethics is a reflective process. One must think about ethical problems and come to a conscientious decision through a process of proper reasoning. For religious traditions, the communal context of ethics is crucial: that one follow the teaching of one's religious community is important. Even so, ethics is not a matter of simply acting upon the orders of authorities—whether these be parents, religious teachers, or political leaders—even though it is appropriate to listen to these authorities and give their suggestions or commands a great deal of deference. That ethics is a reflective process also means that individuals can discuss an ethical problem with others, who give reasons for their views. Others may not change their views, but at least both parties can better understand the sources of the disagreement. Hopefully, by examining the strengths and weaknesses of each perspective, individuals can together build stronger arguments—if not a middle ground, then at least a modified position that responds to some of the concerns of others.

We hope that reading this book and discussing it with others will help the reader better understand the factors that go into a decision for war and, more important, demonstrate that a person need not be an expert before taking a stand. To think ethically about war does not require one to have a fixed attitude. What is required is a thinking attitude. Holding unwaveringly to the rightness of a claim can be valuable as long as reasons for such tenacity are clear and held conscientiously. However, changing or modifying a view can also be valuable, if a person has encountered new information or seen things in a different light. Both ways require one to reflect, discuss, assimilate new information and arguments, and acknowledge mistakes humbly. War is too serious a matter to be thought of uncritically with views that have not been tested.

Therefore, in this book we invite our readers to reflect further on the world, to recognize the urgency of these issues in which millions of human lives are at stake, and to think critically about the religious and cultural traditions in which they are situated. We invite each reader to develop and refine an ethical position on war, so that each can be an informed participant in political debates. We invite our audience to discuss and debate these issues with others as we ourselves will do in the pages of this book.

WHY A CHRISTIAN FOCUS?

One of the main contexts in which most people learn, develop, and interpret their morality is the religious setting. We have chosen to privilege this context, specifically Christianity, in this book. As Christian ethicists and citizens of the two nations that led the military invasion of Iraq in 2003, we feel a great urgency to think about this war—not merely by itself, but for what it represents about the direction of the foreign policy of our nations and the fate of the world in the twenty-first century. We write, first of all, as theological ethicists to fellow Christians, asking them to study their tradition in its complexity and then to take a reflective, critical stand on the morality of war. Of course, very few readers will be developing their ethical position on war on a blank slate. Even those people who are unaware of having an ethical position on war have, very likely, some basic attitudes about the moral implications of faith that—as we will show—bear on the morality of war. Each person probably has some basic views or instincts about the acceptability of violence, at least in certain situations. Would one use deadly force against a home invader? Could one serve on a jury and vote for the death penalty? Was the 2003 war on Iraq a terrible decision or a necessary, though imperfect, decision? We want to take the answers to such questions and hold them to the light of Christian reflection.

Christians have as much reason as anyone to be perplexed about war. Christians of most denominations are raised with the understanding that the

Church sometimes supports "just wars." Many Christians in the United States and some in the United Kingdom supported the 2003 war on Iraq, believing that it was a necessary action to protect themselves and the global community from weapons of mass destruction and terrorism, or to liberate the people of Iraq from Saddam Hussein's rule. Many other Christians in both countries believed their Christian faith required them to oppose the war. The dividing lines went right through some denominations, sometimes between the leaders of the denomination and the membership. So, despite being inheritors of a rich moral tradition, Christians found themselves divided about whether to support the war in Iraq and at odds about the best ways to respond to terrorism.

Facing both a complex tradition and demographic division among Christians today, we strive to shed light on what is shared by Christians and to identify the adequacy of the various ethical stances that divide Christians. Our exploration is located within a Christian context, using the ethical frameworks of just war tradition and pacifism. We aim to illuminate what is at stake between these positions for Christians and for the churches. We try to shed light upon the thinking of Americans and Europeans on the questions of global order. As members of different churches and citizens on different continents, the authors reflect some of the differences running through the debate on the war on terror: between just war supporters and pacifists; between theologians using natural law reasoning and theologians taking a witness-based approach to social problems; between Americans and Europeans; between advocates of military responses to terrorism and rogue states and critics who believe that military reactions to these problems are unwise or even immoral.

In the debate portions of each chapter, Brian Stiltner and David Clough speak from the respective sides of these four polarities. Yet we debate not in order to defeat the other position; rather, sharing a desire to develop a faithful Christian witness appropriate to current realities, we seek to identify what is shared and not shared between the major positions within Christianity. We debate in order to test our views and perhaps to modify some of them in response to persuasive arguments by the other. We will not talk past each other, as too often happens in political and media debates. The concluding chapter will give us a chance to take stock of what can be learned from a constructive debate between just war and pacifism. Of course, any debate has the risk of appearing to represent diversity while excluding other viewpoints. Therefore, in the debates that follow, we will try to be sensitive to what we have in common as well as our differences so we can become aware of our shared blind spots. For instance, a possible limitation in our vision is that we are citizens of nations wealthy enough to fight wars overseas, rather than citizens of poor nations whose peoples are disproportionately represented among those killed and injured in wars.

This book is not only for Christians. We think it will be useful to readers regardless of their religious background or lack of it, because understanding Christianity is vital to understanding the current debate over the ethics of war. We see three reasons for this. First, Christianity is the largest religion worldwide, claiming one-third of the earth's population. The Christian faith is an important shaper of attitudes and actions. Christians are involved in political power and interreligious relations that can bear good or ill for the causes of peace and security around the globe. Although there has been a gradual decline in churchgoing and church membership in the developed world, Christianity, especially in its evangelical forms, remains a rapidly growing religion in the developing world. There it competes for adherents with Islam, which is the second largest religion in the world and is growing even faster than Christianity. To explain and analyze Islam is beyond the scope of this book, but we believe it is crucial for Christians collectively to gain a better understanding of Islam and to develop relationships with its followers. Furthermore, our treatment of terrorism and the Iraq War should be sensitive to differences between the mainstream of Islam and the militant phenomenon of jihadism.

A second reason to study Christianity is that this religion is often criticized, either specifically or as part of a general criticism of religion, as one promoting strife and violence. This challenge has to do partly with war yet goes beyond it. We do not deny that lay Christians and Church leaders historically have wielded violence in some of its most horrible forms. Certain interpretations of Christian beliefs have contributed to violence and still have the power to do so. Support for war is problematic enough, but religious persecution, crusades, and genocide appear in ghastly, lamentable chapters in Christian history. So we must explain, to the extent we can, why Christians have been involved in violence and whether violence is in any way endemic to our faith. We want to face this history of Christianity honestly and show that it must not be the face of Christianity today.

Third, Christianity has been a major influence in shaping the discourses that Western cultures use to debate the morality of war, and political leaders have used this influence to decide when to go to war. The primary discourse with political import is the just war tradition, a body of political-philosophical guides about when military action is justified. The main assumption undergirding the tradition's occasional acceptance of war is that political authority is essential for the right ordering of society. Society must use force when force is the only means available against those who would endanger the common good. This assumption is criticized at the theoretical and practical level, particularly by pacifism; we will be subjecting it to close scrutiny in this book.

Our overarching task in this book is to assess the authenticity and practicality of just war and pacifism from the perspective of Christian faith. Does the just war tradition, which has been the dominant result of Christian reflection on war for sixteen hundred years, deserve to retain this privileged position today? If Christians use just war reasoning, do they inevitably play into the game of rationalizing nationalist self-interests and legitimating the large-scale destruction of life and property that is the inescapable consequence of war? Should Christians, instead, embrace pacifism as the most faithful response to Jesus' call to discipleship, or is pacifism an irresponsible ethic in a dangerous world? These and many other tough questions will be asked of the two traditions on war.

CONTENDING POSITIONS ON WAR

To locate where our debate takes place within Christianity, it will be useful to identify four historical and contemporary positions concerning the obligations of Christians toward war and peace. Because Christianity has been intertwined with the development of Western culture, versions of these positions also appear in secular political thought. Likewise, although it will not be further remarked upon, versions of and analogues to these positions are found in many religious and cultural traditions around the world. These positions are being simplified here for ease of description and, as embraced by actual Christians, they are not always sharply divided from nearby positions.

Christian pacifism renounces deadly violence in fidelity to the teaching and witness of Jesus Christ. Pacifists understand Christian churches as communities whose members try to live as disciples of Jesus Christ, the Prince of Peace. Jesus taught his disciples to "turn the other cheek," that is, not to respond to violence with violence. Pacifists see violence as a terrible be-smirching of God's gift of life; they note that often the vulnerable and de-spised persons in society bear the brunt of violence.

Jesus reached out to such people in his own day and thereby transformed our way of looking at the world. Jesus expressed a dramatically new vision of God's plan for humans in the image of the reign of God. In hopeful anticipa-tion of the reign of God, inaugurated in Jesus Christ and to be fully mani-fested at his return, Christian pacifists strive to live in a way that witnesses to this new order. The early Christian communities were pacifist, as was most of the organized Church until the fourth century. During the sixteenth-century Reformation, organized Christian pacifism enjoyed a resurgence, which saw the birth of the peace churches. The Amish and Mennonites are the best known of the surviving peace churches; a related group known as the Hut-terites will be described in chapter 2. Every subsequent century has seen the birth of new churches and religious movements espousing pacifism. Throughout Church history until today, many organizations, leaders, and theologians have urged Christians to take up the challenge of peacemaking. Despite the social unpopularity that can meet this vision in a time of war and fear, it is a vision that inspires many Christians. We will see, in chapter 2, that there are a number of ways to interpret and apply this vision.

The *just war tradition* of reasoning was taken over from its roots in clas-sical Roman political thought by Saint Ambrose and Saint Augustine in the fourth and early fifth centuries and then developed by a number of Catholic and Protestant theologians in the West. Starting in the late Middle Ages, a secularized strand of the tradition became incorporated into the developing body of international law. Just war tradition is called a "tradition" because it is a historically developing body of reasoning about war. For this reason it is also called just war "theory," "doctrine," "thought," or "reasoning." We will use many of these terms in the book for the sake of felicity but will often use "tradition" as a reminder that just war is more than a rule book and that it has taken distinctive shape in various cultural and religious milieus.

The tradition comprises several criteria against which to judge a case for going to war or to judge an ongoing or completed war. A nation must meet all the criteria for going to war (jus ad bellum) before starting military ac-tions and must rigorously abide by the criteria while fighting in war (jus in bello). Failure to do so makes the nation's actions immoral and often illegal un-der international law. None of the criteria, which will be individually explained in chapter 2, are distinctively Christian, but they are defended by advocates of the tradition as a reasonable way for Christians to decide which wars they should support and which they should stand against given certain assumptions about Christian life and the nature of the world.

The remaining two positions are, generally speaking, more accepting of violence than just war doctrine, but they are quite different from one another. *Christian realism* can be seen as taking just war's insights about the necessity of force in an imperfect world to stronger or—its advocates would say—more consistent conclusions. In its general sense, political realism asserts that we cannot expect virtuous behavior from individuals, and still less from groups. Therefore, realists are prepared to act outside the bounds of standard morality in order to protect the self-interests of their nation or group. The secular version of realism is often characterized, even by its supporters, as amoral, that is, unconcerned with ethical principles. Some thinkers have advanced a Christian version of realism; the American theologian Reinhold Niebuhr (1892–1972) is identified as its contemporary progenitor. Niebuhr did not think of his realism, which he claimed to model on the thoughts of St. Augustine, as amoral but as pragmatic about the limitations of applying moral ideals to political struggles. In contrast to the just war tradition, Christian realism does not regard war as a reasonable action for the sake of the common good but as a tragic use of imperfect methods in a situation of sin. Christian realism is not necessarily more bellicose than Christian just war theory, but it is prepared to consider the use of violence in circumstances and in ways that are beyond the limits that the just war tradition has set.

In a sense, realism—whether secular or Christian—puts a bookend on one side of just war doctrine and pacifism places a bookend on the other side. These bookends set limits on what is acceptable under just war theory, but they also exert an influence on those who support the theory. On the one hand, just war thinkers often are attracted to realists' rhetoric about the need to take action in a dangerous, sinful world; on the other hand, they share pacifists' concerns about the fragility of peace and the horrible destructiveness of war. Whether just war can maintain a coherent perspective between these two positions will be tested in this book.

Since September 11, 2001, the perceived increase in the threat of terrorism and nuclear proliferation has brought out a realist strain in some just war thinkers. Therefore, we will expand on the analysis of realists and their influence, for good or ill, on just war tradition throughout the book. On the other hand, just war theory's high standards for the use of force and its aim of reestablishing peace suggest overlaps with pacifism. Another contemporary strain of just war thinking, which gained increasing popularity during the cold war, articulates the doctrine as starting its analysis from a presumption against violence. This way of thinking about just war has been embraced in official documents from many Christian denominations. We will introduce this issue in chapter 2 and continue to explore the compatibility of pacifism and just war throughout the book.

Finally, the *holy war* position has been a major attitude toward war in Christian history. Another name for this position, the "crusade mentality," derives from the era of the Crusades, which were military campaigns led by various European rulers from the eleventh to the thirteenth centuries to take control of Palestine (the Holy Land) from the Muslim empires. The holy war position believes that God directly commands Christians to fight certain wars. A major reason for war in this view is to spread the Christian faith. In a similar vein, the holy warrior may claim that the faith is under attack, so a defensive war must be fought; yet in doing so, the holy warrior will not shy from creating a political order in which Christianity is favored and other religions are forbidden.

The holy war mentality has also found expression in other world religions, particularly in the diffuse jihadist movement in Islam. There are a number of ideological, psychological, and sociological reasons that some believers embrace extremist movements in their religious community. Chapter 5 will examine the holy war paradigm in the context of terrorism. The holy war mentality drives Islamist extremists to embrace the techniques of terror, but it has also propelled domestic Christian terrorism in the United States, exacerbated Catholic-versus-Protestant struggles in Northern Ireland, and provided a pillar of ideological support for the American and British war on terror.

As theologians and ethicists, we acknowledge there is legitimate diversity in the Christian tradition, so both pacifists and just war thinkers can make legitimate ethical claims in the name of Christianity. Though we both will criticize the overall program of Christian realism, we accept that certain Christian realist claims have warrant in the tradition and that students of Reinhold Niebuhr have contributed useful ideas to the Christian debate over war. However, we are united in completely rejecting holy war as a legitimate Christian ideal. Holy war violates Jesus' teachings on mercy, forgiveness, and humility, and it recklessly confuses God's purposes with human interpretation.

STRUCTURE OF THE ARGUMENT

The first chapter, "Sources and Methods for a Christian Ethic of War," explains how our conversation is located within a Christian context, with Brian Stiltner endorsing just war tradition and David Clough advocating pacifism. We present two divergent manifestations of Christian ethics: thinking from a starting point of reason versus revelation, and speaking to a civic audience versus the church community. These approaches can overlap and complement each other in some ways, but the basic differences generate different ethical assumptions between just war and pacifism. We also survey relevant biblical texts before concluding with a debate between the authors concerning how theological, ethical, and biblical interpretations impact the just war and pacifism controversy. Chapter 2 explains in depth the two ethical perspectives in its title, "Christian Pacifism and the Just War Tradition." We summarize the historical development of these perspectives and provide a guide for understanding them in a modern context, including an innovative typology of pacifist positions. We then discuss the controversial question of the relationship between pacifism and just war theory. The final section of the chapter is again devoted to an exchange of views, this time concerning which position is best rooted in the Christian tradition.

Then follow four chapters treating problems of modern war. In chapter 3, "Does Humanitarian Intervention Pass the Test?" we scrutinize what ought to be the easiest Christian case to make for war: the rescue of innocent third parties from attack. If just war thinkers can maintain a strong case that violence is justified in some of these situations, they vindicate a fundamental claim of their theory. If pacifists identify flaws with just war thinking on this topic, or even show that there are better ways to protect people than to start a war, their argument against other uses of military power will be all the stronger. Because just war thinkers and pacifists both embrace the cause of human dignity, humanitarian intervention is a useful context in which to look for shared assumptions and values between these two perspectives, which are otherwise so often placed at odds. This chapter discusses the challenges of humanitarian intervention with the help of case studies making clear what is at stake. The final debate section confronts hard questions for the pacifist and just war traditions alike.

The problem of chapter 4, "The Challenge of Weapons Proliferation," is as old as human society: Can groups agree to forgo the use and possession of weapons and then abide by the promises they make? Following the historical presentation of this problem—via four case studies on bows and arrows, chemical and biological weapons, nuclear weapons, and conventional arms— we consider how Christian theologians and churches have addressed weapons proliferation, relying upon pacifist, just war, and realist reasoning. Then we make a frank assessment of the political and ethical challenge of weapons proliferation today before launching into a debate over whether and how it can be achieved.

Chapter 5, "Political and Holy Terrorism: Frameworks for Analysis and Action," analyzes the responses to terrorism offered by pacifism and just war theory. We examine four case studies of different kinds of terrorist attacks: the Oklahoma City bombing, the bombing of Pan Am flight 103, republican and loyalist violence in Northern Ireland, and al Qaeda's jihadist terrorist campaign. We offer an original scale for understanding the similarities and differences between these attacks in terms of the relative role played by nations, terrorist groups, and individuals, and use this to illuminate the discussion of appropriate responses to them. The debate section looks at alternative ways of understanding the motivations of terrorists and the options for formulating an effective response to them.

In chapter 6, "Spreading Democracy or Asserting National Interests? The Case of the Wars on Iraq," we critically assess the use of just war theory in the debates over the Persian Gulf War of 1991, the period of sanctions during the 1990s, and the Iraq War of 2003. We aim to shed light on how just war doctrine was used or abused in these debates. A fundamental ethical question in this chapter is whether preventive war represents a new and acceptable category of just war, or whether it is simply a new way to dress up the assertion of national self-interests. The analysis of this chapter will contribute to a deeper ethical understanding of the ongoing violence in Iraq and address challenges that will shape international relations in the decades ahead.

The concluding chapter, "A Christian Agenda for a Warring World," summarizes and extends the reflection of the previous chapters concerning the viability, coherence, and development of just war theory and pacifism. We bring the ethical and theological status of the two theories back into the foreground, asking whether these positions can work together or, conversely, whether a Christian must choose between them. Judging that the positions have important shared goals and values, we set out a peacemaking agenda for all Christians in the twenty-first century.

CHAPTER 1

Sources and Methods for a Christian Ethic of War

I n this chapter we set out some key building blocks upon which much of the debates in the following chapters are built. First, we describe two approaches to Christian ethics; the differences between these approaches are highly relevant when it comes to issues of war and peace. Next, we explore the question of how the Bible can be used in the debate. We conclude with a discussion between us about the merits of the different methodological options explained in the chapter.

TWO APPROACHES TO CHRISTIAN ETHICS

Christians have taken many approaches in deciding how they should act according to their faith. Generally speaking, all approaches draw upon four sources—that is, four places to look for the vision, values, and rules that can provide answers to the questions: "What does God want of us and how shall we live?" These sources are the Bible, Church tradition, reason, and experience. Christian ethics begins with a careful reflection on the Bible as a record of God's word to God's people who have gone before us. It will be important to attend to the continuing experience of the Church after the completion of the Bible at the beginning of the second century to learn how wise and holy—and not so wise and holy—members of the Church in the past reflected on God's word to them. Resources such as creeds, Church declarations, canon laws, sermons, histories, lives of the saints, and writings of theologians are all part of this Christian tradition. Yet ethics is always a contextual question, a question of what to do in a particular situation, so Christians need to learn all they can from human knowledge of the world in all its many forms: the physical and human sciences; the humanities; and the creative insights of art, music, and literature. These insights from human learning are applications of our reason, and they must be guided by the ethical understanding that emerges from the first two sources. Finally, we must also recognize our own location in a given situation and appreciate our place both in the church community and as individuals: the particular range of experiences that has shaped us and the particular insights and blind spots we have as a result. This recognition allows for a humble and self-reflective application of the ethical values and principles that emerge from the first three sources.

The foregoing is a very brief description of a complex process, for there are many options for interpreting each source and for relating them to others. In this section, we present two alternative accounts of how Christian ethics should be understood. The approaches differ in the choices they make about which sources to privilege and how to interpret and relate them to each other. The approaches overlap in many ways, but their central difference lies in the source they privilege. The first approach emphasizes the sources of reason and human learning so Christian ethics can make contact with the problems facing society; the second approach stresses that Christian ethics begins with the Bible and the distinctive vision of community found there.

Christian Ethics via Reason

In deciding how to act ethically, Christians in every age have been aware that their moral norms and practices can be compared to the norms and practices of other cultures and religions. Sometimes Christians have focused on the differences and stressed the need for moral behavior that departs from the status quo, such as when the early Church opposed the Roman practices of abortion and infanticide. Yet Christians have also been aware that some of their moral norms and practices are similar to or the same as those of non-Christians. This similarity is most obvious with Jews and Muslims, with whom Christians share scriptures and a belief in God's covenant. Christians have also recognized what they have in common with people belonging to other faiths or even people of no faith. Theologically, this common ground is rooted in the affirmation that God, the Father of Jesus Christ, is the Creator and Lord of the entire universe. Nothing is outside of God's plan and control;

therefore, God's laws hold true even when people do not acknowledge God. This recognition is evident in Paul's letter to the Romans, in which he argues that the Gentiles are without excuse before God for immoral actions because God's power and nature have been made plain to them (Rom 1:18–22).[1]

Paul is pointing to an order of the created world that Christian theologians later called the "natural law." Natural law reasoning (often called "natural law theory," both terms referring to the method of reasoning ethically from the fact of natural law) is an ethical method with a long and varied history. We can summarize it through one of its greatest expositors, Thomas Aquinas of the thirteenth century. Aquinas drew together the notion of created order suggested in the Bible, the writings of great theologians before him, and the philosophy of Aristotle into a systematic account of natural law. "Natural law" can be defined as an ethical framework that does and should guide human conduct, based on goals that are derived from the order of natural inclinations and the participation of human reason in God's reason. The order of inclinations refers to the tendencies of created things to act in a way that fulfills their nature and that perfects them. It includes the tendency of living things to preserve their existence; of all animals to seek food and shelter and to bear and protect offspring; and of humans to live in community, to seek knowledge, to play, and to act necessarily and properly as rational beings.[2] The last part of the definition adds an important qualification: natural law is to be understood as the way that human reason has a share in or participates in God's reason. Humans are not driven by natural instinct; they have to use their reason to understand and properly act on their inclinations. To use an example from the ethics of warfare, the twentieth-century natural law philosopher Jacques Maritain claimed that human nature reviles against genocide "as incompatible with its general ends and innermost dynamic structure: that is to say, as prohibited by natural law."[3]

Whether the fact that the judgments of the natural law tradition are subject to disagreement reflects poorly on natural law reasoning and is a matter for debate. Some natural law thinkers—and many who are critical of the tradition—do natural law a disservice by assuming that it refers to a complete Christian morality or to a human morality that is self-evident and unquestionable. Regarding the first charge, natural law thinkers do not deny the deleterious effects of sin on human reason, but they do believe that the power of reason is not completely marred by sin. Moral education by parents, fellow Christians, and church leaders, along with guidance from the Christian tradition, are essential for a well-developed and mature use of natural law. Regarding the second charge, several late-twentieth-century Catholic theologians have explained why natural law methodology cannot be as specific as it sometimes appears in the teaching of the Catholic Church. These theologians have argued that instead of reading objective moral norms from an obvious order of nature and formalizing these through Church teaching, natural law thinking requires the individual moral agent to reason about the application of moral norms in concrete circumstances. These natural law ethicists see right reason as the "port of entry" into natural law. Natural law is respected when a person makes a conscientious, well-reasoned decision in a particular case. The insights of natural law are also gradually unfolded through moral development in an individual's life or in the moral maturation of the human race.[4]

Characterizing ethics as based in reason is, obviously, a simplification. The point of putting it this way should be clear by now. This approach to Christian ethics identifies continuities between Christian moral reasoning under the light of faith and other sources of moral wisdom. This approach believes that any behavior that respects human dignity and that promotes what is good is finally attributable to God's grace. The benefits of this approach to Christian ethics are that it provides a framework for dialogue and cooperation with other religious believers and nonbelievers; it encourages Christians to be humble and to be willing to learn moral insights from those outside their tradition; it brings Christian reasoning into dialogue with other theoretical frameworks, which can test and strengthen Christian reasoning; and it gives Christians a way to understand the contributions their morality can make to ethical deliberations and projects in a pluralistic society. This is ethics through reason only in part because human beings certainly need more than natural law in order to live out their deepest calling and to be truly happy. They need the good news of Jesus Christ. Christians themselves should never be satisfied with reason alone as a moral source. Rather, they must use it to help refine and apply the insights of their faith in a complicated world.

Christian Ethics via Revelation

"The knowledge of good and evil seems to be the aim of all ethical reflection," observed Dietrich Bonhoeffer. He continued: "The first task of Christian ethics is to invalidate this knowledge."[5] This statement clearly suggests an approach to Christian ethics that strongly contests the approach we have just described. Where a natural law methodology in Christian ethics begins with the presumption that significant common ground in ethics will be found with all people of good will, of any faith or of none, a revelation-based view expects Christian ethical reflection to lead to a distinctive way of life for the Church such that Christians will act differently from others in society. Revelation refers to the understanding that humans gain God's will for them. It may also be described as God's word to them because the first and most important conduit for revelation is the Bible. The Bible is a specific and authoritative revelation, but revelation also comes to individuals and to the Church through prayerful reflection on their lives and the world around them under the guidance of scripture and Church teaching. Christians following this approach have no less confidence than advocates of the first that their insights are true for the whole of society—this is not an "each to his or her own" moral relativism—but they are much less optimistic that those who do not belong to the Church will be able to share their ethical vision.

When talking about this approach to ethics, it is most natural to speak in the first-person plural: What is God asking of us who are disciples of Jesus Christ? For the Church to live as the body of Christ is demanding; it requires actions that are surprising by the world's standards.[6] This is most evident in the seemingly foolish Sermon on the Mount (Mt 5–7). Christian disciples are called to turn the other cheek, not resist evil, and to reckon with a moral scale in which lust and anger are equated with adultery and murder. The world under the reign of God is a world turned upside down, where the first are last and the meek will inherit the earth. For Bonhoeffer and other theologians who have challenged the reason-based approach, for human beings to try to discern right from wrong apart from God's word to them is the primeval sin of Adam and Eve who wanted to know good and evil as God knows it.[7] Human beings must, instead, recall their status as creatures: They are finite, sinful, and forever tempted with the hubris of claiming that they can work out ethics for themselves.

Although this approach emphasizes that human beings are dependent on God for knowing right from wrong, this does not mean they can merely wait for instruction to be delivered to them. The task of all Christians is to discern, through prayerful reflection, where God's will for God's people might lie. The task of church leaders is to discern God's will and to instruct Christians about it in a spirit of freedom. The task of Christian ethicists is to reflect critically yet sympathetically on all modes of reasoning as a service to the discernment of the Christian community. God's word to us is always mediated through the world around us; there is no other way creatures like us can communicate. In some respects, then, behaving ethically in this way will not look very different from some versions of a natural law approach. Yet in contrast to that approach, theological ethics in this mode will be concerned first with the life to which members of the Church are called. Moral discernment is rooted in God's self-revelation to a group of wandering Jews and then to a Jewish group that came to believe two millennia ago that Jesus of Nazareth was the Messiah.

The historical particularity of this faith means that the Church cannot expect everyone to think the same way it does. The Church is in possession of crucial wisdom into what it means to be living as human beings in this world and this universe, yet beyond the context of the stories and history that have formed it, this wisdom may often appear to be mere foolishness. If our ethical insights are shaped by the story we have received, rather than solely by reflection on the world as such, we cannot be confident that those who belong to different traditions will agree with us. This fact, however, is no excuse for the Church to keep itself separate from the world; it should have an urgent passion both for sharing what it has learned of God's will and for shaping the world in ways that are good for human beings and all of creation. The Church exists in a political context, and building consensus with those beyond the Church will always be an essentially political task. For this reason, the common ground that Christians discover in discussion with others is to be celebrated. It is celebrated, however, precisely because it cannot be taken for granted.

BIBLICAL TEXTS ON WAR AND PEACE

Although they differ in how they understand the Bible's primacy and sufficiency alongside other sources, both approaches to Christian ethics would have us turn to the Bible in order to understand fully God's will for us. When it comes to peace and war, what do we find in the Bible and how should we interpret what we find there?

What Is the Bible?

For Christians, the Bible is the Word of God, proclaiming the good news of a loving God who is Lord of all. It is a salvation history that starts with the creation of all things; continues through the redemption from sin made possible through the life, death, and resurrection of God's son, Jesus Christ; and culminates with the final realization of God's purposes in the new creation. The Bible is also the story of God's people, narrating the history of the covenant made between God and them and the way they responded to the loving faithfulness of God with both faith and lack of faith.

The Christian Bible is made up of two parts: the Old Testament, or Hebrew Bible, which is the scripture of Judaism; and the New Testament, which tells of Jesus Christ and the beginning of the Church. (Christians sometimes refer to the Bible as "scripture." Most religions have scriptures, that is, central and authoritative holy texts. The Bible is the official scripture of Christianity.) The Bible is a diverse collection of texts, composed over a period of around seven hundred years and comprising many different literary genres. Over the first four centuries after Christ, the churches of the Christian world gradually recognized twenty-seven books of the New Testament as inspired by God and, thus, as authoritative. Decisions by Church councils established these twenty-seven books and the thirty-nine books of the Old Testament as the canon—the official list of biblical writings—although the branches of Christianity differ regarding the exact list of the Old Testament.[8]

Despite holding to slightly different canons, all Christians believe the Bible has a key role to play in guiding decisions about how to act. Yet how are we to understand the Bible as God's word, and how are we to allow it to speak to us? In the Bible, we find instructions as diverse as do not eat the blood of animals (e.g., Lv 17:14), do not consult wizards (Lv 19:31), do not work on the Sabbath (e.g., Lv 23:3), tear out your eye if it causes you to sin (Mt 5:29), and do not resist an evildoer (Mt 5:39). We also find more general instructions, such as those of the Decalogue, or Ten Commandments (Ex 20:1–17; Dt 5:6–21), choosing life (Dt 30:19), and loving your neighbor as yourself (e.g., Lv 19:18). More generally still, we are encouraged to follow the example of the faithfulness of the patriarchs (Heb 11:1–12) and to act like the Good Samaritan (Lk 10:25–37). Above all are the overarching stories that provide the general shape of the Bible's message: stories of creation, fall, redemption, judgment, and new creation.

We have just given examples of biblical teaching in four categories, ranging from the most concrete to the most general. Richard Hays terms these four ways that the Bible can inform our ethical thinking "rules," "principles," "paradigms," and "worldviews."[9] Clearly, not all rules issued to the

Israelite nation will be applicable in different contexts twenty-five hundred years later. Not eating the blood of animals, for example, has commonly been attributed to the ceremonial law of Israelite religion; thus, it is understood as no longer relevant for Christians.[10] Biblical commandments such as "do not steal," "do not commit adultery," and "love your neighbor" seem· less clearly tied to an immediate context and so serve as generally applicable principles. Yet especially in the case of the love commandment, it is harder to interpret the meaning of biblical principles in a modern context. Detachment from context and generality more extensively characterize paradigms such as the parable of the Good Samaritan, and worldviews such as the creation and the fall. Each of these four modes of address properly influences the development of our ethical understanding, but it should already be clear that interpreting these modes in particular cases is often a challenge, especially where their applications appear to conflict.

Appreciating the complexity of the task makes clear we cannot escape the difficulty of interpreting the meaning of the Bible in the context of ethical issues. In the past, biblical texts were used to justify slavery, racism, and apartheid, and the current univocal rejection of these interpretations by churches worldwide should not undercut our appreciation of the need to take care that we are not merely reading our own prejudices into the Bible. Different churches are still wrestling with the meaning of biblical texts for male and female roles and for expressions of gay and lesbian sexuality. Christians must remain committed to the centrality and authority of the Bible as God's word to us while recognizing that interpretation of its meaning for our situation requires a demanding two-way conversation between our scripture and our world.

In relation to the issues of war and peace, the first and fundamental point to note is that from the beginning of the history of salvation in the Garden of Eden to its end in the new Jerusalem, the Bible's witness is to the profound value of life and peace. God in Genesis 6 causes the great flood because of human corruption and violence and afterwards announces that a reckoning will be demanded of any person—or animal—that takes human life, because humans bear the divine image (Gn 9:5-6). The Bible looks forward to a time when there will be no more violence, notably in Isaiah's vision of God's holy mountain where no life of any kind will be destroyed (Is 11:6-9) and in the revelation of St. John of the new heaven and earth where God will wipe away all tears and where "mourning and crying and pain will be no more" (Rv 21:4). Isaiah and Micah share the vision of a time when

God "shall judge between the nations, and shall arbitrate for many peoples; they shall beat their swords into plowshares, and their spears into pruning hooks; nation shall not lift up sword against nation, neither shall they learn war any more" (Is 2:4; compare Mi 4:3).

The New Testament Witness to Peace

Much of the teaching in the New Testament concurs with this vision of peacefulness as both original and ultimate. This idea is expressed most clearly in Jesus' teaching in the Sermon on the Mount that the peacemakers will be called children of God (Mt 5:9) and that disciples must not act aggressively:

> You have heard that it was said, "An eye for an eye and a tooth for a tooth." But I say to you, Do not resist an evildoer. But if anyone strikes you on the right cheek, turn the other also; and if anyone wants to sue you and take your coat, give your cloak as well; and if anyone forces you to go one mile, go also the second mile. Give to everyone who begs from you, and do not refuse anyone who wants to borrow from you. You have heard that it was said, "You shall love your neighbor and hate your enemy." But I say to you, Love your enemies and pray for those who persecute you, so that you may be children of your Father in heaven; for he makes his sun rise on the evil and on the good, and sends rain on the righteous and on the unright-eous. (Mt 5:38–45)

In a time and place that was anything but peaceful—a land under occupation by an aggressive military superpower—Jesus tells his disciples that they are not to use violence against their oppressors. Some have suggested that turning the other cheek would have been a gesture of defiance, rather than submission, so Jesus might be counseling nonviolence as a strategy rather than as an absolute rule.[11] Yet even if there is merit in this, it cannot defuse the force of "offer no resistance to one who is evil," especially given the dramatic exemplification of this teaching by Jesus during his Passion.

This imagery of peace continues beyond the Gospels. Paul's Letter to the Romans echoes the Sermon on the Mount:

> Bless those who persecute you; bless and do not curse them. Rejoice with those who rejoice, weep with those who weep. Live in harmony with one

another; do not be haughty, but associate with the lowly; do not claim to be wiser than you are. Do not repay anyone evil for evil, but take thought for what is noble in the sight of all. If it is possible, so far as it depends on you, live peaceably with all. Beloved, never avenge yourselves, but leave room for the wrath of God; for it is written, "Vengeance is mine, I will repay, says the Lord." No, "if your enemies are hungry, feed them; if they are thirsty, give them something to drink; for by doing this you will heap burning coals on their heads." Do not be overcome by evil, but overcome evil with good. (Rom 12:14–21)

The Letter of James also echoes Jesus' praise of peacemakers: "A harvest of righteousness is sown in peace for those who make peace" (3:18). The Letter to the Hebrews calls on church members to "pursue peace with everyone" (12:14). Throughout the epistles, Christians are exhorted to find not only an example of peacemaking in Jesus but also to receive the power to become peacemakers by relying upon the grace of the "God of peace" (1 Thes 5:23) and the sanctification of Jesus, the "king of peace" (Heb 7:2). Even the cosmic work of Christ is described as making peace, most obviously in Colossians: "Through him God was pleased to reconcile to himself all things, whether on earth or in heaven, by making peace through the blood of his cross" (1:20).[12]

There are a few New Testament texts that sit oddly with this consistent emphasis on peace. According to Luke, John the Baptist did not tell soldiers to leave the army (Lk 3:14), and Jesus told the disciples at the Last Supper that they should buy swords if they do not have them (Lk 22:36–38). Furthermore, the astonishingly violent imagery of war in the Book of Revelation must give us pause, as John recounts his vision of God defeating God's enemies and the destruction of swaths of humankind. None of these passages, however, should lead us to set aside the strong witness of the New Testament against the use of violence. The astonishing feature of the story of John the Baptist is that Roman soldiers as foreign occupying forces paid any attention to him at all. At the Last Supper, Jesus is warning the disciples of the opposition they will face in the next phase of their ministry; any more literal interpretation is ruled out by Jesus' lack of patience with the attempted violent resistance of the disciples later that evening when a crowd came to arrest him (Lk 22:49–51). Finally, the message of Revelation is that Christians should endure and trust in God's power to redeem them; the book cannot be cited to support Christians bearing arms.[13]

Those who look to the New Testament for an affirmation of the use of force cite two key texts. The first is Romans 13, where Paul affirms the right of the authorities to use force:

> Let every person be subject to the governing authorities; for there is no authority except from God, and those authorities that exist have been instituted by God. Therefore whoever resists authority resists what God has appointed, and those who resist will incur judgment. For rulers are not a terror to good conduct, but to bad. Do you wish to have no fear of the authority? Then do what is good, and you will receive its approval; for it is God's servant for your good. But if you do what is wrong, you should be afraid, for the authority does not bear the sword in vain! It is the servant of God to execute wrath on the wrongdoer. Therefore one must be subject, not only because of wrath but also because of conscience. (Rom 13:1–5)

There is clearly no permission for Christians to use violence here, and the passage just cited from the preceding chapter of Romans confirms that this was not Paul's intention. However, he does affirm the need for the state—that is, sovereign government—to use force, which meant that when the Church found itself to be the official religion of the Roman Empire after Constantine's conversion, this text became an important one. It continues to be relevant in contexts where Christians share political responsibility for the nation to which they belong, such as in democracies.[14]

The second New Testament text cited in the tradition to support the use of force is an implicit rather than direct reference. As we will see in the next chapter, many have argued that Jesus' command to love your neighbor as yourself (Mk 12:31 and parallels) means that weaker neighbors should be defended against those who attack them.

The Complex Status of War in the Old Testament

Alongside the Old Testament vision of peace as the fulfillment of God's purposes and the New Testament witness to faithful nonviolence, we find the Bible wrestling with a world that is anything but peaceful. This is clear in the

Ten Commandments: "You shall not murder" (Ex 20:13; Dt 5:17). This commandment is sometimes taken as a rationale for rejecting killing in all its forms—particularly when translated as "Thou shalt not kill"—but reflection quickly shows a much narrower prohibition than initially appears. "Murder" is a better translation than "kill" because, although the precise meaning of the Hebrew term is uncertain, the commandment should probably be taken to refer only to killing within the community of Israel. In any case, it is clear that this prohibition intended to leave open the possibility of legitimate killing both in warfare and capital punishment because these actions are allowed at other places in the same biblical books.[15] A further text that suggests a moderate position—recognizing the legitimate use of force but setting limits on it—is Amos 1:3–2:3. Here the prophet criticizes unjust conduct in war, such as when Damascus "threshed Gilead with threshing sledges of iron" (1:3) or when Gaza "carried into exile whole communities, to hand them over to Edom" (1:6). It is not a stretch to see in this passage the distant origins of the just war tradition.[16]

The most disturbing texts relating to warfare in the Bible are the parts of the law documenting how the Israelites are to fight and the stories of their slaughter of neighboring tribes at the command of God. Deuteronomy 20 sets the standards of expected conduct. For distant nations, Israel is to offer peace. If the offer is accepted, the population is subjected to forced labor; if it is not accepted, after the battle all the males are to be killed and the women and children taken as spoils of war (vv. 10–15). For nations living within the land that God has given Israel, an even harsher standard applies: "You must not let anything that breathes remain alive" (v. 16). Alongside these breathtaking texts, we must place the narrative of 1 Samuel 15, where God commands Saul to slaughter the Amalekites "both man and woman, child and infant, ox and sheep, camel and donkey" (v. 3). Saul spares the king and the best of the animals and, as a result, loses favor with God. Finally, an example of Yahweh's violent action is the Exodus story. After the Egyptians have been drowned in the Red Sea, Moses celebrates that "the Lord is a warrior; the Lord is his name. . . . Your right hand, O Lord, glorious in power—your right hand, O Lord, shattered the enemy" (Ex 15:3, 6). There is no escaping these difficult texts—all the more disturbing given our familiarity with genocidal crimes in the last century in Nazi Germany, Rwanda, and elsewhere. How are we to interpret them? Of the many interpretative issues relevant to these texts, we want to identify three key points: the social and political context of the biblical books, the impact of Israel's cultic concern for purity on its discussion of warfare, and the prophetic question of who fights for Israel.

One key difference between the contexts of the New and Old Testaments is the political situation of the communities in which the texts were written. Israel is a theocratic nation with no dividing line between its religious and nonreligious aspects. It is a nation among other militarily powerful nations and suffers catastrophic defeats in battle as well as dramatic successes. Furthermore, Israel is heir to a promise from God that it will have as its possession a land flowing with milk and honey (see, e.g., Ex 3:17). The contrast between the social location of those writing the New Testament texts and those who wrote the Old Testament is stark. The authors of the New Testament start out as adherents of a small, new Jewish sect under persecution from the Jewish religious authorities, who themselves belong to a nation under foreign occupation by Rome, the world's superpower. The leaders of this sect found small communities of Gentiles around the Mediterranean world— communities that are likewise socially marginal and subject to persecution. These communities have no role in political authority and little stake in the questions it raises; their only concern is how to survive as a people subjected to authority.

This difference in social location between the Old and New Testaments can be used in two main ways, depending on how they are seen in relation to our own context. The first is to say that the Old Testament is our main resource for relating the Bible to questions concerning political authority and the choices it forces upon us. As citizens of modern nations, we are faced with these questions as Israel was, but as the New Testament authors were not. The Old Testament shows us God's will for the conduct of the nation of Israel, and so it is the best guide for how we should think about our involvement in national affairs. From this perspective, war is recognized in the Old Testament as an appropriate way for nations to defend their interests, so we should accept this judgment and admit war as legitimate for modern nations, too.

The second way of discerning the relevance of the different contexts of the Old and New Testaments leads to a very different conclusion. It points to the theocratic aspect of Israel as a strong contrast with modern states and sees the location of churches today as much closer to that of the New Testament communities: removed from political power and more concerned with their communal practice than large-scale political questions. These contrasting readings of the relevance of the social and political context of the biblical texts clearly lead to very different conclusions about how to interpret what the Bible says about war and convince us that judgments about context are a key interpretative issue. A considered view must appreciate both the relevant continuities and the relevant discontinuities between each text of the biblical canon and the various political positions of Christian churches at the beginning of the twenty-first century.

The second interpretative issue for understanding the Old Testament texts we have surveyed is their relationship to the concern for purity in the religion of Israel.[17] Israel is a people chosen by God that shows its faithfulness by keeping itself pure and undefiled, obeying God's command to be holy. The book of Leviticus is fundamentally concerned with what it means to be God's holy people: "You shall not do as they do in the land of Egypt, where you lived, and you shall not do as they do in the land of Canaan, to which I am bringing you" (Lv 18:3); "You shall be holy, for I the Lord your God am holy" (Lv 19:2). The injunctions to slaughter whole peoples and their livestock have a clear rationale in this context, a rationale specified by the author of Deuteronomy 20: Israel must obey the command so that the enemies "may not teach you to do all the abhorrent things that they do for their gods, and you thus sin against the Lord your God" (Dt 20:18). The violence commanded is not based in cruelty or unbridled aggression but in a struggle to keep a people holy and separate from those around them. We should also recognize that these texts may represent the theoretical application of purity law to the conduct of warfare rather than a practice that ever took place. Because this purity law is one that Christians have set aside in any case, it would be strange, indeed, if we took these texts as an authoritative basis for right conduct in war. There is no reason for those taking a just war or a pacifist position to differ here.

The third interpretative question raised by the Old Testament texts is, Who fights for Israel? We have already cited the Exodus story in which the Lord defeats the Egyptian army. Deuteronomy also makes clear that it is the Lord who acts for Israel. Chapter 2 demonstrates this by recording that all the warriors of Israel had died out before God brought the nation victory in a series of important battles. The book of Joshua similarly celebrates the power of the Lord fighting for the Israelites: "For the Lord has driven out before you great and strong nations. . . . One of you puts to flight a thousand, since it is the Lord your God who fights for you" (Jo 23:9–10). This direct action on the part of Yahweh is a key component of the holy wars in the Old Testament. Without Yahweh, Israel is weak and can achieve nothing; with Yahweh, all nations fall before Israel. The prophets of Israel frequently criticize the Israelites for not trusting sufficiently in the saving purposes of God. Perhaps the clearest example is this passage from Isaiah (30:15–16):

> *Thus said the Lord God, the Holy One of Israel:*
> *In returning and rest you shall be saved;*
> > *in quietness and in trust shall be your strength.*
> *But you refused and said,*
> *"No! We will flee upon horses."*

Horses are representative of military might here. Gerhard von Rad and commentators following him have seen this and similar texts as indicating a close link between prophecy and the holy war tradition.[18] At a time when the monarchy was building up standing armies, a prophet recalling Israel to the time when it depended on the might of Yahweh alone was a critique of a nation that had lost faith in its God. This insight puts the doctrine of holy war in Israel in a surprising perspective, suggesting that it functioned importantly as a divine criticism, rather than as a divine endorsement, of the building up of military power.

This brief survey has shown that relating biblical texts to the ethics of war and peace is a complex interpretative task. We have seen a clear and univocal testimony to God's will for peace among God's creation and the promise of a time when there will be no more killing. New Testament texts suggest that the early Church perceived in the teaching of Jesus a call to anticipate this vision for the end of history by renouncing violence now. The Hebrew Bible celebrates Yahweh's fighting for Israel as part of the fulfillment of the covenant, but it also identifies illicit means of fighting and criticizes reliance on human military might. In interpreting these two different visions, we have noted the need to attend to the context of the communities in which the texts were written; the early Church did not have to face issues of the legitimate use of force by peoples and empires, and the theocratic character of Israel distinguishes it from most modern states. The fault lines of subsequent interpretation are not hard to see. Was Jesus' teaching about violence a central part of his message or a short-term measure only appropriate for the Church in a particular time and place?

Has the era during which Yahweh takes sides in battles ended, or may we, like Israel, call on our Lord to help us win battles?

The fundamental question is about relating our responsibility to God's plan for history: Given the biblical vision of peace and justice among the human and nonhuman creation, are we called to anticipate it now by renouncing violence? Or are we to recognize that the vision is not yet realized, so we must, for now, engage actively with the world as we find it, using force where necessary? This question implies competing interpretations of *eschatology*, which is the theological interpretation of the purpose of history based on its final goal. The term is based on the Greek word *eschaton*, meaning "the end times." Eschatology figures in the overarching Christian narrative of history, but it does not mean that all Christians think the world will end in a cataclysm that is literally predicted in the Book of Revelation, although some Christians do embrace that apocalyptic eschatology. In keeping with the mainstream of Christian theology, we believe that the eschatology is about how believers respond to Jesus' proclamation of the "reign of God," which is a reality that is already present in human history and contemporary experience.[19] Theologians and biblical scholars use the term "inbreaking" to express the way Jesus saw the reign of God as presently entering human history at the time of his earthly ministry and as demanding an immediate response from people. At the same time, taking account of the entire Bible, theologians holding an "already/not yet," or "proleptic," version of eschatology consider that God has a goal for history: Jesus Christ will bring God's reign to fulfillment, at which time the joy and peace that are described figuratively in the Bible (e.g., the wolf lying down with the lamb in Isaiah, the holy city being built in Revelation) will become realities. But are Christians called to live in strict fidelity to the values of God's reign now, or do different standards hold as they await the return of Jesus? That is the eschatological question that bears on the ethics of war.

DEBATING THE ISSUES

We have interpretive tools in hand now to begin answering some of these questions. We now explore the strengths and weaknesses of ethical options and methodological choices by speaking in our own voices, explaining and defending the assumptions that lie beneath our respective positions on war: pacifism for David Clough (DLC) and just war theory for Brian Stiltner (BES).

The Starting Point and Method of Christian Ethics

DLC Of the two starting points for Christian ethics that we have outlined, my vision is close to the second. My opening definition of Christian ethics is *a discernment of the shape of the life the Church is called to live in response to the salvation we have received from God.* The continuity or discontinuity with other forms of ethical reflection, such as secular moral philosophy, is very much a secondary issue. To see Christian ethics as a subset of some larger enterprise of ethics threatens to limit our ability to attend to God's call to us. Another slant on this is whether Christian ethics is primarily intended to inform the behavior of the Church and its members or the behavior of all people. It may be that my background within the Protestant tradition inclines me toward the first of these options, and yours within the Roman Catholic tradition inclines you toward the latter. This distinction is absolutely crucial for the topic of the ethics of war: The only strands of the Christian tradition that have adopted pacifism are those with an ethic that focuses on what Christians should do, rather than what will work for society at large. Finally, there are questions about how the Church relates to the world around it—about how much its teaching should be influenced by its sociopolitical location and how far it is responsible for shaping the political world it happens to live in. That is a major theme that will run throughout this book; one of its methodological aspects is what Jesus' proclamation of God's inbreaking reign means for the way Christians live their lives here and now.

BES Then let's explore our differences concerning the continuity of faith-based reflection with other sources of moral insight and the ways that we interpret and apply the Bible on such matters as faithfulness to Jesus and responding to his proclamation of the reign of God. My opening definition of the process of ethics is *reflection on values and principles that determine which acts to commit and which to avoid, and what kind of person to be, to which standards we hold ourselves and our community.* I do not think that this is a complete definition of ethics for

Christians, but in starting this way, I assume that ethical reflection for anybody—whether Christian or non-Christian—involves deciding what to do and striving to develop a good character, doing so both as an individual and along with the many communities in which one participates. I believe that Christians draw upon two distinct sources—scripture and tradition—but they use these together with what they learn from reason and what they gain from reflecting on their experiences throughout life.

I know you use the same four sources, but we differ in how we see these sources working together. I think that God gave us the power of reason, a power that is hampered but not destroyed by sin, and that reason yields many insights into God's plan for humanity. The use of reason—or natural law as the Catholic tradition puts it—is very helpful for having a dialogue with persons of different religions and cultures and for coming to partial agreements with them. This assumption of a common human moral law is borne out, I believe, in the agreements that the nations of the world have made on human rights conventions, conventions guiding warfare, and the institutions of international law. I don't pretend that these agreements can eliminate war, but without them, I think the world would be much worse off.

DLC I'm much less optimistic than you that human beings have access to the common moral understanding that most accounts of natural law require, and I don't think the examples of international conventions and institutions make your point. Of course, the international community—like any other—has a need to come to agreements about what kinds of actions are acceptable and unacceptable. But we don't get to agreements by different nations reflecting together on their common understanding of humanity and what it means for how we should act towards each other. Instead, each nation brings to the table its own understanding of norms of behavior, and reaching an agreement is a political process in which commonalities and differences are debated, concessions made, and eventually a consensus is reached on what can be jointly affirmed. Although there is a wide consensus on the basic minimum of what protections should be given to individuals, countries interpret it very differently. For example, China's understanding of individual rights and responsibilities is very different from that of Western societies. When we get to the rules of war, things are much more uncertain, as was evident in the different assessments of Arab and Western media about the conduct of the 2003 war in Iraq. International agreements just show we have to have rules to get along with each other, not that we all share a substantive moral vision. It would be great if all people could agree on what's right and wrong. Unfortunately, it's very clear that they don't.

BES I don't deny that there is a large measure of pragmatic negotiation with a view to national self-interest that goes on when these conventions are developed, nor do I deny that the world's major civilizations interpret them through very different lenses. That all happened in the development of the Universal Declaration of Human Rights. Still, that document lays out an ambitiously broad account of civic and social rights as ideals toward which human beings want to strive. Sure, there's no way to enforce it, but the Universal Declaration paved the way for more specific and more enforceable conventions in the future; it gave energy to human rights work; and it can still hold a nation's feet to the moral fire. The Universal Declaration of Human Rights reflects a wide consensus on the minimum, as you say; it reflects a considerably shared sense among cultures of what most basically matters for human well-being. Like Maritain, I think this achievement testifies both to natural law and to pragmatism, and we don't have to pose a sharp dichotomy between the two ways of looking at it. When it comes to rules of war, conventions are based on mutual self-interest ("both our countries will be in trouble if we set off biological weapons"), but the content of these conventions largely reflects the judgments of the Western just war tradition as it was gradually codified into international law. My view, in sum, is not that natural law reasoning can work out a whole system of moral rules for the global community but that Christians' acknowledgment that there is a natural law allows us to understand why it is worth the effort to work on cross-cultural agreements.

DLC I don't think that we need to believe that there's a natural law to realize that we need international agreements. I also think there's a real danger in assuming that other nations not only will but should agree with what we think because of natural law; it can become a very good reason for not taking seriously views that differ from our own. But my main concern with natural law thinking is that it starts us off by looking for moral norms that will be universally applicable, whereas I want to start by listening for what the Church that I belong to is called to do and what my part in that calling should be. The first place I look for this guidance is to the Bible, and it's clear that many of the instructions Jesus gave his disciples don't make good social policy. Take the Sermon on the Mount (Mt 5–7): Blessed are the poor, those who mourn, the meek, the persecuted? Anger is tantamount to murder? Lust is as bad as adultery? Don't resist evil? Love your enemies? Jesus' teaching contradicts any kind of shared commonsense morality. The ethic he calls us to is unnatural, a new kind of living that runs counter to everything we thought we knew. We are faced with a choice between what we think is reasonable and what the Bible tells us is faithful. Christians have to choose the latter.

BES We saw in the section on two approaches to ethics that the use of reason and the use of revelation are not mutually exclusive. Both of us are trying to take the Bible seriously, and both of us acknowledge that it has to be interpreted properly, which often means not strictly literally. Some of the teachings from Jesus' Sermon on the Mount seem to be about setting the right kind of inner disposition ("don't get angry") in a way that is not humanly possible but pushes us to go beyond where we are and where we think we can go. Many of his teachings set us on a certain way of looking at the world and involve a great deal of judgment when trying to live them out. So I would say, let us follow the command to "love your enemies," but let us recognize that it doesn't answer every practical question we face. Therefore, reason will be a necessary tool for answering questions as we apply the biblical vision to our lives and our world today.

Interpreting the Bible: Eschatology and Faithfulness to Christ

DLC Certainly, rational reflection must be part of ethics, but I'm less convinced than you that we can appeal to it as some sort of independent norm.[20] Another crucial element in interpreting the Sermon on the Mount, of course, is thinking about its eschatological context. Many interpreters—most famously Albert Schweitzer and Johannes Weiss—have argued that Jesus only made these extreme demands on his disciples because he expected the end of the world to come very soon.[21] If we accepted this view, we could happily discount the strange things the Sermon asks of the disciples on the basis that Jesus was aiming to prescribe not long-term societal norms but only an interim ethic for a short time. I don't agree with this interpretation, and I imagine you don't either, but I think eschatology is a cause of divergence between our positions. I want to use the formula of the reign of God as both "already" and "not yet" to recognize that the life, death, and resurrection of Jesus Christ inaugurated a new time in which God's reign will be made known. For now, we live in a world that does not acknowledge this new reality, and the Christian vocation is to witness to where it breaks into a world deeply compromised by sin. One of the ways we do this is by living lives in response to the teaching and example of Christ; living without recourse to violence is a crucial component of such discipleship.

BES The eschatological context is significant for Christian teaching on war. It remains relevant today, though we will have to admit that its significance doesn't strike home for many Christians. That's a blanket criticism in which I include myself. It is easy to get wrapped up in everyday living and forget to ask: "Where is my life going? Where is this world going? Are God's priorities my, and our, priorities?" Christians, then, should look to God's announcement of the future that God has planned for us to take our bearings. It is a future in which "the wolf shall live with the lamb, the leopard shall lie down with the kid" (Is 11:6) and in which "mourning and crying and pain will be no more" (Rv 21:4). But, as you say, we are not there yet. My own take on eschatology is, like yours, that the reign of God is both "already" and "not yet." Just war thinkers typically point to the tension between "already" and "not yet" to open a space for Christians to participate in war because the world is not yet transformed to the reign of God. We have to reckon with this space; otherwise, as Martin Luther observed, "if the lion lies down with the lamb, the lamb must be replaced frequently."[22]

One way to develop this insight is through the Christian realism of Reinhold Niebuhr, which boldly embraces the tension between God's reign and our times and says that we cannot live by the values of God's reign. I think that is far too pessimistic. I say that Christians should live by values of peace and solidarity that reflect the goal to which we are called. More specifically, Christians should express mutual forbearance, forgiveness, and caring; they should reject domination and be reluctant to use coercion as a means to achieve social ends. At the same time, there are features of living in this order between the times that make it unchristian to avoid all coercion and force. We are called to relieve suffering and protect God's lowly ones. We also live with political authority, which has a responsibility for providing social order. The eschatological position of contemporary Christians is that, in an imperfect world, we can't forswear responsible attempts to intervene in order to protect the innocent and we are called to responsible participation in, or at least cooperation with, political authority.

DLC So where does this leave us in relation to interpreting the Bible on these issues? It seems that how we understand this eschatological question is crucial. We both recognize that the Old Testament has no difficulty with a nation of God's chosen people going to war with God's support, but that the New Testament, written for a persecuted social minority, mandates the followers of Christ to abandon the sword. Your position seems to be that the Church was right subsequently to come to a different view: to decide, after gaining influence in the Roman Empire, that peace sometimes needs to be enforced by military means. This relies heavily on interpreting the teaching of Jesus as not being wholly adequate for living during the already-but-not-yet, as needing a more realistic supplement. My position is that the later development of just war doctrine sits uncomfortably with the teaching of the gospels, that Jesus' teaching was for Christians living in the real world, and that we cannot defer faithfulness to gospel teaching until the eschaton.

BES Does the New Testament in fact mandate followers of Christ to abandon the sword—all followers of Christ in all situations and all times? I don't see that it does. First of all, the few texts addressing this topic are enigmatic. I would characterize Jesus' statement about turning the other cheek as what is popularly called one of his "hard sayings"—an enigmatic statement that is not meant to be taken literally but to challenge the audience's way of thinking. Jesus' statement is not an absolute ban on forceful self-defense any more than his sayings that disciples should leave their families to follow him (such as Mk 10:28–30 and Lk 9:58–62) and that he came to set family members against one another (Mt 10:34–36) are a mandate for all disciples to forsake their families and become celibate. These teachings—even though each is a little different from the others—get their full meaning only in the context of Jesus' imminent eschatology. That eschatological context must be accounted for when we interpret the teachings today. Although the eschatology that emerges from the Bible as a whole, when interpreted through subsequent Christian tradition, is a balanced already-but-not-yet, Jesus' own eschatology leans heavily toward the not-yet-but-very-soon. The apparent aim behind Jesus' difficult and paradoxical sayings was to develop a community of disciples that preached and modeled the reign of God right then. Jesus called his closest followers to sacrifice a great deal—to give up families and jobs, to live on alms, and to share goods in common. He saw this community, along with his healings and exorcisms, as dramatic signs of God's inbreaking reign. The reign of God was inaugurated with Jesus, yet it is not fully realized. To be faithful to this reign, Christians must respond every day to the teachings we have been talking about. Yet the response can take various forms.

So I would not say that Jesus' teachings were inadequate for later Christian ethics but that, by necessarily focusing on his day and age, Jesus could only address certain questions and draw a limited range of explicit implications when instructing his disciples. Jesus taught vision, values, and ways of discernment that Christians could keep using. He also left certain prerogatives to the developing community. His statement in Matthew, "I will give you the keys of the kingdom of heaven, and whatever you bind on earth will be bound in heaven, and whatever you loose on earth will be loosed in heaven" (16:19), expressed the early Church's understanding that Jesus gave it authority to develop and interpret moral rules.

DLC   We have to be very careful not to use the category of "hard saying" as a way of ignoring sayings of Jesus that we find hard to accept or obey. I agree that any number of particular problems are not directly addressed by the Bible and that Christians have to discern a response to a current ethical problem using all the sources of ethics. But you seem to let Jesus only set us out on a vague direction of being responsive and responsible. Christians can find more determinative content than that in

Jesus' teaching; they are called to a distinctive way of living that is the practical working out of our identity as persons created, redeemed, and reconciled by God. This means that we start our ethical thinking by reflecting on God's love shown to us in Christ and the new possibilities arising from our salvation. We have heard God's good news for us: What does it mean for the way we are to live?

To answer this question we need to attend to God's word to us, primarily in scripture, but also through the witness of other Christians through the history of the Church, through our reasoned reflection on these sources, and through our own experience of how God works in our lives and the life of the world. This will mean we take responsibility for doing all we can for our neighbor and our enemy, as well as having concern for the welfare of nonhuman creation. But there are limits to what we can do. For me, the New Testament makes clear that part of what will make Christian life distinctive in a violent world is that Christians refuse to participate in its violence, instead making themselves subject to it. This is most explicit in the example of Jesus Christ, who could have brought more than twelve legions of angels to his aid (Mt 26:53) but chose instead to allow himself to be subject to the feeble human powers of the Jewish and Roman authorities. It is clear from his teaching that he intended this example to be a way of life that his disciples followed, too.

BES   I am glad you noted the Jewish and Roman authorities, because eschatology isn't the only component of Jesus' social context. His nonviolent ethic must be understood in light of those who wielded socioreligious authority and political authority in his day. My view is that the nonviolent but socially visible nature of the community of Jews that formed in response to Jesus' proclamation was a rebuff to the opinions of various Jewish groups of his day: the Zealots, who wanted to fight the Romans in a guerrilla war; the Essenes, who withdrew from society; and the Sadducees, who collaborated with the Romans' taxation and granting of perquisites to the favored.[23] Like almost every Palestinian Jew, Jesus would have detested Roman rule. But he denied both violent response (which would have been suicidal, in any case) and capitulation. Jesus took no stand on what it would mean for his later followers to respond to most political questions, including the question of policing or warfare if they were involved in the operations of government. It would have been very difficult for a Jewish disciple of Jesus in first-century Palestine to imagine serving in a police organization that was accountable to the populace and that operated under rules that limited the use of force.

But what Jesus taught and did, in his context, set boundaries and directions for later political engagements by Christians: aggressions with the aim of instituting a political messiah, as the Zealots did, is out; simple avoidance of political confrontation, as the Essenes did, is out; and collaboration with unjust political authorities, as the Sadducees did, is out. Living out the ethic of love with the goal of inclusive solidarity is mandated, even when that threatens the power structures of society and brings risk to those who practice love.[24]

DLC   I agree that Jesus decided that none of the options represented by the Zealots, Essenes, or Sadducees was legitimate, but we differ about how to interpret his example beyond this. This is another key difference between us. What you're trying to do is describe Jesus' actions in sufficiently wide terms to justify very different actions in another context. I think that's too much of a stretch. We have clear teachings that Jesus forbade his disciples from using violence. Even confronted with his own death, he chose not to respond violently. In innumerable cases, martyrs in the early Church understood that this response was demanded of them, too. There are some questions in ethics that are hard to resolve based on the teaching and example of Jesus; whether Christians can legitimately use violence is not among them. If you want to justify warfare, I'm still left thinking you have to go beyond the New Testament and appeal to the later judgments of the Church, which we'll look at in the next chapter.

CONCLUSION

In this chapter we have set out some of the background for a theological discussion of whether warfare can be considered legitimate. These themes will be taken up in a variety of ways in the chapters that follow as we grapple with how Christians ought to think about warfare in more detail. The next chapter is devoted to a discussion of the two main approaches Christians have taken toward war: pacifism and the just war tradition.

CHAPTER 2

Christian Pacifism and the Just War Tradition

The question of whether war can ever be morally legitimate has been given two major answers in the Christian tradition. "Pacifist" is the umbrella term for those who answer "no"; "just war theory" describes the position of those who answer with a qualified "yes." In the introduction we noted that holy war ideology and Christian realism are two other positions that have concluded that Christians may support warfare. Holy war cannot be considered seriously as an acceptable tradition of Christian moral thinking about warfare—although in the case of the Crusades, regrettably, the Church had not always taken this view. Christian realism is a recent divergence from the just war tradition that both just war thinkers and pacifists have felt obliged to engage, given its appropriation of important thinkers and themes in Christian history. However, in our opinion, it does not stand alongside the others as a full-fledged tradition of reasoning. In this chapter, therefore, we focus on pacifism and just war, making comparisons to Christian realism when it raises a significant challenge to the two traditions. We summarize these traditions' historical development and provide a guide for understanding them in a modern context, and then we address the relationship between them. The final section of the chapter is again devoted to an exchange of views, this time concerning which position has the best claim to be Christian.

PACIFISM

Christian pacifists believe that a life of Christian discipleship means renouncing the use of violence. As we shall see, pacifism was, with few exceptions, the

39

doctrine of the Church until the beginning of the fourth century. Since that time, the mainstream view of the Church has been that Christians can serve as soldiers. Yet there has been a consistent witness by a minority of Christians that this position cannot be squared with the example and teaching of Jesus or with a proper understanding of what it means to love one's neighbor. "Pacifism" refers to any ethic that aims to promote peace and to limit violence. One of the marks of pacifism is nonviolence, that is, the refusal to use deadly force or any level of force that might cause physical injury. Nonresistance is the extreme practice of giving no forceful opposition to an evildoer. As we will see, Christian pacifists broadly support nonviolence as a personal lifestyle, but only a few Christian movements and thinkers have embraced nonresistance. Rather, they usually explain how Christians can challenge purveyors of injustice using techniques of nonviolent resistance. On the political level, most pacifists encourage governments to take nonviolent actions to achieve their goals, but only some believe that governments should be completely nonviolent.

Pacifism in the Early Church

For the first Christians, renouncing violence and living in peace was an important part of the new life of discipleship to which they had been called. They interpreted the teaching of Jesus, which we surveyed briefly in the last chapter, as prohibiting the use of any kind of violence. As a persecuted religious sect, Christians would not have had to face questions of military service, but as early as the middle of the second century, we find a clear statement of the link between Christian faith and living in peace. Justin Martyr (c. 100–165) claims the peacefulness of Christianity fulfils Isaiah's prophecy of swords being beaten into plowshares: "We who formerly used to murder one another do not only now refrain from making war upon our enemies, but also . . . willingly die confessing Christ."[1] At the end of century, Clement of Alexandria (died c. 215) similarly contrasts war and peace: "It is not in war, but in peace, that we are trained. War needs great preparation, and luxury craves profusion; but peace and love, simple and quiet sisters, require no arms nor excessive preparation."[2] In another work he instructs the rich to gather "an unarmed, an unwarlike, a bloodless, a passionless, a stainless host."[3] Tertullian (c. 160–c. 230) addresses the issue of military service forthrightly: "But how will a Christian man war, nay, how will he serve even in peace, without a sword, which the Lord has taken away?"[4] He also asks, "Shall it be held lawful to make an occupation of the sword, when the Lord proclaims that he who uses the sword shall perish by the sword? And shall the son of peace take part in the battle when it does not become him even to sue at law?"[5] Origen (c. 185–c. 253) is similarly uncompromising, explaining that Christians "no longer take up 'sword against nation,' nor do we 'learn war any more,' having become children of peace, for the sake of Jesus, who is our leader."[6]

Roman soldiers were required to take part in military religious rites, and some historians have suggested that early Christians' objection to idolatry, rather than to killing, was the motive for prohibiting military service. Others have pointed to examples where Christians did serve in the military in the second and third centuries, notably those who fought for the "Thundering Legion," whose prayers (according to Tertullian and others) led to a miraculous rainfall that rescued a campaign in the year 173.[7] It is clear, however, even from this brief survey, that Christians objected to military service on the grounds that use of the sword was prohibited to them as well as out of concern about participation in military cultic rites. Although these objections were not uniformly successful in preventing Christians from enlisting in the Roman army, they were the established view of the Church into the fourth century, as represented in Church discipline manuals and the writings and sermons of many Church leaders.[8]

It is important to note that objections to Christians using force in the second and third centuries were based on the belief that such activities were prohibited for the followers of Jesus, rather than the belief that the exercise of force could never be justified. Just as Paul affirms the right of political authorities to wield the sword in Romans 13, so Tertullian and Origen defend the Church against its Roman critics on the basis that it offers prayers for the security of the empire and on behalf of armies fighting in righteous causes.[9] We find, then, support for the defense of the empire by military means alongside an affirmation that, on the basis of the teaching of Jesus, Christians are not permitted to participate in this activity and must, therefore, render their service to the empire in other ways.

Christian Witness to Nonviolence after Constantine

The breathtaking change in the social location of the Church following Constantine's conversion to Christianity and his edict mandating toleration of the religion in 313 led to a major upheaval in Christian thinking about war. Christians, suddenly finding themselves transformed from a persecuted sect to a prominent position of influence within the Roman Empire, had quickly to come to terms with their new status. For Ambrose (c. 339–397), Bishop of Milan, recognizing the Church's common interest in the empire's defense against barbarians was not difficult: "Not eagles and birds must lead the army, but thy name and religion, O Jesus."[10] Only clergy were forbidden to participate in the military; former soldiers—together with civil magistrates and murderers—were forbidden to enter holy orders.[11] Ambrose was not uncritical of the empire and was himself involved in nonviolent disputes with imperial forces as well as in effective challenges to the excessive violence of Theodosius I. By 416, however, the shift in Christian thinking made it possible for Theodosius II to issue an edict specifying that only Christians could serve in the army.

Even though attitudes in the Church toward military service before Constantine were somewhat diversified, we must recognize continuing differences of views once approval of military service had become mainstream. Thousands of Christians were dissatisfied with the consequences of the new relations between Church and empire, and, led by individuals such as Anthony the Hermit (died c. 356), many left their communities in search of a place where they could live in fidelity to the literal teaching of Christ. Pachomius (died c. 346) and Martin of Tours (c. 315–c. 397) were prominent examples of Christians who left the army because they considered it incompatible with their calling. As a young man, Martin was forced to serve in the army but asked his commander for permission to leave, saying, "I am a soldier of Christ and it is not lawful for me to fight."[12] Accused by the commander of cowardice, Martin offered to stand on the frontline, armed only with a cross. Even in the context of the widespread barbarian attacks suffered by Christian communities, leading to the sack of Rome in 410, there are many accounts of nonviolent acts of witness by Christians, which often led to the conversion of those threatening violence. Despite the permissive shift following the conversion of Constantine, clear evidence suggests that a significant minority of Christians continued to believe in the illegitimacy of violence. Although this belief was largely expressed in the prohibition of military service for the clergy and monks, we should not conclude that the Christian laity was unconcerned about the issue; many decided to become monks because they were impatient with what they perceived as compromises in Christian teachings once Christianity gained favored political status.[13]

In following centuries it remained the stable view that it was permissable for ordinary Christians to engage in warfare. The tension caused by the juxtaposition of this policy with the New Testament precepts, however, gave rise to a series of movements expressing dissatisfaction with this status quo. Notable are the following:

- The Peace of God and Truce of God movements in the tenth and eleventh centuries sought to limit the permissible targets and occasions for armed conflict.
- Condemnation of the Crusades or of the abuses committed by crusaders was voiced by Peter the Venerable in 1122, the Franciscan philosopher Roger Bacon in 1271, and other Church leaders.[14]
- The Franciscans and other monastic tertiary orders imitating Jesus' peaceful way of life became popular in the thirteenth century.
- Sects such as the Waldenses, the Lollards, and the Hussites—though controversial and flawed in various regards—embraced pacifism and challenged the comfortable compact that the medieval Church had made with political power. These groups presaged the radical wing of the Protestant Reformation, including its pacifist churches.

These examples make clear that many Christians did not have an easy conscience about wielding the sword in the name of their faith. However, many of these initiatives clearly could not withstand the powerful societal pressures toward the use of force; the Peace of God and Truce of God movements were appropriated by the feudal aristocracy into violent tools, and many of the sects who initially espoused pacifism later turned to arms to defend themselves. Even the monastic witness to peace was corrupted through the creation of military orders of knights.[15]

Since the Reformation, however, the growth of the peace churches represents a renewed witness to the nonviolent demands of the Christian gospel. The Anabaptists, followed by the Mennonites, Hutterites, Quakers, and the Brethren, all bore witness to the incompatibility between bearing the sword and Christian discipleship. Although they have faced difficult choices regarding the demands of government—such as military conscription and payment of war taxes—they have succeeded in sustaining a clear pacifist vision, which in the past century has given rise to a wide range of peace organizations objecting to warfare and supporting conscientious objection.

From this brief survey of the pacifist strand of the Christian tradition, the diversity in the motivations and aims of those who considered the use of arms to be illicit for Christians should be clear. For Tertullian and Origen, pacifism was a Christian vocation with few implications for wider society; they were happy, for example, to offer prayers for the success of the Roman armies. Following Constantine's patronage of the Church, however, Christians began to reflect on the import of the gospel for the affairs of nations. Although this reflection led many Christians to justify war in some circumstances, many others were inspired to espouse a Christian teaching of peace as part of a broader vision for society than had been possible before Constantine. Movements such as the medieval Peace of God were aimed not just at ensuring that Christians did not engage in violence themselves but also at reducing the incidence and destructiveness of warfare. Later movements for reform of the Church were different again, often prioritizing the achievement of faithful Christian practice by means of withdrawing from the world and leaving it to its own sinful devices. Thus, pacifist Christians took a range of positions with regard to the wider world: some accepted the appropriate use of force by others, others tried to make the wider world more peaceful, and others separated from the wider world they thought had gone astray.

Modern Versions of Pacifism

Events in the twentieth century changed the context for thinking about pacifism significantly. Even before World War I, labor unions protested against sending workers to die in a war they had no stake in. The mass killing of troops during the war gave rise to a widespread disillusion about warfare as a means of resolving conflicts and to a consequent growth in peace movements in Europe. Concurrently, clear evidence of the efficacy of nonviolent action was demonstrated in the campaign led by Mahatma Gandhi against the British Empire in India. Gandhi's peaceful protests inspired many pacifists to believe that they did not have to sacrifice effectiveness in combating injustice when they rejected the use of violence.

The issue of effectiveness provoked hard questions for the peace movement: Should nonviolent action be promoted as the most effective means to address particular kinds of conflicts, or was it a moral demand irrespective of the consequences? World War II persuaded many that nonviolence was not likely to be effective against all opponents, though nonviolent action was politically important after the war in the shape of antinuclear protests in Europe and anti–Vietnam War protests in the United States. Many different peace organizations flourished during the century, including the International Peace Bureau (formed in 1891), the International Fellowship of Reconciliation (1919), War Resisters International (1921), and the Peace Pledge Union (1934). Within this broad movement, quite different perspectives about aims and methods were soon apparent. Some argued for the formation of an international police force to resolve disputes between nations, whereas others sought the destruction of all weapons, by direct action if necessary.

To comprehend the wide variety of perspectives and motivations of positions that are termed pacifist—John Howard Yoder has identified twenty-nine variants of religious pacifism alone[16]—it is helpful to consider four scales onto which particular pacifist positions can be mapped.

Principled or Strategic? A *pacifism of principle* is motivated by the belief that violent acts—or particular kinds of them—are unacceptable whatever the results of using or not using them are likely to be. Renouncing violence is an unconditional ethical demand that must be observed irrespective of any other considerations. Christians who believe that Jesus' teaching of turning the other cheek means that Christians are prohibited from using violence clearly exemplify this principled pacifism, though many have derived similar commitments from other faiths or nonreligious philosophies.

Strategic pacifism, in contrast, renounces violence on the basis that the use of violence is illegitimate in some contexts but legitimate in others. Emil Brunner, for example, wrote in 1932 that war could have been justified some decades ago but has now "outlived itself," having become "so colossal that it can no longer exercise any useful function."[17] In the same spirit, the 1980s saw many Christians identify themselves as "nuclear pacifists," meaning that they believed the destructive potential of nuclear weapons made any resort to war illegitimate. The key difference with the principled position is that strategic pacifism is rooted in the belief that violence is illegitimate because of its likely results rather than because of any absolute prohibition. There is obvious continuity between this view and the just war tradition, which also recognizes that in some circumstances the use of violence is counterproductive.

The difference is finally one only of degree; for an individual who believes that no modern war is likely to be justifiable, "pacifist" seems a better label than "just war advocate."

Another group to be noted here is that which turns to nonviolent methods of resolving conflicts or causing political change because it judges that such means are more likely to be effective than using violence. The use of nonviolent means is then a strategic choice rather than one based on principle, often where a popular movement is confronting a regime of overwhelmingly superior military power. Obviously, principled pacifists can use nonviolence in an effective way, following the example of Gandhi and Martin Luther King Jr. But strategic pacifists would be prepared to consider violent methods if nonviolent ones are not thought to be effective; the choice of the African National Congress (ANC) in South Africa to turn to limited violent attacks in the 1960s, 1970s, and 1980s after many decades of nonviolent protest is one example of such a choice. (It is worth noting that the ANC's greatest effectiveness arguably coincided with Nelson Mandela's return to a strategy of nonviolent resistance in the 1990s.[18])

Absolute or Classical? *Absolute pacifists* are those who renounce any use of force, whatever the circumstances. This prohibits participation not only in warfare but also in the criminal justice system. Count Leo Tolstoy, the Russian novelist and social commentator, believed that the Christian gospel required an absolute pacifism of this kind:

> I now understood the words of Jesus: "Ye have heard that it hath been said, An eye for an eye, and a tooth for a tooth: but I say unto you, That ye resist not evil." Jesus' meaning is: "You have thought that you were acting in a reasonable manner in defending yourself by violence against evil, in tearing out an eye for an eye, by fighting against evil with criminal tribunals, guardians of the peace, armies, but I say unto you, Renounce violence; have nothing to do with violence; do harm to no one, not even to your enemy."[19]

This is a demanding and strongly countercultural position. On the personal level, Tolstoy commends a lifestyle of nonresistance, not simply nonviolence.[20] On the political level, although Tolstoy never espoused anarchism, it is clear that no conventional state could exist with his radical pacifist vision.

Recognizing this difficulty with absolute pacifism, many pacifists have adopted instead a *classical pacifism* that distinguishes between the legitimate use of force in policing and its often illegitimate use in wars between nation-states. This conviction rests on the belief that there is a morally relevant difference between a state's use of police force to preserve order within its borders and its use of military force against other nations. This point is contested by many just war theorists, who argue that military action is merely a continuation of policing. Classical pacifists resist collapsing all forms of force together. But because they recognize the need to use limited force in restraining evil, they could support an international force to police disputes between nations. UN peacekeeping operations—even when soldiers are used—would be justifiable to classical pacifists.

Separatist or Politically Engaged? *Separatist pacifists* seek an existence at a distance from the concerns of the world. Christians should seek, as far as possible, to avoid the taint that involvement with the world inevitably brings. Separatist pacifists, therefore, often form communities that literally separate themselves, living as self-sufficiently as possible outside normal social structures. Because they do not acknowledge political responsibility in the wider society, they recognize no necessity to consider what a nation needs from them in order to thrive. This commitment to pacifism is straightforward and uncomplicated by external demands—unless community members are conscripted or attacked. When that occurs, separatist pacifists tend to practice nonviolent resistance or nonresistance; for instance, they will go to jail rather than fight, even if they are drafted. Separatism was a mark of some of the Reformation peace churches and is still seen in Amish communities today.

Politically engaged pacifists believe their faith requires them to take an interest in the ordering of the common life of the nation-state. They do not see Christians as excused from political responsibility. Christians should, therefore, engage in reflection and conversation about how law and government should be ordered nationally and internationally. These pacifists clearly have much in common with just war thinkers on the matter of political responsibility, but they believe that using violence is not a proper way to participate in political life. This politically pacifist engagement can take a variety of forms; Tolstoy's pacifism drove him to be involved in the causes of protection for Russian pacifist dissenters and opposition to the Sino-Japanese War. His writings and his correspondence with Mohandas Gandhi profoundly influenced the latter's nonviolent movement against British rule in India, though Tolstoy would have disapproved of some of Gandhi's later political activities.[21] Others are drawn to adopting classical pacifism by their political engagement. Both are distinguishable from separatist pacifists, however, in their concern for the life of society as a whole.

Communal or Universal? *Communal pacifists* believe that pacifism is demanded of their own community but not of everyone in society. This is true, for example, for Christians who believe that nonviolence is a requirement of Christian discipleship but is not a wider moral demand. *Universal pacifists* believe that pacifism is a moral demand on everyone irrespective of their beliefs. At first glance, this fourth scale seems related to the previous one. It is certainly the case that separatist pacifists are most likely also to be communal; they have little expectation that the wider society will share their commitments. However, communal pacifists can equally well be politically engaged, believing that the prohibition on violence only applies to Christians while having an interest in the order of society. Origen and Tertullian are good examples of this position: prohibiting Christians from joining the Roman army while recognizing the essential role of the imperial forces in maintaining peace, and praying for their victory in battles.

Pacifism has been most commonly espoused in a Christian context by communal pacifists, those who believe it is a demand on the Church rather than society at large. Universal pacifism has more often been proposed by idealistic humanists. This is partly because most Christians have less optimism about how far they will be able to transform the world, given human sinfulness. Making the case for pacifism is also easier in its communal form, which does not require facing hard questions such as, what would be the fate of an unarmed nation-state?

With the spread of democracy and its broad approval by the churches in the twentieth century, it has proven somewhat easier for Christians to maintain a communal stance in their attitude toward the Church and to work for peace in political affairs. The middle of the spectrum could be phrased this way: Christians must be pacifist, and the world might become more peaceful through Christian witness and activism in cooperation with other pacifists.

To see how these scales can be used to identify particular pacifist positions, it may be helpful to take some specific examples, which are summarized in table 2.1.

TABLE 2.1

Mapping Examples of Christian Pacifists

Representative Authors or Groups	Principled or Strategic	Absolute or Classical	Separatist or Engaged	Communal or Universal
Origen and Tertullian	principled	classical	engaged	communal
Hutterites	principled	absolute	separatist	communal
Leo Tolstoy	principled	absolute	engaged	universal
Emil Brunner	strategic	classical	engaged	universal

1. Origen and Tertullian believed that Jesus prohibited Christians from taking the sword, so their pacifism was principled rather than strategic. There is no evidence that they were displeased with Christians participating in other civil roles, such as policing, in the Roman Empire, so their position was classical rather than absolute. They affirmed the support of Christians for the Roman Empire, so their pacifism was politically engaged rather than separatist. However, as noted earlier, they only applied the prohibition on the use of the sword to Christians, so their position is communal rather than universal.

2. The Hutterites were one of the sixteenth-century Anabaptist groups that formed their own settlements in order to live out the Christian life more consistently. They believed that pacifism was a biblical teaching, so were principled rather than strategic. They did not believe that Christians should use force in any form, so they were absolute rather than classical pacifists. Their desire for new settlements indicates that they were separatist rather than politically engaged, and their belief that the teaching of Jesus applies only to Christians indicates that they were communal rather than universal in orientation.[22]

3. Leo Tolstoy believed that the gospel made a radical demand for nonviolence on all Christians. He also considered, however, that the whole of society would be better off if everyone adopted nonviolence, and he was prepared to accept the implications for a very different view of political authority as a result. His pacifism was, therefore, principled rather than strategic, absolute rather than classical, politically engaged rather than separatist, and universal rather than communal.

4. We noted earlier that Emil Brunner was an example of a strategic pacifist because he believed that war was justified in the past, but given the destructive power of modern weaponry, it was no longer an effective tool. Brunner had no problem with use of force in policing, was concerned for the implications for the whole of society, and thought everyone should take a similar view of war. His pacifism, therefore, was strategic rather than principled, classical rather than absolute, politically engaged rather than separatist, and universal rather than communal.

Clearly, then, there are considerable differences in the versions of pacifism adopted by various groups of Christians, both in the past and in the present. This makes clear that the pacifist strand of the Christian tradition is a diverse and complex phenomenon and not all arguments either in favor or against pacifism will apply to each alike.

JUST WAR TRADITION

Most people—Christian or not, pacifist or not—accept that Jesus taught and lived a nonviolent ethic. That Jesus was regarded by the early Church—and is widely regarded now—to have been pacifist seems to pose an insuperable obstacle to a Christian ethic of justified war. However, the mainstream of the Catholic and Protestant traditions has held to the just war tradition for 1,600 years, and the majority of Christians today accept the moral necessity of some wars. How Christians could contemplate this possibility needs to be explained in a way that neither contorts Jesus in order to make him a promoter of war nor dismisses his teaching as constrained to its historical circumstances and, therefore, irrelevant today. The former option is hardly plausible, though it rears its head in unreflective statements by Christians all the time, with the holy war mentality lurking close behind. The latter option is one that many Christians disavow, but it is always possible that we simply rationalize away the hard teachings of Jesus.

The path between these extremes is to place the moral authority of Jesus in the full context of Christian convictions about God, humanity, social order, and eschatology. Advocates of the just war position need not deny that Jesus lived and taught nonviolence, nor should they deny that peace is God's goal for humanity and the essence of the Christian life. Rather, they affirm that the path from Jesus' ethic to God's goal runs through an earthly life that is between the times and that requires political acts and judgments appropriate to this eschatological position. The Anglican theologian Oliver O'Donovan defends the just war position along these lines. His starting point is an affirmation that peace is the original and actual truth of God's creation, it is God's goal for history, and it is a practical demand laid upon us. Every human conflict is subject to God's judgment that there must be peace.[23]

The us-versus-them mentality that is a common attitude in war should never be blessed with the language of justice. So how can Christians be called to peace and yet accept just war? O'Donovan acknowledges that Jesus does, indeed, call Christians, as witnesses to the Gospel, to the practice of peace, to "the winning peace out of opposition," through the service of reconciliation.[24] However, God has also provided humanity with a time to live on earth before the coming of the reign of God; this is a time and place in which humans together, Christians and non-Christians alike, make judgments about how to live in a manner that is as orderly, fair, and humane as possible. To develop and guide the ordering of social life, Christians are called to be involved in politics; therefore, they are involved in making judgments and laws, some of which are aimed at the restraint of crime and violence.

Just war emerges as a corollary to the Christian call to political participation; it is a rare but sometimes necessary extension of the activities that Christians are always doing as citizens or allowing leaders to do in their name. O'Donovan sums the point this way: "Armed conflict can and must be reconceived as an extraordinary extension of ordinary acts of judgment; it can and must be subject to the limits and disciplines of ordinary acts of judgment. In the face of criminal warmaking, judgment may take effect through armed conflict, but only as armed conflict is conformed to the law-governed and law-generating shape of judgment."[25] This tightly worded claim is worth explaining; let us do so through examples. Consider the kinds of everyday political judgment in which you have a direct or indirect voice. Citizens of a town vote to increase educational funding through an increase in property taxes. The legislature votes to increase spending on prenatal and infant health care, supported by an increase in sales taxes. The legislature requires airlines to improve the security of aircraft, and the increased costs are added to fares. A robbery suspect is arrested, tried, and sentenced to prison. A riot breaks out after a sporting contest; police control the crowd with batons and make several arrests. All of these examples are "ordinary acts of judgment." All of these ordinary acts involve a measure of coercion; the decision forces some people to do what they otherwise would not do—often it is to pay taxes. This coercion is widely accepted as legitimate if it was decided upon in a fair manner and if there are good, public reasons for the action. In a democracy, these conditions are usually satisfied when laws are made and enforced, and if not, there are legitimate mechanisms for addressing the problem. The actions of police and the decisions of courts involve overt coercion, including arrest and incarceration. This coercion is not wanted and often not accepted as legitimate by the person so coerced, but still, it operates out of a broad consensus that a system of policing and judging is beneficial for society. Again, all actions need to be carried out under rules that ensure fairness and justice.

Now consider this example: The president or prime minister commits troops to a humanitarian intervention in response to a United Nations Security Council resolution; the troops fire on armed rebels who are attacking unarmed civilians. O'Donovan's point is that this set of actions is continuous with the preceding examples. Military actions and wars sit at the far end of the spectrum of coercive judgments. They are "extraordinary" because they involve the explicit and intentional use of force and because they cause more harm to all involved than most other acts of judgment. However, they do not differ in kind: They employ deadly force, as does policing, and they employ coercion, as all the examples do. Because military action is similar in kind to ordinary political acts, it must be controlled by similar moral rules. Historically, this insight led the Christian moral tradition to develop rules for the proper use of force; the list of these rules are often labeled "the just war theory." O'Donovan cautions that this term "is a misnomer, since it is not, in the first place, a 'theory,' but a proposal of *practical* reason; and it is not, in the second place, about 'just' wars, but about how we may enact just judgment even in the theatre of war."[26] These rules were developed through four historical stages—three stages in which the rules were gradually expanded in number, specified, and codified, followed by a fourth in which just war theory has been challenged to incorporate insights from pacifism.

Four Historical Stages in the Development of Just War

How did the Christian Church come to the point of involving itself in political judgments, a place far removed from its social location in the first three centuries of its existence? We saw how, once its political fortunes changed in the fourth century, the Church tried to accommodate soldiering as a viable vocation for Christians. The Church's developing appreciation of worldly responsibilities influenced its interpretation of biblical teachings, which in turn led the Church into new forms of thinking about political life. One of the tasks the Church undertook was to explain the conditions that made a war right or wrong in order to give guidance to the Christians who now led and fought wars.

Ambrose and Augustine. Augustine (354–430), the North African bishop who is a towering figure in both the Protestant and Catholic branches of Christianity, is usually considered the father of the Christian just war tradition. However, he built his theory on the ground prepared by his mentor St. Ambrose. "Prior to becoming the Bishop of Milan, Ambrose occupied the position of Roman governor of northern Italy, essentially a military post. He viewed the Roman Empire as the warder of peace, the pax romana, and preached that the ongoing assaults on the empire by Germanic tribes were divinely inspired as retribution for Roman paganism."[27] Ambrose drew upon the philosophy of Cicero by making justice the highest social virtue. Assuming a virtuous Christian citizen would fight when called upon by the state (because governmental power is part of God's dispensation, even if the ruler is pagan), Ambrose applied the virtue of justice to the conduct of fighting, calling on soldiers to risk their lives to protect the innocent. He distinguished their responsibility on the battlefield from the obligations of the leaders to call for war. His aim was not to provide guidance to rulers about how and when to wage war but to instruct Christians of their civil duties, which include fighting in wars for the protection of social order.

Augustine made similar assumptions about a Christian citizen's duty to obey political authority and contribute to the tasks of the civic life. His account of political order is complex. From a negative perspective, government is a necessity for restraining evil and injustice; Christians have to endure this essential function of government, even if it is headed by a pagan or unjust ruler. From a positive perspective, Christians have a common interest with non-Christians in the peace and order of worldly society; therefore, Christians should be prepared to cooperate with government for the sake of peace.[28]

Like Ambrose, Augustine's writings on war drew upon Cicero. But he moved beyond Ambrose by providing rudimentary criteria for determining when war may be justly waged: The cause of war must be just, the legitimate political authority must declare the war, and the authority must be rightly motivated in doing so.

> A great deal depends on the causes for which men undertake wars and on the authority they have for doing so; for the natural order, which seeks the peace of mankind, ordains that the monarch should have the power of undertaking war if he thinks it advisable, and that the soldiers should perform their military duties in behalf of the peace and safety of the community.[29]

The natural order that God ordained is a state of peace; the only credible justification for war is to restore peace and the order that brings peace. Augustine does not want the ruler to rush to this solution, for "it is a higher glory still to stay war itself with a word, than to slay men with the sword, and to procure or maintain peace by peace, not by war."[30] This is a caution to rely on war only as a last resort. Augustine applies the requirements of justice and compassion to soldiers as well, but, like Ambrose, he distinguishes levels of responsibility. Hence, a solider must obey orders even from an unjust ruler.

Lisa Sowle Cahill explains the complicated strategy these authors used to accommodate Jesus' teaching about turning the other cheek:

> Christian authors have progressively restricted the practical force of New Testament sayings against violence ("turn the other cheek," "go the second mile," "love your enemies") by making one or more of the following assertions: the sayings define a "higher" Christian life (for example, of the clergy) but need not be taken literally on the "lower" plane (for example, by the laity); that they must be interpreted strictly regarding actions on one's own behalf but not if one is removing or preventing harm to others; that they apply to the inner realm of loving intention but not to the outer realm of just action; that they apply to the decisions of private citizens but not to those of public authorities acting in an official capacity (who have the right to command their subordinates, for example, soldiers).[31]

All four of these strategies can be found in the works of both Augustine and Ambrose. The "inner/outer" distinction is perhaps the most surprising and controversial. Augustine interprets Jesus' command to turn the other cheek to require "not a bodily action, but an inward disposition."[32] The soldier outwardly gives physical obedience to the ruler while giving inwardly a spiritual obedience to Christ's law of love. Augustine counsels the Christian soldier—or indeed, any Christian required to use force—to be "prepared" to love the enemy and to maintain an attitude not of anger and selfishness but of justice and objectivity. So the Christian can continue to love the enemy in combat by distinguishing the sinner from the sin and by directing the use of force toward the sinner's bad actions. At the same time, both authors apply the "for oneself/for others" distinction to self-defense. In a situation of personal attack outside the context of a civil role (such as police officer or soldier), a Christian is still expected to turn the other cheek literally, by refusing to respond with deadly force.

Aquinas. Thomas Aquinas (c. 1225–1274), a Dominican monk from Italy and influential teacher at the University of Paris, was the great systematizer of the theological tradition in the Middle Ages. He was likewise a systematizer and developer of the just war tradition. He unified the tradition before him into three clearly listed criteria: that the war be just, be waged by a legitimate authority, and fought with the right intention. In addition, he advanced the moral principles of proportionality and double effect, which laid the foundation for the later systematization of criteria for just conduct in war (jus in bello).[33]

Proportionality emerged when Aquinas justified some kind of resistance or rebellion (the actual options and means for which were not clear) against a tyrannical government. When a leader or group (probably a local magistrate or prince leading citizens against a tyrant) has cause to fight, fighting is not morally acceptable unless it also promises to bring about greater good than harm. Like Augustine and all the proponents of the just war tradition, Aquinas seeks peace and just order as the goal. Notice that this rudimentary acceptance of rebellion reflects a departure from Ambrose's and Augustine's requirement to obey an unjust ruler.

Recalling the four strategies for reconciling New Testament teachings on nonviolence to the social necessity of war, Aquinas maintained that loving the enemy and turning the other cheek apply as inner dispositions, and he affirmed the higher/lower distinction that barred clergy from fighting (this ban was, by that time, part of canon law). However, he departed from Ambrose and Augustine by reconciling the responsibilities of public and private life and accepting the just use of force both in defense of others and of oneself. Aquinas justified self-defense on grounds that were not open to those fourth-century theologians because they thought the urge to defend one's own life was motivated by selfish desire. Instead, Aquinas saw the preservation of life as reasonable, as part of the natural law. Provided that the action (rebutting the aggressions of an attacker) is not evil in itself and that the intended effect is to preserve one's life, one can fight back against the attacker even if one foresees that the attacker might die.

This reasoning became known as "the principle of double effect," which states that an act with good and bad effects may be done if four conditions are satisfied:

1. The action itself is not evil.
2. The bad effect is not intended.
3. The bad effect is not a means to the good effect.
4. There is a serious ("proportional") reason for allowing the bad effect to occur.

A person may perform the action and tolerate the bad result as long as the aim is the good result, which is sufficiently good to justify causing the bad result. Notice that for self-defense to be justified by the principle of double effect, the aim to kill the attacker must not be the intention. The principle of double effect is not splitting hairs; in fact, it makes an important distinction between, on the one hand, fighting with the least force necessary to deter an attack or taking an available alternative to fighting (for example, running away or calling the police) and, on the other hand, aiming to kill the attacker whether or not it is essential to the self-defense.

Systematizing and Secularizing Just War Doctrine. The third stage of the historical development of the just war was one that specified the basic criteria, added additional ones, and systematized the doctrine into legal form. Several major figures in the Late Middle Ages built the just war tradition into a complete set of criteria and established these precepts into the nascent body of international law. Francisco de Vitoria (c. 1486–1546) was a Spanish Dominican whose two short books on just war were derived from the lecture notes of his students.[34] *On the Indians* and *On the Law of War* wrestled with Spain's conquests of the indigenous peoples of the Americas—a military and political campaign that greatly disturbed Vitoria and some other churchmen. These works developed an account of the rights and wrongs in war according to the natural law because the Indians were protected neither by European law nor by Christian fraternity. Vitoria gave particular attention to developing standards for noncombatant immunity and proportionality in the conduct of war, standards that forbade the inhumane treatment of the Indians at the hands of the Spaniards. He also explicitly discounted religion as a reason for waging war, a position toward which the medieval theologians had been moving. Vitoria's student Francisco Suarez (1548–1617) transferred Vitoria's ideas into the language of the canon lawyers, further setting the stage for their codification into international law, and expanded the criteria of last resort and noncombatant immunity.[35]

Hugo Grotius (1583–1645), a Dutch Protestant lawyer, is regarded as the founder of international law for compiling and interpreting the diverse laws, compacts, and legal writings of the preceding centuries into a body of law. His major work, *On the Law of War and Peace*, developed an account of the "law of nations" or "peoples" (*jus gentium*). At the time that Grotius and other international lawyers were systematizing the body of international law regarding war, the Protestant Reformation was seizing Europe. The feudal system was breaking up, and the concepts of limited government and democratic accountability were taking root in Europe. In this context Grotius extended restrictions on the authority of monarchs, reduced the causes for war to self-defense, and systematized for the first time the rules regarding the protection of civilians and prisoners.[36] He considered the rules of war to be founded on God-given natural law, but it was a notion of natural law distanced from the control of the Church and even of God ("it cannot be changed even by God himself").[37] Grotius's systematizing and secularizing of just war doctrine laid foundations in international law that endure today.

Late Twentieth-Century Rethinking of Just War. Until the mid-twentieth century, only marginal Protestant and Catholic groups and thinkers challenged the assumptions of the just war doctrine. Several mainline Protestant denominations, acting through the Fellowship of Reconciliation organization, supported a peace-based agenda in response to World War I, but Reinhold Niebuhr's scathing attacks on their positions helped to mute Protestant criticism of just war theory for another several decades. Likewise, most Catholic commentators during World War II disparaged pacifists, charging them with propagating a false and dangerous idea.[38] Dorothy Day's Catholic Worker movement, which maintained an absolute pacifist position during both world wars, was given the cold shoulder—and worse—by Catholic leaders and citizens in America. It was not until the late 1940s, when people around the world were sizing up the devastations of World War II and glancing apprehensively at the advent of the nuclear age, that a peacemaking agenda gained momentum within Christianity.

More Christians began to value the pacifist witness and its support for practices of conflict resolution, even if not agreeing with the position as a whole. Most Christian denominations strengthened their pronouncements for causes of peace and began creating parachurch organizations that worked for peace and reconciliation in various ways. The churches generally supported the creation of the United Nations, the promulgation of the UN Declaration of Universal Human Rights, and the negotiation of treaties to eliminate nuclear weapons. A dramatic example of the shift in thinking can be seen in official Catholic teaching. In his Christmas Message of 1956, Pope Pius XII forbade Catholics to claim conscientious objection;[39] yet in 1965, the Second Vatican Council "praise[d] those who renounce the use of violence in the vindication of their rights . . . provided this can be done without injury to the rights and duties of others or the common good."[40] This statement is emblematic of the greater respect that Catholic, Protestant, and Orthodox churches began showing for their pacifist members and movements.

This shift in attitude about pacifism went hand in glove with Christian rethinking of the just war tradition. Both just war and pacifism are developing traditions; in this post–World War II stage, they have increasingly influenced each other through the dialogue and cooperation within a context of improving ecumenical and interreligious relations. This fourth stage of development is still underway; the paths it may take are still open. What seems likely, though, is that Christian just war thinkers and Church leaders will continue to

- converse and cooperate with Christian pacifists,
- resist a punctual approach to warfare in favor of making ethical judgments on the root causes of social conflicts,
- take a critical attitude toward governments that claim the mantle of just war,
- recover the theological foundations of the just war tradition, and
- apply the tradition's criteria strictly.

TABLE 2.2
The Just War Criteria

Just decision (jus ad bellum)

The war must have a just cause.

The war must be waged by a legitimate authority.

The war must be fought with a right intention.

The war must be a last resort.

The expected results of the war must be proportionate.

There must be a reasonable hope of military success.

Just conduct (jus in bello)

The weapons and acts of fighting must be discriminating: noncombatants may never be intentionally targeted.

The weapons and acts of fighting must be proportionate.

All the legal rights of enemy soldiers and civilians must be honored.

Naturally, all of these characteristics are subject to debate; they are at issue at various points throughout this book. An ongoing debate concerns how to specify and apply the just war criteria. We turn next to a summary of the content of these criteria, which are listed in table 2.2.

Just Decision Criteria—Jus ad Bellum

The war must have a just cause. A just cause is one that protects one's nation or innocent third parties from harm and restores a state of peace and just order. Richard Regan categorizes six types of potentially just causes, including some that are strongly affirmed in the tradition and others that have a foothold in the tradition but that are also controversial.[41] The substantial causes are

- defense of national territory and international space,
- preemptive attack against imminent aggression,[42] and
- the rescue of one's citizens unjustly held by another nation.

Nations have also invoked the grounds of

- rectifying economic injury,
- vindicating territorial claims, and
- punishing and preventing terrorism.

Only the first of the six is explicitly allowed in the United Nations Charter, although the second can be covered by the first, as long as the threat that provokes preemption is genuinely imminent. For any claim of national self-defense to hold weight, the offense by the aggressor must be actual, intentional, of substantial importance, verifiable, and unilateral.[43] If there is good reason to hold nations accountable on one of the other grounds, military action, as a matter of international law, is supposed to be taken only upon authorization by the United Nations Security Council. Economic and territorial claims should almost always be handled by less aggressive means than war.

The war must be waged by a legitimate authority. Historically in the West, the legitimate authority was one who was the supreme sovereign for a territory, a monarch who received power by inheritance or brute conquest. Concepts of legitimacy based on the justice of rule became increasingly important in the Middle Ages. Aquinas held that a just ruler was one who took care of the common good; based on this principle, he and others began to allow for revolt against a despot.[44] Over time the democratic concept of legitimacy flowered, holding that the ruler is accountable to the citizenry as a whole. In modern nations—particularly, but not only, those shaped by the Western political tradition—the legitimate authority for a nation is a leader who justly holds office by constitutional procedures and is accountable to the people through democratic means. The legitimate-authority criterion has always excluded war by private citizens. But that does not mean that citizens have no say; in the modern democratic system, the populace itself has responsibility for deciding whether war waged in their name is just.[45]

The war must be fought with a right intention. Right intention, along with just cause and legitimate authority, is one of the earliest just war criteria. However, it has also been one of the most difficult criteria to apply because intentions are opaque, sometimes even to oneself. From its inception the criterion has stipulated that leaders waging war search their hearts to ensure that their true motive is to ensure justice and that they are not acting on the basis of passions. Augustine, for instance, wrote that "the real evils in war are love of violence, revengeful cruelty, fierce and implacable enmity, wild resistance, and the lust of power, and such like."[46] A contemporary statement of the criterion provides that "ulterior motives, such as a power or land grab, or irrational motives, such as revenge or ethnic hatred, are ruled out. The only right intention allowed is to see the just cause for resorting to war secured and consolidated."[47] Just war theorists have realized, though, that they should be realistic regarding leaders' mixed motives; they should not expect that political and strategic considerations never come into play—indeed, sometimes these considerations are necessary in order to ensure that military success is possible (which is another jus ad bellum criterion). This awareness of mixed motives does not entail that it is impossible to judge leaders' intentions. In fact, some just war thinkers claim that right intention should be given greater prominence, provided that its use is objectively connected to a theory of political justice.[48] Right intention can and should be objectively tested by asking whether the decision makers have honored all the other just war criteria—a question that can be answered by interpreting available evidence.[49] A positive answer suggests that the war was pursued with a right intention; a negative answer indicates that the leaders' intentions were corrupt.

The war must be a last resort. Other means of resolving a quarrel between nations such as negotiation, mediation, and arbitration, must have been tried or carefully considered and rejected as unworkable with good reason. If no alternative means to secure the just cause remains, a declaration of war must be made so that the warring nation is accountable to the world community and so the opponent can sue for peace on the stated ground.[50] There has been a vigorous and still unresolved debate among contemporary thinkers particularly in light of the 2003 Iraq War—as to how far authorities must go to exhaust options short of war.

The expected results of the war must be proportionate. Proportionality is a principle that appears in both the ad bellum and in bello criteria. As a criterion for decision, it requires that the authorities ask whether the proposed war can reasonably be expected to bring about more good than the evils of destruction that are to be suffered by all sides. Although this determination cannot be made with surety in advance, leaders are required to research the facts, seek good counsel from advisors, make sound judgments based on past examples, and consider the long-term impact of their planned campaign.

There must be a reasonable hope of military success. This criterion is implied by the proportionality criterion. If a political leader cannot reasonably

expect to win against a more powerful foe, it is wrong for the leader to subject citizens to the evils of destruction, even for a just cause. Obviously, in
wars such as the two wars in Iraq, there was no doubting that the U.S.-led
coalitions could achieve military victory. The criterion has more influence
with nations that clash with opponents of similar power, for nations that face
the use of nuclear weapons, and for liberation movements that are up against
a national army. But is any nation or group, when it is strongly convinced of
its justice and influenced by ideological motives, willing to forgo a fight because the prospects for success are murky? As with all the criteria, unethical
outcomes result when cool heads do not prevail.

Just Conduct Criteria—Jus in Bello

*The weapons and acts of fighting must be discriminating: Noncombatants
may never be intentionally targeted.* The principles of *discrimination* and
noncombatant immunity—sometimes separated, often combined into a single criterion—are central to the just war tradition. The principle is simply that
those who are not fighting are technically innocent of aggression and so must
not become the target of an intentional attack. There are two key questions
involved in this criterion. The first is who counts as a combatant? The category of the innocent basically comprises all those people who are not fighting. Combatants are enemy soldiers—those currently engaged in a military
campaign and specifically those actively fighting. Therefore, soldiers have a
legal and ethical duty to capture—not kill—surrendering soldiers; it has even
been considered unseemly in military culture to fire upon enemy soldiers
who are not dressed and ready to fight.[51] All other citizens are immune from
attack. As the nature of warfare has changed, questions have been raised
about who counts as a combatant. For instance, what of those citizens who
support the war effort economically? In the two world wars, whole nations
were mobilized into war production. Should the cities that held the factories
that made the munitions be objects of attack? Just war thinkers have not been
willing to give ground and consider those involved in military production as
combatants.[52] Another difference is that armies once met on remote battle-
fields. Sometimes that still happens, yet the twentieth century saw frequent
guerilla wars, in which an insurgent enemy hides among noncombatants.

   This development leads to the second key question raised by the criterion: Are foreseeable losses of civilian life morally acceptable? Under the

principle of double effect, soldiers may shoot on legitimate military targets anticipating that some innocent civilians may die, as long as the deaths of civilians is not their intention and the action meets the standard of proportionality (discussed following). Much controversy attends this stipulation. If too loosely applied, this "foreseeing but not intending" can become an easy justification for the killing and injury of civilians. The tradition tries to keep the application strict through several stipulations. First, intention is determined by the nature of the action, not the wishes of the soldiers or commanders. Second, the types of weapons used and the way they are used must be subject to measured control.[53] Third, the attack on the military target must be necessary in the prosecution of the war.[54] According to most just war thinkers, nuclear, chemical, and biological weapons inherently violate the second stipulation so there is no way their use can be morally justified.

The weapons and acts of fighting must be proportionate. Leaving aside indiscriminate targeting and uncontrollable weapons, what is to be said of military actions and strategies that do not intentionally target civilians but result in the deaths of many of them? Does double effect not become a subterfuge allowing armies to kill civilians as long as they don't wish to? To prevent such a result, the principle of proportionality—that one must reasonably expect to achieve more overall good than harm—also applies to the fighting of the war. For example, an attack that would possibly stop the advance of an enemy battalion on an army's position while also risking the death of a dozen civilians could be proportional and discriminate, but an attack on a building that probably houses a handful of guerillas while running the risk of killing fifty civilians in an adjacent building might be discriminate (because the guerillas are the target) but not proportionate. There is no numerical formula for determining when proportionality is violated; rather, it is a prudential judgment one should consider along with other factors. Michael Walzer argues that even this principle can be insufficient; it becomes eroded unless the military practices "due care," which is "a positive commitment to save civilian lives," even when that means soldiers put themselves at risk.[55]

All the legal rights of enemy soldiers and civilians must be honored. A number of customary practices and Church-mandated practices regarding the rights of soldiers and civilians were codified into international law by Grotius and others. In the last century, a number of important treaties and conventions have been adopted by the vast majority of nations, the most significant being the Geneva Red Cross conventions of 1864, 1906, and 1929; the Hague conventions of 1907; and the four Geneva conventions of 1949.[56] It is incumbent upon all belligerents to respect these rights scrupulously, even though the means for punishing violators remains inadequate.

THE RELATIONSHIP BETWEEN THE TRADITIONS

Now that we have surveyed both pacifism and just war theory within Christianity, it makes sense to ask about the relationship between these traditions. We cannot do so adequately without reintroducing Christian realism, which we earlier noted as an important third party in the debate among Christians regarding war and peace. Realism in its secular form is often treated as a rival tradition to pacifism and just war. We do not believe that a Christian form of realism can or should be accorded such status. Nevertheless, the Augustinian (as opposed to Thomistic) strain in the just war tradition and Reinhold Niebuhr's modern revival of what he called "Augustine's political realism"[57] exert a force on just war thinking. When deliberating on immediate questions of war, many Christians feel obliged to deal with the so-called real world and thus are tempted by realism's pragmatism. Similarly, realism aims to prevent terrible results from happening, which strongly appeals to human nature under stress. Few people want to believe that they would call all moral bets off, yet the risk of Christian realism is that it gives permission to a way of thinking that leads precisely to that situation.

Consideration of the jus in bello criteria of discrimination and proportionality in the context of the bombing of Japan by the United States is a good place to see where the Christian realist approach to warfare departs from most interpretations of the just war tradition. More than one hundred thousand civilians were killed in the attacks, a similar number were injured, and the nuclear radiation had serious long-term effects on the survivors and their children. Nonetheless, the use of the atomic weapons against Japan is often defended with the claim that it prevented even greater suffering and death on the part of American soldiers and Japanese soldiers and civilians. Without the bombings, the argument goes, Japan would not have surrendered, which would have led to further conventional air attacks on Japanese cities and a long and desperately difficult campaign by sea and land, with numerous casualties on both sides. This appeal is made in terms of proportionality; the attacks were justified because, although the destruction they caused was appalling, they prevented a situation that would have been still worse. Now even if we were to accept the judgment that using atomic weapons to destroy Hiroshima and Nagasaki was proportionate (which we dispute in chapter 4), the attacks remain unjustifiable according to the mainstream of the just war tradition because they are a clear and flagrant breach of the criterion of discrimination between combatants and noncombatants.[58]

Some Christians could be dissatisfied with a judgment that the option that brings about the best results is rendered illegitimate by the criterion of discrimination; at this point Christian realism has the potential to depart from just war thinking. Reinhold Niebuhr was ambivalent about the decision to drop the bombs, but conceded that the attacks were probably necessary in the final analysis (his qualified support will be further explained in chapter 4). This position is evidence of realist skepticism about the possibility of adhering to absolute moral norms. As we have hinted, however, not all interpreters of the just war tradition take a view of noncombatant immunity that rules out targeting civilians in all circumstances. Walzer, a secular just war theorist, suggests that the British firebombing of German cities until 1942 could be justified as the only response to a "supreme emergency," though the bombings of Hiroshima and Nagasaki could not be so justified.[59] For Jean Bethke Elshtain, a Christian political theorist, this permissiveness indicates that "just war discourse is hard to distinguish from modified realism."[60]

When we ask where the dividing line is between Christian realism and the just war tradition, therefore, we need to recognize the diversity among just war thinkers. Those who interpret the criterion of discrimination, together with other criteria, as inviolable principles are at a clear distance from realist thinkers such as Niebuhr. Other thinkers, such as Walzer, who judge that such principles may sometimes need to be overridden, have more in common with a realist position. Among modern Christian thinkers who claim the theory of just war, we can detect this commonality with realism in Methodist Paul Ramsey's questioning of strict noncombatant immunity in the Vietnam War because the Viet Cong guerillas were not playing by the rules;[61] in George Weigel's desire to see Catholic teaching on war be more accepting of the first use of force when the United States and other nations believe a rogue state has become a threat;[62] and in Elshtain's plea that Christians reclaim the legacy of Niebuhr in response to jihadist terrorism.[63] We believe that realism's tug on just war tradition presents risks for Christians who want to abide faithfully by the comprehensive Christian witness to peace. We will not prematurely rule out the validity of the Christian realist position, but we will test it carefully in our debates.

In our interpretation, then, Christian pacifism and just war theory agree in criticizing realism's sacrifice of principle for the sake of consequences. But do they share anything else? The traditions seem to present an either/or situation: either war is never a legitimate way of resolving conflicts for Christians or, under certain conditions, war can be a virtuous and responsible choice. Furthermore, we have seen that these two positions are opposed in their interpretation of New Testament teaching. Finally, the traditions stand in some tension on matters such as the legitimacy and role of political authority, whether Christian ethics aims to guide communal practice or establish universal norms, how engaged Christians should be with social and political life, and whether Christians are required to be effective in guiding world events.

Recently, however, many have suggested that despite these points of difference, there is a considerable degree of overlap between just war and pacifist positions. In particular, James Childress and others have claimed that they are each committed to a presumption against violence. Just war as a system points to a duty that persons in general as well as leaders of political communities have not to attack the lives of other persons. This obligation is neither absolute nor a mere rule of thumb. It is a strong duty that sometimes needs to be overridden, given that there are other moral obligations that pull on us. Each criterion in the theory—starting with legitimate authority, which identifies who has the right to decide a war is justified—can present a reason for overriding the presumption against attack on human life.[64] Just war theory and pacifism then share the view that the circumstances under which states take recourse to violence should be limited as narrowly as possible. Childress argued that just war theory and pacifism were complementary: Pacifists remind just war theorists of the presumption against war; just war theorists help pacifists with a framework for reflecting on particular wars and ways of restraining how wars are fought.[65]

One recent outworking of the approach that emphasizes the common ground between the pacifist and just war traditions is the *just peacemaking theory*, a collection of ten practices providing practical alternatives to war that was developed by pacifist and nonpacifist Christian ethicists working collaboratively.[66] These authors claim that the practices, if used with patience, can establish a peaceful and just resolution of conflicts using bloodless means. Table 2.3 lists these practices. Although few would wish to question whether both pacifists and just war theorists can agree on the value of such initiatives, some theologians have claimed that this is an example of superficial agreement masking a profoundly principled difference between pacifism and the just war tradition. They reject the idea that just war theory is best understood as a set of conditions for when a presumption against war can be overcome, and they argue that it is fundamentally rooted in an understanding of the providentially ordained role of political authority, exercising force where necessary to preserve peace. Although pacifists and just war theorists may happen to agree on particular ethical judgments from time to time, this agreement is more coincidental than rooted in any commonality of approach.[67]

To make sense of this divergence of view about the common ground between just war theory and pacifism, it is important to recall the breadth of positions each term can include. We have seen that pacifists can be motivated by a strategic assessment of what will work or by a belief about what the gospel requires; they may be absolutely opposed to all use of force or prepared to allow for the use of force in policing; they may have leanings to separatism or political engagement; and they may believe that the renunciation of war is just for the church community or applicable universally.

TABLE 2.3
The Practices of Just Peacemaking

Initiatives
  Support nonviolent direct action.
  Take independent initiatives to reduce threats.
  Use cooperative conflict resolution.
  Acknowledge responsibility for conflict and injustice, and seek repentance
    and forgiveness.
Justice
  Advance democracy, human rights, and religious liberty.
  Foster just and sustainable development.
Love and Community
  Work with emerging cooperative forces in the international system.
  Strengthen the UN and international efforts for cooperation and human rights.
  Reduce offensive weapons and weapons trade.
  Encourage grassroots peacemaking groups and voluntary associations.

What may be less clear is that there is similar diversity under the just war banner. There are those, for example, who interpret the just war criteria to indicate that few or none of the wars fought in the past fifty years were legitimate and who campaign against proposed wars as actively as pacifists. Others consider that—on grounds of humanitarian intervention or for self-defense—too few wars are fought, and so they attempt to lower the threshold for embarking on war in order to make it more common. It is unsurprising, then, to find that some pacifists and some just war theorists find they have more in common with each other than they do with those in their own camp. For example, we have seen that Tertullian and Origen supported with prayer the Roman armies in battle. They would, therefore, have a great deal in common with just war theorists who believe the Roman Empire was justified in its military campaigns, only differing on whether Christians should be permitted to serve in the armed forces. Other just war theorists might find it hard to assent to such Roman imperial ambitions, however, and might find more sympathy with those in the fourth-century monastic movement who sought to live apart from the compromises of living subject to a newly Christian empire.

Alongside the breadth of pacifist and just war positions, a second reason for different views about how far apart pacifism and just war theory stand is the relative importance given to theoretical underpinnings versus judgments on specific situations. More pragmatic types set greater store by the question of what we should do and so may support initiatives such as the just peacemaking practices. If pacifists and just war theorists can agree on where they stand in current debates, then the different rationales for their judgments seem less significant. Those who participate in the just peacemaking project temporarily set theoretical disagreements to one side and focus on what practical measures they can support. So do Christians of different perspectives when they engage in one of the practices, such as nonviolent direct action and grassroots peacemaking. Often, they join other religious believers and nonreligious persons in action on a certain political or social cause. Those who interpret pacifism or just war theory in such a way as to give little potential for such an overlapping consensus are more likely to see the disparate judgments in the context of their theoretical underpinnings. Such differences in temperament are worth keeping in mind as concerned Christians follow debates about war—and take their own stands on them.

DEBATING THE ISSUES

Many questions and concerns are raised when pacifism and just war vie to be understood as the most authentic Christian tradition. Here we try to answer some of the fundamental objections that are perennially raised against each position and to keep shedding light on the assumptions that lie beneath our respective positions. We aim to be clear about where the disagreements lie while keeping in view the possibilities for cooperation between Christians who embrace different ethics of war.

Tough Questions for Pacifists

BES Because we started the chapter with pacifism, let's put that position on the hot seat first. The best place to start might be with the most common question posed as a challenge to pacifists. Is it morally right—indeed, is it morally obligatory—to use deadly force to defend oneself and other individuals, such as family members, from an attacker who is about to use violence?

DLC In the first place, we need to get real. What kind of deadly force do you imagine me using? If you're suggesting a gun, I think that the risks of having a firearm in the house, the demands of keeping in training to be able to use it with accuracy, and the risk of provoking additional violence with its use, all mean that in the United Kingdom or the United States this is not a realistic means of self-defense, whatever one's beliefs. This balance of risk and benefit is recognized in the gun-ownership laws of the United Kingdom and most other democracies—though not in the United States.

Similarly, should I get training in how to kill with a kitchen knife or baseball bat? I'm sure I couldn't use these effectively otherwise. But if I was so trained, I'd be much more likely to use violence even when nonviolent means would be more effective. I don't find this a hard case personally because the most effective response I could make to an attack on my family would be to challenge an aggressor nonviolently. The Christian vocation to peacemaking includes confronting evil wherever possible, and could include restraining the use of force, by holding back a person about to hit another, for example. The boundary marker between this restraint of force and self-defense is when attacking the aggressor, rather than restraining him, is the only way to stop him. At that point, the action becomes violent: We decide that we would rather see violence done to the aggressor than allow him or her to be violent. For me, this is the kind of intervention that is incompatible with Christian discipleship; it's the kind of intervention Jesus rebuked Peter for using at his arrest.

BES At first blush, people suppose that just war tradition is gung ho for personal self-defense. But just because the tradition allows violent self-defense doesn't mean that it encourages it. The tradition probably saw the need to articulate the principle of private self-defense in the social conditions of prior centuries when people could not rely upon a regular police force. The moral recommendation to defend with deadly force belongs properly to the political authorities, that is, to the police. So I can very much agree with what you say about the problems of preparation, especially at the individual level. To prepare for self-defense by owning a gun is, for most individuals, almost always disproportionate; the gun is much more likely to be used against the owner or to be the occasion of a tragic accident than it is to be used in successful self-defense.[68] From society's point of view, allowing lightly regulated, extensive ownership of personal firearms is disproportionate. My country suffers an obscene number of handgun deaths annually as a result of our unwillingness to strike a more reasonable balance between individual rights and the common good.[69] Yet if a Christian's legitimate aim is to avoid harms and to restrain attacks against others when the police are unavailable, then there are some preparations that are proportionate, such as classes on self-defense against sexual assault, martial arts classes, carrying pepper spray, and installing an alarm system. And if, as can infrequently happen, a victim saw the chance to seize an attacker's gun or whack the attacker with a pipe, or whatever—I think her use of force would be just.

DLC The difficulty with the criterion of proportionality is that it is subject to a vicious circle: Bad acts from bad people lead good people to act in ways that would in other circumstances be considered bad. If everyone has big sticks, then it's proportionate for the Christian to get one; if everyone has guns, then it's proportionate for the Christian to get one; if everyone has nuclear weapons, then it's proportionate for the Christian to get them, too. Proportionality offers no escape from this downward spiral into chaotic mutual destruction. Pacifism never gets trapped in this cycle; it refuses to take the actions of others as justification for our own actions. Of course, just war theory attempts to place limits on the operation of the principle of proportionality; you should never deliberately target noncombatants, for example. But there is always pressure on these deontological norms, and so proportionality often gets to operate virtually unfettered, with disastrous consequences. For a pacifist, any legitimate use of force—in policing, for example—must be subject to tight principles not subject to proportionalist dilution.

BES   I would like to pause on the police for a moment, because their role is the middle ground between the individual and the nation on this question of self-defense. The ethics of policing in Western democracies draws on the same basic vision and principles as just war.[70] It's notable that the use of force by the police has recently been held up to stricter scrutiny. Ask any police officer, especially one who has matured into the job, and he or she will tell you that it is his or her aim never to fire a gun. An officer once told me, "If I have to fire, that means I have failed in my job." This attitude is now being thoroughly incorporated into police training. The use of deadly force is circumscribed at the private, police, and military level by the same basic principles: the just war criteria and related norms. So although I see just war as providing a coherent analysis at all three levels, I wonder if you can defend pacifism as applicable at all three. If a Christian wants to practice nonviolence as a personal ideal for himself or herself, that is fine. But as long as there are "bad guys" in the world, we will need governments to use their police powers domestically and military power internationally to protect people from harm and to bring evildoers to justice. If pacifists always recommend a path of negotiation and nonviolent responses to aggression, aggressors are sure to take advantage of that situation. A state simply can't act on the advice of pacifists—at least not all the time. To think otherwise is irresponsible. How do you respond to that charge?

DLC   Let's start by recognizing that to be human is to be vulnerable to the actions of others, and that to live humanely requires a strong element of trust in the goodwill of those about us. Driving on an undivided two-way road, for instance, requires a significant act of faith both in the ability of those traveling the other way to control their vehicles and in their desire to avoid collisions. Passing someone on the street similarly expresses considerable confidence that he or she doesn't intend to injure you with some concealed weapon. Of course, such trust is not always justified. Some people are incompetent or irresponsible drivers and cause accidents; some people attack strangers for gain or even without reason. But what makes life possible is that almost all of the time we can trust this basic level of nonmaleficence on the part of our neighbors. The key point I want to draw out of this observation is that if we want to live anything like the lives we are used to, we cannot—pacifists, just war theorists, realists—guarantee protection of ourselves, our families, or our neighbors. We can provide disincentives for antisocial behavior through policing and punishment, and we can remove those guilty of offenses from society temporarily or permanently, but fundamentally we depend for our safety not on policing but on the goodwill of our neighbors.

Moving to the level of states, pacifists would, therefore, seek to influence policy towards those actions likely to bring about peaceful living in the long term. Canada doesn't maintain big defenses against the United States, or vice versa; England and France no longer fear attacks from one another. This security is not built on force of arms but on mutual trust. In short, military action overpromises; it can neither guarantee protection of the innocent nor create peace in the long term. A pacifist response is to challenge the solutions militarist thinking proposes as shortsighted and inadequate. It's obvious that the urgent priority for keeping everyone as safe from violence as possible is to build familial, social, and international relationships and institutions that make it as unlikely as possible that citizens or nations will attack their neighbors. This is the task of building for peace. It is no wonder that the peacemakers are picked out in the Beatitudes (Mt 5:9); the primary and only reliable defense of the innocent is the patient building of a peaceful society.

BES   I appreciate your fine testimony to the need for mutual trust. I think the just war perspective has a similar vision at its core. But what about when governments are aggressive and untrustworthy? I hate to throw out the overused and emotional example, but here goes: What would pacifists have recommended the community of nations do in response to Nazi Germany? I will preemptively agree with you that our nations do plenty to let tyrannical leaders grow in power and to let humanitarian crises fester; I still won't agree that there will never be a need for governments to use force when—for whatever mix of culpabilities—a nation aggresses on a neighbor or its own people. You acknowledge that peacemaking does fail and that some kind of restraint of evildoers is warranted. So what methods should governments use in response?

DLC It is crucial to recognize that serious mistakes were made in international relations with Germany between the wars; it was clear that its economic situation was untenable. Its citizens were reduced by successive currency devaluations to taking wheelbarrow loads of money to buy ordinary necessities; they were demoralized and, therefore, susceptible to the allure of the false hopes of Nazism. But you're right that we have always to start from where we are. To answer your question directly, when it really comes down to it, and an implacable enemy is about to invade your nation, and all peaceful means of resolving the conflict have been found unworkable, I believe the New Testament calls Christians to endure, rather than violently resist the attacker. Where a foreign aggressor is grossly maltreating its citizens or exterminating them as the Nazis did to the Jews and other minority groups, then all other nations should seek to intercede as strongly as possible on their behalf with nonviolent means. This may seem unlikely to be successful, but there were very many nonviolent means used to allow Jews to escape the Nazis and—very regrettably—they were probably the only effective response offered. Even a full-scale war, fought largely without just war constraints, was unable to prevent the deaths of six million Jews.

BES But I am sure that the consequences of fighting no war at all would have been even worse. It's entirely conceivable that the whole of European Jewry would have been eradicated—in other words, about another three million Jewish persons, plus yet more Eastern European prisoners. I don't discount at all the bravery of those ordinary citizens who helped Jews and others escape, but they couldn't liberate the concentration camps. That's not to say that the American or British leaders had only humanitarian motives in mind, and it's certainly not to say that the means of the war fully abided by justice. Justified wars still involve grave losses. World War II was this kind of war, not just in the sense of good or holy, but justified in the sense of being the necessary and lesser evil.

Tough Questions for Just War Thinkers

DLC I want to press you on your strategy of defending the overall benefits of World War II in the face of its violations of discrimination. How much space is there between just war theory and the realist position when it really comes down to it? Isn't it almost as idealistic to suppose that nations would stick to its criteria as to think they'll turn pacifist? Can you cite a single example of a nation renouncing a means of fighting a war because, though it would be the only means of securing victory, it would contradict just war principles? World War II is often cited as the obvious case of a just war, yet the Allies' direct targeting of civilians in their firebombing of German and Japanese cities and their atomic bombing of Japan was obviously a wholesale breach of the criterion of discrimination. Isn't this what war has always been like: When it really counts, any means is justified by the end of winning?

BES Although there are vague borders between just war and realism in some of their ways of thinking about war, you're right that just war ought to make a difference when it comes to discrimination. It is vital that just war theory distinguish combatants from noncombatants and that it not elide the difference for the sake of an end that supposedly justifies the means. However much the atomic bombing of two Japanese cities may have seemed the best hope for ending World War II without protracted loss of life, it is—or it should be—repugnant to just war theorists to justify those bombings. (I don't think that for American leaders to wrestle with the option of nuclear bombing in the context of the time was obviously repugnant, but I think they made a very wrong decision and one that we should not justify in retrospect.) I think your question about renouncing a means of fighting is not fairly posed. We should not hold just war theory to standards different from other ethical frameworks. That nations almost inevitably fall short does not, in itself, cast doubt on the standards, any more than high divorce rates in the United States or United Kingdom cast doubt—for Christians—on the standards for marital commitment. Actually, I think there are examples of nations that aspire to just war doctrine constraining their conduct and their choice of weapons. For instance, most nations, including our own, have chosen to forgo the development of biological and chemical weapons. It's often the case that individual nations don't want to foreswear a means unless everybody does; fortunately, nations have come together several times in the last two centuries to agree on conventions banning various weapons. The process is imperfect and problematic, but there have been real advances as well.

DLC We can agree in celebrating any effective multilateral agreements that succeed in limiting the spread of arms while regretting they are much too rare. You cannot claim them as victories for just war theory, though. Even the most Machiavellian of leaders would sign up to such agreements if they considered them to be in their own self-interest. In order to show that just war theory has the potential to work, you'd need to find an example of a nation prepared to suffer a unilateral disadvantage for moral reasons. And just war theory does have to demonstrate that it provides this kind of constraint in practice, because it's used by leaders to justify wars. If it serves to justify wars without morally restraining them, then we'd clearly be much better off without it: Just war theory is then just a moral fig leaf for immoral wars.

BES Let me clarify how three kinds of moral agents are expected to act according to the just conduct criteria. The first are soldiers who make immediate decisions about the conduct of their fighting. The second are field commanders who order their soldiers to act or refrain from acting in certain ways. The third are top-level military commanders and civilian political leaders—such as presidents, prime ministers, and secretaries of defense—who authorize broad strategies that involve just-conduct questions. Soldiers are trained and operate under rules of engagement that are shaped by the principles of discrimination and proportionality. We could find in military histories and first-person war narratives many examples of both restraints and violations of these moral guidelines. Nevertheless, I'm willing to take at face value the claims of professional soldiers from democratic countries that they do all they can to live up to rules of engagement and standards of honor. Next are field commanders who command their troops to raid that building, or shell that hillside, and so on. A great deal of responsibility falls on field commanders to certify that noncombatants will not be targeted or placed at undue risk as they make decisions under tight constraints of time and information. Again, I believe that their intentions are to strive to abide by the criteria, even to suffer some disadvantages to their military aims in order not to harm civilians. But again, I acknowledge that the historical record and current practice are a mixed bag.

DLC I am particularly concerned with how the top decision makers act, because if they are routinely hypocritical, the whole notion of a politically effective just war doctrine is called into question. It is clear that at the level of strategic planning, the history of warfare is rife with incidents of the rules of war being violated. In *Just and Unjust Wars,* Michael Walzer not only provides numerous examples but addresses the "sliding scale," his term for the prevalent attitude that "the more justice, the more right," that is, the more justice we have on our side, the more right we have to bend the rules of war.[71] Although Walzer thinks the sliding scale can be controlled, the behavior of nations proves that it can't be.

BES The intellectual efforts of just war ethicists and the practical efforts of international conventions and war crimes trials put breaks on this sliding scale—or at least tries to. I believe just war doctrine has teeth, but in practice it gets a looser bite on the initial decision making than on the subsequent judging of rights and wrongs. We have seen that the public can judge wars like Vietnam and the current Iraq war by ethical standards (the just war principles in essence, if not always in name), and, if the public perceives a large gulf between ethics and reality, it can put pressure on leaders to change course. Coming back to decisions about forgoing certain weapons or certain uses of weapons, an important trend has been the development of precision-guided ordnance and the attempt by the United States since the 1990s to be more discriminating than was previously possible in aerial campaigns. Do you believe that this development has been able to prevent ethical abuses?

DLC I can place no confidence in precision-guided ordnance if the possessors of these weapons used them improperly, which they routinely do. Isn't it true to say that the principle of discrimination has been weakened significantly in the last one hundred years, notwithstanding how much it's talked about? It used to rule out attacks on commerce, industry, and population centers, yet cities are now routinely targeted. Even those working in a Serbian broadcasting station were said by NATO to be legitimate targets. The civilian deaths in Iraq in 2003 belie the claims advanced for so-called smart weapons. War has become much more dangerous for noncombatants than ever before. For me, this is another example of how just war criteria are too flexible to get real purchase on the realities of war. This leads to a dangerous divide between how peoples in different nations see the same actions: The U.S. population believes they are fighting morally with advanced and discriminating smart weapons, and the Arab audience of Al Jazeera television just sees the thousands of civilian casualties in Iraq and is understandably skeptical about moral claims.

BES   Yes, regrettably, there has been some serious slippage throughout the twentieth into the twenty-first century as to the legitimate targets of military action. Most of the problem, when practiced by Western nations, comes not from intentional and overt violations of discrimination—the fire bombing of German and Japanese cities and the atomic bombing of Japan being the major exceptions—but from violations of proportionality. War has become more and more inclusive of every sector of society. Given the high stakes and global scale of World War I and World War II, all sides accepted the sliding scale mentality, leading to huge civilian losses. More recently, the use of precision-guided ordnance provides some hope that a war of humanitarian intervention could be discriminate and proportionate, but it will still require a great deal of discipline to resist the sliding scale. The NATO bombing of the Serbian radio station—although NATO justified it as an attack on a command-and-control communications network—appears to me unjustified. It is the result of the sort of sliding scale righteousness that infects even largely upright military interventions.[72]

So I would still say that just war theory in the hands of religious leaders and ethicists has been doing good service in holding the line, but it is disconcerting how politicians can abuse it. You say that the international community would develop the conventions and procedures whether we had a just war theory or not. I say that the value of just war theory lies in supporting a cultural discourse that keeps the practices of civilian protection on a moral footing, rather than simply a pragmatic one. Even though this discourse is politically abused, we are better off for having the standards than none at all. It's very similar to human rights discourse; by itself, it doesn't hold back brutal leaders, but it shifts the defaults in international relations, gives energy to grassroots reform movements, adds pressure for nations to live up to their rhetoric, and gradually takes hold in law. For these benefits, it is reasonable for Christians to join human rights efforts and just war discourse.

The Church's Priorities

DLC Based on the previous chapter, it's very clear that the New Testament, at least, sees Christian discipleship not as reasonable but as distinctive and prophetic, pointing to a new way of relating to God and to one another that has little relationship to this kind of calm theorizing. Christians are called by Christ to witness to the inbreaking of the reign of God, a reign that will countenance no violence, however worthy the motive. We have to recognize that this witness takes place in the context of a world that is violent, of course, and that's where the debates begin. We can't start from a position of trying to think about how we might make sure the world is orderly and lawful; as John Howard Yoder notes, we're not responsible for making things turn out right.[73] We are responsible for being faithful disciples of Christ, which, among other things, rules out killing people, including Germans, Serbs, and Iraqis.

BES In the passage to which you allude, I appreciate Yoder's insight that the compulsiveness to make history come out right can infect Christians' thinking. But does that mean we have no responsibility for the way the world goes? If we try to keep the whole of the biblical witness in view, there is a cumulative case for Christians to be involved in shaping the world toward the goal of justice, for instance, to establish policies for economic justice in the spirit of ancient Israel's Sabbath and Jubilee laws. We noted in the previous chapter that the early Christians expected the imminent end of the world in a context where they had no political power and were vulnerable to persecution. At that time, they would have read the political implications of their faith differently than would make sense later. But combining the paradigm of shared political responsibility from the Old Testament and the responsibility that Jesus handed on to his followers in the New Testament, Christian discipleship carries a concern for responsibility and for changing the world, so far as possible and with licit means.

DLC Another angle on what leads us to different positions on the issue of war is how we think about the Church. For me, the primary reason to do Christian ethics is for the Church to work out how it should live out its common life and for individuals to work out the implications of this discernment for their lives as members of the body of Christ. Because the Church and its members exist inescapably in a political context, theological ethics cannot avoid ethical questions about how nation-states should behave. As citizens and voters, they should have a view about how their country should order its affairs and its relations with its neighbors; they should take responsibility to participate in debates about these issues. But neither the nation-state nor the international community can be the starting point for ethical reflection; that would tempt us to think we could do ethics from first principles and ignore our identity as those called to follow Christ. We must begin by attempting to discern God's call to the Church. Only then can we consider the political implications of this calling.

BES When it comes to Church life, I embrace a classically Catholic both/and approach in distinction to your classically Protestant either/or approach. Social teachings from the Catholic Church in the last thirty years have given us the best of both worlds when it comes to the two approaches to ethics. On the question of war, for example, the U.S. bishops' statement in 1983 was taken quite seriously in the American political debate about the nuclear arms race. It gave moral leverage to political and social movements that challenged President Reagan's military buildup. More recently, Pope John Paul II, who was probably the most widely respected religious leader speaking on the matter of the Iraq war, argued strongly against the war. In both cases, these religious leaders used just war language and other commonsense claims. But they did not hide their religious vision. They called Christians to be peacemakers. Although it can be a little challenging to speak both ways at once, often the discourses complement each other. On one hand, the Church calls the nations to stop warring because there are better, more prudent ways to resolve disputes. On the other hand, it points to a vision of peace that lies beyond politics, a vision that the Church believes can stir hearts even outside its walls. I appreciate your strong attention to that ecclesial dimension because just war thinking is strengthened by it. Without it, Christians may think of just war theory as simply some philosophical language that Church leaders use to talk in political debates. If just war thinking is connected to the rest of the Church's life and vision, including its vision of peace, I believe Christians will be more cautious in support of war. I hope we will see in the course of this book that the pacifist and just war traditions have important things to learn from each other, despite their differences.

CONCLUSION

We said at the beginning of the chapter that pacifism and just war tradition have long vied to be understood as the most authentic tradition of Christian reasoning on war. Obviously, we cannot provide a resolution to that debate because we stand on different sides of it. What we hope to have achieved so far is to give a clear explanation of how each position is deeply rooted in the sources and methods of Christian ethical reasoning, to model a thoughtful use of each position, and to show how each position might respond to the other's criticisms. In the remainder of this book, it will be clear that, as authors on different sides of this fence, we share some common ground in relation to some practical judgments. It should also be clear, however, that these judgments are usually based on different underlying positions and these underlying positions also generate sharp disagreements in other cases. Therefore, we recognize the importance of pacifists and just war theorists making common cause in peacemaking initiatives, but we also believe that this shared interest neither points toward convergence in the short-term nor diminishes the importance of continuing to debate foundational differences of perspective.

CHAPTER 3

Does Humanitarian Intervention Pass the Test?

ntervening for a humanitarian reason is a duty that governments are reluctant to assume. This is understandable because no nation wants to sacrifice its troops, especially when the strategic and economic reasons for doing so are questionable or unclear. Still, the idea is affirmed by the leadership of the major world powers and of the United Nations. Facing the Kosovo crisis in the late 1990s, U.S. President Bill Clinton said, "Whether you live in Africa or Central Europe or any other place, if somebody comes after innocent victims because of their race, their ethnic background or their religion, and it's within our power to stop it, we will stop it."[1] UN Secretary-General Kofi Annan has spoken similarly: "Why was the United Nations established, if not to act as a benign policeman or doctor? Our job is to intervene: to prevent conflict when we can, to put a stop to it when it has broken out, or—when neither of those things is possible—at least to contain it and prevent it from spreading."[2]

The last fifteen years alone have seen major humanitarian crises in Somalia, Rwanda, East Timor, Bosnia, Kosovo, Liberia, Haiti, and the Darfur region of Sudan. When should the crisis be seen as more than a domestic matter, giving legal basis for the United Nations to act? Even if the crisis occurs solely within national borders, is it not wrong to leave civilians to the whims of a dictator? Do people as people, as citizens of the world, have a right to protection? How serious and widespread must injustices be before nations intervene? May nations intervene only with the approval of the United Nations, or may an individual nation or group of nations act without UN mandate if they believe that the UN is forsaking its responsibility to act? Although those who take opposing stands on foreign policy debates often ask these questions rhetorically, suggesting that the answers are obvious, knowing what to do in a humanitarian crisis is by no means easy.

A situation calling for the defense of others is inherently difficult for Christian ethics, as it brings into tension the quest for peace and the desire to help one's neighbor. The late Paul Ramsey put a pointed twist on the Good Samaritan parable: "What would Jesus have the Samaritan do if he came upon the robbers still at their fell work?"[3] To be sure, the strategy of nonviolent resistance as preached and practiced by pacifists and numerous Christian social movements reveals that we have more options than to kill or let someone else be killed.[4] Still, most Christians, including most of those who promote nonviolence, do not condemn as morally corrupt all forms of coercive intervention for the protection of others; the maintenance of a domestic police force is the obvious example. Should the policing concept be extended to just policing of the international community? How is it possible to structure and limit governmental power so that the claim of a humanitarian motive does not become a subterfuge for self-serving, inhumane military action? And who should act, in the famous phrase, as "the world's policeman"?

Our purpose in exploring these questions is to scrutinize what ought to be the easiest Christian case to make for war: the rescue of innocent third parties. If just war thinkers can maintain a strong case that violence is justified in some of these situations, they vindicate a fundamental claim of their theory. If pacifists raise plausible problems with just war thinking on this topic, or even show that there are better ways to protect people than to start a war, their argument against other uses of military power will be all the stronger. And because just war thinkers and pacifists both embrace the cause of human dignity, humanitarian intervention is a useful context in which to look for shared assumptions and values between these two perspectives, which are otherwise so often placed at odds with one another.

THE LEGAL AND POLITICAL CONTEXT OF
HUMANITARIAN INTERVENTION

To begin, let us clarify the meaning of "humanitarian intervention": "The common factor in all cases of humanitarian intervention is that the intervening nation(s) uses its armed forces in a coercive role to cause some effect in the internal affairs of another nation and, after this humanitarian objective is achieved, the intervening force withdraws."[5] This category of military action occupies a middle ground between the nonhostile placement of peacekeeping forces or troops that are delivering aid or engaging in rebuilding and related efforts and formally declared war by one nation against another. Humanitarian intervention shares with peacekeeping (in theory) an altruistic intention, and it shares with warfare the methods of hostile force. Given the shared methods, humanitarian intervention with armed forces is legally and ethically subject to the same just war restrictions on conduct (jus in bello) as other forms of warfare.[6] From the outset, we should note that some pacifists, realists, and just war thinkers object to the phrase "humanitarian intervention." Pacifists generally deny that war can bring about an overall humanitarian benefit. Many pacifists and some just war thinkers believe that interventions are rarely altruistic, and most realists believe that interventions should not be altruistic. However, because humanitarian intervention is a well-known term, we will use it, but we will often add a reminder that what is under discussion is military intervention in a (purported or actual) humanitarian crisis.

The unsettled questions in international law largely concern the legality of deciding to intervene under jus ad bellum. "Humanitarian intervention" is a term that has been in use only for a few decades; the concept was adopted by the United Nations and other regional international bodies after struggling for a method for collective intervention in cases of genocide and regional conflagration. The United Nations has recognized the concept of humanitarian intervention and has assumed that, like other uses of force, it must be approved by the UN Security Council. International lawyers in recent years have recognized and affirmed the concept, but as of yet, there is no consensus in international law on the exact criteria for a justified intervention or what bodies have the authority to intervene. It will take some time for a settled concept of and procedure for humanitarian intervention to be established in international law. This establishment will occur in four overlapping steps:

1. International lawyers will analyze and clarify the concept;
2. The United Nations and regional organizations will engage in interventions and the public will reflect on the long-term successes and failures of these events;
3. The United Nations will provide procedures and declarations; and
4. The nations of the world will affirm these procedures and declarations.

There is movement now on all four fronts, but mostly on the first two. Still, it will take some time to work out the conceptual and practical challenge framed by international lawyer Nico Krisch: "The main problem of human-itarian intervention consists in the divergence of law and morality: while considerations of justice and human rights demand the recognition of a right to intervention, international law prevents this by anachronistically re-lying on order and on state sovereignty."[7]

Military action under the rubric of humanitarian intervention has three features that are not as common as they are in traditional warfare: It is an in-terference within national boundaries instead of a response to an act of out-ward aggression; it typically involves several nations acting cooperatively; and it aims to defend the human rights of citizens of another nation who face severe threats to their lives, health, and safety. Since 1945 these three fea-tures of humanitarian intervention have usually been present when interven-tion has been contemplated, but each one is controversial. First, because international law is built on the foundation of the nation-state system, the presumption has always been that nations should not intervene in each other's domestic disputes. Hugo Grotius and subsequent international lawyers established this principle, even as they recognized some rare excep-tions.[8] The United Nations Charter requires that all members "refrain from the threat or use of force against the territorial integrity or political inde-pendence of any state" (Article 2).[9] Yet because the UN's primary purpose is to provide a cooperative and peaceful framework for relationships among nations, the Charter also reserves for the Security Council the right to call upon the military forces of member nations to "maintain or restore interna-tional peace and security" (Article 42). This right of the UN to act in the in-terests of international peace and security is the touchstone for the contemporary discussion of humanitarian intervention. Everyone agrees that Article 42 of the Charter allows the UN Security Council to authorize intervention into a conflict that has spilled outside national borders or that imminently threatens regional security. What has been recognized of late is the need for citizens sometimes to be protected within the boundaries of their sovereign state from their own government. Yet it has proven diffi-cult to secure consensus about the legal warrants for such intervention.[10] The thinking of the international community on this topic has recently been taken further with the publication of the report *The Responsibility to Protect*, which argues that when a state fails to protect its citizens adequately, other nations have a right and duty to intervene that overrides the presumptive principle of nonintervention.[11]

Second, the principle of collective action is controversial because nations often violate it while ostensibly accepting it. Since the cold war era—during which the United States and the Soviet Union intervened in many nations for reasons of bald self-interest despite claims to the contrary—the idea of intervening in other nations' affairs has been widely regarded as both wrong and counterproductive. Few Americans want to repeat the experience of Vietnam, and few Russians the experience of Afghanistan, though both nations have found themselves in analogous situations—in Iraq and Chechnya. The Persian Gulf War of 1991 and the Iraq War of 2003 are instructive examples of the complexities of collective action. In both wars the United States has been recognized as the prime political mover for military action with the United Kingdom as an important secondary mover. In both wars, the United States could claim that it was a part of a coalition of nations. However, only the Gulf War involved Arab nations in the coalition, and only the Gulf War proceeded under clear approval from the UN Security Council. Even so, the Gulf War remains controversial among ethicists and political commentators as to whether it really constituted a legal, free decision by the community of nations for the international common good (see chapter 6). When the United States and the United Kingdom tried to transfer the appearances of collective action to the 2003 war, they were widely condemned by domestic opposition and by other nations for acting unilaterally and without legal basis. Perhaps the difference between the two wars shows that the principle of collective action is somewhat effective, but the controversy is far from settled.

Third, human rights, though not controversial in the same way as the previous two features, present a dilemma for action nonetheless. The United Nations was founded in the wake of World War II, which required many nations to band together to defeat Nazi Germany, fascist Italy, and imperial Japan. The Allies' declarations of war were clearly acceptable under international law as defensive responses to the aggressions of the Axis powers. But each of the Axis nations also treated atrociously both their own citizens and the peoples they claimed the right to control. The horror of six million Jews together with other minority groups murdered in the Holocaust—and the many other genocidal, colonial, and military casualties of the World War II era—impressed on the world the need not only for security and stability but also for protection and justice for the world's citizens. The former pair of concerns almost always overrides the latter, but the concept of the right of every person to be free from political tyranny and related abuses gained international political footing at the end of the war and has grown steadily ever since. The United Nations Universal Declaration of Human Rights and other conventions have given these rights the force of law.[12]

Several problems plague the effort to conform political action to the ideal of human rights. One problem is what kinds of violations constitute a humanitarian crisis? Sadly, violations of human rights are legion in the world, especially if we consider the full set of economic rights that have been described in covenants, such as the right to adequate education. Clearly, not all these violations justify military intervention. Violations have to be serious and widespread to render the use of force morally plausible, although there is presently no consensus on what violations are sufficiently serious and widespread. Still, the broad parameters have been coming into focus over time. Legal and ethical analyses typically conclude that, for a significant proportion of a population, peoples' lives, health, and/or physical safety must be under attack by a willful plan of a government or some group. The following situations meet those criteria and thus are commonly regarded as humanitarian crises.

- *Genocide*: Acts committed with the intent to destroy, in whole or in part, a national, ethnic, racial, or religious group.[13] Genocidal campaigns have become more frequent since World War I. The genocide in Rwanda in 1994 claimed between half a million and a million lives, and the ongoing genocide in the Darfur region of western Sudan has caused around four hundred thousand deaths.[14]
- *A nation's repression of a disputed territory*: When a nation controls a territory that is claiming independence, it often uses brutal measures to repress the people. Often a rebel group fights against the government, a context in which many innocent civilians are killed. If the situation develops toward the previous or the next category, nations consider military intervention but are usually stymied by practical worries such as the reluctance to sacrifice their own troops and the legal obstacle of state sovereignty. The crisis in East Timor in 1999, leading up to its independence from Indonesia, was an example of this type.

- *Civil war or mob violence in a failed state*: A civil war is usually the locus of many human rights violations. When the nation's government cannot restore order, is failing in its basic functions, or is rendered impotent by internal power struggles, outside nations and the UN consider intervention, though they are usually reluctant to insert themselves into a deadly morass. The on-again, off-again crises in Haiti have kept that nation teetering on the edge of this category for over twenty years. A failed intervention in this category was the United States' abortive engagement in Somalia in 1993, recounted in the book and film *Black Hawk Down*. On the successful side was the United States' deployment of troops to Liberia in 2003 and the United Kingdom's deployment to Sierra Leone in 2000. In both cases, a modest deployment at the right time restored order and helped establish a ceasefire that eventually led to full resolution of hostilities.
- *Totalitarian regime killing its citizens*: A government's abuse of human rights and killing of its citizens need not be based on a genocidal plan or be evidence of social collapse in order to be a situation that demands justice from the outside world. Certainly, the reigns of terror of Idi Amin in Uganda in the 1970s, Pol Pot in Cambodia in the 1970s and 1980s, and of Kim Jong-il in North Korea today have been situations from which citizens should be rescued—somehow. But intervention is unlikely for the same reasons of practicality, fear, and sovereignty.
- *Systematic war crimes*: In either a civil or an external war, a nation might abuse civilians and captured combatants on such a scale that it forfeits its claim to be a legitimate belligerent. In the Balkan wars, Serbia's shelling of civilian areas, forced relocation of ethnic groups, rape of female prisoners, and establishment of concentration camps were systematic war crimes that strengthened the case for intervention by the international community.

A second problem is determining who may and must defend human rights. Whose duty is it to act? The logical answer is that the responsibility falls on the community of nations because these are rights of persons as such and not as citizens of certain nations. Presumably, the UN should be the body that defends these rights, just as the World Court and various human rights tribunals and war crimes tribunals, which are constituted through the UN, prosecute violators of these rights. The UN has acted to defend rights by condemning violations, engaging in conflict resolution, establishing ceasefires, and inserting peacekeeping troops. When these methods fail, member states should call upon the UN Security Council to approve an intervention. The Security Council has approved some engagements but at other times has simply not stood in the way of individual states taking action—often these states fail to ask for approval in the first place. If humanitarian interventions are to become more effective and legitimate, the international community must establish clear criteria for violations and for determining who acts.[15]

CASE STUDY: THE NATO INTERVENTION IN KOSOVO

To analyze the complex problems described earlier in light of Christian pacifism and just war theory, we will take as a case study the situation in Kosovo, which was the site of the final Balkan conflict of the 1990s. Serbia threatened to annex Kosovo as Kosovo angled for independence. Serbia sent its army to terrorize and displace ethnic Albanians from the region in 1998. The North Atlantic Treaty Organization (NATO) decided to intervene against the Serbian army in the spring and summer of 1999 with an aerial bombing campaign. Was this intervention justified—both in how it was decided and how it was conducted? Was it the best and most humane way to protect the Kosovars?

First a brief primer on the Kosovo crisis is necessary.[16] The Balkan region of southern Europe comprises a wide range of ethnic and religious groups living within shifting national borders. For centuries the Balkans were all part of the Ottoman Empire of the Turks. In the middle of the twentieth century, it was known as Yugoslavia and was under the rule of Communist strongman Josip Tito from 1945 to his death in 1980. Kosovo lies at the western end of the former republic of Yugoslavia; Serbia borders it to the east and Albania to the west. Ethnic Albanians constitute the majority of its population, with Serbs/Montenegrins as the second major ethnic group. However, the balance shifted sharply after the breakup of Yugoslavia. In the 1950s, the balance of Albanians to Serbs/Montengrins in Kosovo was 67 to 28 percent; by 1999, it was 90 to 10 percent.[17]

The region has been politically volatile for centuries. The Balkans have been a key region where Muslim cultures have alternately coexisted and struggled with western Christian cultures. The historical memory of peoples in the region is long. The Serbian kingdom fell to the Ottoman Turks in 1459, but the Battle of Kosovo in 1389 marked a turning point that grew in symbolic significance over the centuries.[18] The mythology of the Battle of Kosovo is that the noble Serbs, temporarily subjugated by the Muslims, would one day reclaim the land of Kosovo. The region was geopolitically highly significant throughout the twentieth century. The assassination of Archduke Ferdinand—the proximate spark of World War I—occurred in Sarajevo in 1914. Yugoslavia, under the rule of Marshall Tito, constituted one of the buffers between the Soviet Union and Western Europe.

Serbian President Slobodan Milosevic rose to power in 1989. The breakup of Yugoslavia began in 1990, when Slovenia voted to secede. Former geographic regions with a predominance of a given ethnic group began asserting claims to self-determination: Slovenia, Croatia, Bosnia-Herzegovina, Macedonia, and Kosovo. If all of these regions broke away from Yugoslavia, only Serbia would be left. Milosevic did not want to lose this territory, so he initiated a nationalist program to incorporate all of the Balkans into Greater Serbia. This program included military attacks upon the two largest neighbors—Croatia and Bosnia. In the Serbian media, a hostile campaign of dehumanization against Bosnian Muslims was initiated. In Bosnia, the Serb army practiced brutal and unjust kinds of military attack, including shelling of civilian areas, relocating non-Serb ethnic populations, gathering civilians into concentration camps, and raping women. This complete program of brutalization was termed by Serbia itself as "ethnic cleansing." It was state-sponsored genocide—a program to rid Bosnia of non-Serb ethnic groups. To be sure, there were violations of military ethics on all sides in the Balkan conflict, including by the Croatian army and Bosnian resistance groups. Yet we take the position of most ethical commentators that Serbia was the most flagrant aggressor and the one with the most power and the greatest ability to end the violence during these years. This first wave of the wars of Yugoslav secession lasted from 1991 to 1995, ending with the peace accords negotiated by the United States with Milosevic and the presidents of Bosnia and Croatia in Dayton, Ohio, in November–December 1995.

But the wars were not over. The final major military conflict in this period was Serbia's aggression against Kosovo in 1998–1999. Owing to the population dislocations caused by the Balkan wars, Kosovo had become, by this point, heavily ethnic-Albanian, and thus primarily Muslim. Citing ancient territorial claims, Milosevic aimed to control Kosovo and to push its ethnic-Albanians into Albania. The Kosovars were largely defenseless. A small resistance group, the Kosovo Liberation Army (KLA), succeeded in raising money from émigrés and smuggling in arms, but it failed to recruit many Kosovars.[19] "The tide turned in March 1998, when the KLA gunned down several Serbian policemen and Milosevic struck back so violently that popular support for the KLA soared."[20] Serbia increased its troop presence in Kosovo throughout 1998. Despite agreeing to a ceasefire on October 12, 1998, Serbia directed its troops to keep fighting against the KLA and attacking civilians. One of the final determining events for the international community occurred on January 15, 1999. "After pounding the small town of Racak with artillery fire for three days, Serb paramilitary and police units rounded up and executed forty-five Albanian civilians, including three women, a twelve-year-old boy, and several elderly men. The Serb forces left the bodies of those executed facedown in an icy ravine."[21] The United Nations and many of its member nations condemned these actions. The Clinton administration was particularly enraged; U.S. Secretary of State Madeleine Albright pushed hard for intervention. As with the earlier Bosnian conflict, the UN Security Council was unable to speak in a unified voice or take meaningful action because Russia stood behind its longtime ally Serbia and China was uninterested in taking a strong stand. These nations simply issued statements of dismay and calls for diplomacy.

Therefore President Bill Clinton and several European leaders worked diplomatically through NATO to establish terms under which Serb forces would withdraw from Kosovo, allowing Kosovars to return to their homes. NATO is a security alliance comprising the United States and European nations, which was formed in 1949 as a counterbalance to the Soviet bloc. In the 1990s it began admitting some former Soviet satellites, such as Poland. Because NATO was concerned with Europe's security, European leaders reasoned that the Kosovo crisis—as one more stage of the Balkan crisis—threatened Europe's political stability. The United States and European nations had been slow to act in the Bosnian conflict, so probably part of their motivation this time was to be more decisive.

Even as Serbia kept promising to abide by ceasefires, it displaced tens of thousands of people from their homes. By February 1999, when NATO brought Serb and Albanian Kosovar representatives to a summit in Rambouillet, France, thousands of Kosovars had been killed and at least one hundred thousand had been displaced from their homes. At Rambouillet, NATO representatives pushed for a ceasefire accord that would grant autonomy to Kosovo. The Serb army would have to withdraw and the KLA stand down under a NATO peacekeeping force. Neither side agreed to this plan. A few weeks later, though, on March 18, the Albanian representatives agreed to the accord. American diplomat Richard Holbrooke traveled to Belgrade, Serbia, on March 24 to convince Milosevic to agree to these terms under threat of NATO bombing. That having failed, NATO forces, under the command of General Wesley Clark, began an aerial bombing campaign against the Serbian army on March 24. The combination of Serb attacks and NATO fire drove even more refugees from their homes. In total, 1.5 million Kosovars became external refugees or internally displaced persons.

During the seventy-eight days of the NATO bombing, the prospects for a successful outcome were murky. Many people and groups were angered by the NATO attacks. Serb citizens expressed bitter anger even though they were by no means happy with their president by that time.[22] Russia objected vigorously, and citizens protested in a number of NATO and non-NATO countries, especially in front of U.S. embassies. The bombing gave the Serbian army rationale to step up its attacks on Kosovars. The army perpetrated more crimes against humanity during the bombing than before the bombing. This aggression and the threat posed by NATO bombs precipitated a large refugee crisis, adding to the ethnic cleansing that had already occurred. Each week the campaign dragged on increased the risk that when the cold weather returned in the fall, thousands of homeless Kosovars would die from exposure.

Eventually, Milosevic relented. On June 9 the thirty thousand Serbian forces agreed to turn back and so NATO ceased its bombing. The United Nations' Kosovo Force (KFOR) was able enter the area to hold the ceasefire, and humanitarian aid began pouring in. Some combination of the military, legal, political, and diplomatic pressures led Serbia to concede, even though Milosevic claimed victory in the Serbian media. What factors were most decisive is a matter of ongoing conjecture. Although Milosevic never cared about NATO's resolve and its plans for ground troops, Russia apparently came to realize that NATO would stay the course. Russia may have reassured Milosevic that he could be protected from the war crimes tribunal; it also appears that Russia planned to occupy part of Kosovo in the occupation, which would have allowed control to revert to Serbia. Because the NATO nations of Hungary, Bulgaria, and Romania refused Russia landing rights in their countries, Russia was unable to realize these plans.[23]

On May 27, 1999, during the bombing, the UN's International War Crimes Tribunal indicted Milosevic and four other Yugoslav officials for crimes against humanity. They were accused of "being responsible for the deportation of 740,000 ethnic Albanians from Kosovo [during 1999] as well as the murder of more than 340 identified victims."[24] After the bombings ended, mass graves of executed Albanians like the one in January 1999 were discovered by UN investigators. "The UN tribunal has received reports that some 11,334 Albanians are buried in 529 sites in Kosovo alone."[25] In 2000, Milosevic was defeated in the Serbian presidential election and, in March 2001, his own government turned him over to UN peacekeeping forces. Milosevic stood trial at the International Criminal Tribunal for the Former Yugoslavia (ICTFY) in The Hague. Proceedings dragged on for several years until his death on March 11, 2006. Founded in 1993 by a UN Security Council resolution, the ICTFY has indicted approximately seventy leaders and belligerents from the Balkan wars. Almost all of them are former Serb or Bosnian Serb political leaders, military commanders, soldiers, and detention camp authorities. A few Croats and Bosnian Muslims were charged, including three members of the KLA who were indicted. The outcomes have been varied. Some criminals have been sentenced to many years in jail, some served time for lesser charges, some were released early for cooperating against other defendants, some were acquitted, some are still on trial, and some remain at large—most notably, Bosnian Serb leader Radovan Karadzic.[26] Some war crimes convictions have occurred outside the scope of the ICTFY.

THE JUST WAR CASE FOR MILITARY
INTERVENTION IN KOSOVO

Just about everyone is pleased to see war criminals successfully convicted. However, was the military intervention the ethically sound way to proceed? The fundamental just war argument—Christian or secular—for humanitarian intervention is premised on four key conditions. In deciding whether these conditions apply in a given case, differences can emerge among just war thinkers despite their common wish to see the crisis resolved justly. Many, perhaps most, just war thinkers supported military intervention in Kosovo. Some thought it was too little, too late; others debated the process that brought about its implementation. Just war thinkers would apply all the just war criteria to this and any other case. Yet the following conditions bring the criteria together in a configuration that highlights the particularly debatable issues at the heart of third-party intervention.

There exists a serious and urgent crisis that endangers a nation's citizens. Milosevic's army unjustly attempted to annex Kosovo, caused a massive refugee crisis, and killed and raped innocent civilians. These were the same, well-documented practices that had been perpetrated in Bosnia just a few years earlier. Rev. J. Bryan Hehir, a Catholic priest who specializes in international affairs, wrote at the start of the NATO bombing in Kosovo, "Over one million people [have been] driven from their homes by brutal methods of killing, rape, burning and looting of their villages. . . . In Kosovo, the world . . . knows exactly what is happening and who is responsible. If the product of this planned rationality does not constitute just cause, it is difficult to know what the category means."[27] The possibility for yet further genocide on the European continent was seen by NATO leaders as a moral outrage that should not stand. Vaclav Havel, president of the Czech Republic, said at the time, "If it is possible to say about a war that it is ethical, or that it is fought for ethical reasons, it is true of this war. . . . [NATO] is fighting in the name of human interest for the fate of other human beings. It is fighting because decent people cannot sit back and watch systematic, state-directed massacres of other people. Decent people simply cannot tolerate this, and they cannot fail to come to the rescue if a rescue action is within their power."[28]

The Christian argument for humanitarian intervention sees the NATO action as a rescue of innocent third parties. Recall Paul Ramsey's hypothetical question: "What would Jesus have the Samaritan do if he came along while the robbers were still at their fell work?" The robber Milosevic was at his work, and with the failure of ceasefire talks, no other remedy was immediately in sight. Because these innocent parties included a belligerent group—the Kosovo Liberation Army—it is important to the just war argument that the KLA agreed to ceasefire terms, but Serbia did not.

The nation to be entered by force lacks an effective and just sovereign government to end the crisis. Kosovo had no sovereign government of its own. It was a country struggling to become independent. It also had no means to defend itself. So the international community had reason to act on its behalf. As far as could be discerned, Kosovars as a whole wanted the international community to come to their aid. Although they could hardly be happy about the risk to their lives from the bombing, many expressed gratitude for the intervention. In regard to Serbia, its government forfeited all claims to legitimate sovereignty over Kosovo by regularly flouting international laws and rejecting diplomatic overtures.

Multiple nations acting through an international body are willing and able to serve as the agents of rescue. If this is impossible, a few nations or a single nation may intervene if its intentions are right. The UN Security Council was incapable of forceful action because Russia, as one of the five permanent members, would have vetoed any military intervention. It was not until some weeks after NATO took matters into its own hands that Russia started to put real pressure on Serbia. It is an open debate in the just war community whether the sole legitimate authority for authorizing humanitarian interventions is the United Nations. Some just war thinkers and many church leaders affirm this position. Other just war thinkers hold that, although it might be ideal if the UN were the final authority on humanitarian interventions, unfortunately, we cannot make that a necessary condition under the current structure of the UN. Michael Walzer commented on this aspect of the Kosovo debate: "Many people on the left yearn for a world where the UN, and only the UN, would act in all such cases. But given the oligarchic structure of the Security Council, it's not possible to count on this kind of action: in [many cases], UN intervention would have been vetoed by one of the oligarchs. Nor am I convinced that the world would be improved by having only one agent of international rescue."[29]

Even if substantial reform of the UN occurs, just war thinkers such as Walzer want to retain more than one route to humanitarian intervention. Invoking an analogy that isolationists use to avoid intervening—"America can't be the world's firefighters"—Walzer argues for multiple institutions: "The men and women in the burning building are probably better served if they can appeal to more than a single set of firefighters. . . . From a moral/political perspective, I don't think it matters much if this particular fire isn't dangerous to me and mine. I can't just sit and watch. Or rather, the price of sitting and watching is a kind of moral corruption."[30] A reasonable conclusion, then, is that the United Nations is the first choice to act as firefighter. If the UN fails, other firefighters may consider intervention, but they ought to be regional associations (e.g., NATO or the Organization of African States) that are relevant to the crisis. Single-nation intervention or ad hoc coalitions should be considered only in the last resort, and usually only if they are specifically requested by some legitimate representatives of the party in need.

The third party nations, having explored all feasible nonmilitary means, are capable of using military intervention to improve the situation for both the immediate and the long term. The just war criteria of last resort, reasonable hope of success, and proportionality introduce elements of pragmatic, consequentialist reasoning into the decision to intervene. Can we make things better by intervening? If the situation would be much worse on account of intervening, we need to find another way. This pragmatic note opens just war reasoning to criticism. Pacifists criticized the Kosovo intervention with reference to the United States' failure to intervene in Rwanda and other places; in essence, they said that the United States was being too pragmatic and not sufficiently humanitarian. Many realists criticized President Clinton for getting involved (Clinton was not being pragmatic enough about national interests) and then for not being more aggressive for a military victory once engaged (it was a pragmatic necessity for NATO to save face and not lose its first war).

Amid such competing expectations, the challenge is to focus on the right kinds of consequences: the cessation of the unjust aggression, the restoration of peace, and creation of a context for just, legitimate governance in the countries affected. The bad consequences to be avoided are an extreme loss of life on either side, significant environmental destruction, and the creation of political instability that makes long-term peace and justice less likely. The just war criteria do not require political decision makers to be sure that everything will turn out well, but to test their decision to intervene against practical realities. They should at least have good reasons to believe that more lives will be saved by intervening than by not intervening.

There was reason for such confidence in the Kosovo case, based on everything that was known about the Serb army's ongoing crimes against civilians as well as the past behavior and current demeanor of Serb leaders. This side of the argument concurs with Samantha Power, who wrote a powerful and widely lauded study of the problem of genocide in the twentieth century. Of the Kosovo intervention, she concludes, "As high as the death toll turned out, it was far lower than if NATO had not acted at all. After years of avoiding confrontation, the United States and its allies likely saved hundreds of thousands of lives."[31] She makes this claim despite her overall thesis that most genocides could be prevented or abated by leaders taking timely, resolute, and consistent action on political fronts, and despite finding that most of the military interventions that the United States finally undertakes suffer from strategic and moral flaws. The immediate greater good was achieved. While it is hard to predict the long-term consequences of the NATO intervention, it is plausible that the resolve European and American leaders showed against Milosevic—in contrast to their delaying and endless negotiation earlier in the 1990s—stifled his ambitions and accelerated the demise of his political viability in the region. NATO and the UN followed through with refugee services and development efforts that gave the Kosovars the chance to rebuild their society.

PACIFIST RESPONSES TO THE INTERVENTION IN KOSOVO

Pacifists see a strong connection between their principled objection to killing and the practical truth that killing is a shortsighted, narrow, and usually ineffective response to a problem. As pacifists see it, just war advocates think far too narrowly. They wrongly phrase the question as "Should we support our government's acts of military killing in order to save some innocent people?" rather than as "What should we and our government be doing on a regular basis in order to prevent humanitarian crises from occurring?" This broader way of thinking can be traced out through four claims that stand in contrast to the just war arguments. These claims can be affirmed by any of the variations within pacifism presented in the last chapter. To use them altogether in serious dialogue with the just war position and with the aim of moving political actors toward a just peacemaking model reflects the concerns of engaged, more than separatist, pacifism. Other than that difference, pacifists raise the following objections to military methods of intervention.

Nations rarely act altruistically, so we must be suspicious of this claimed motive. In the case of Kosovo, European and American leaders claimed that the prospect of yet more genocidal ethnic cleansing moved them to act. But none of these nations moved to intervene in the Rwandan genocide that unfolded in the summer of 1994. Indeed, case after case can be adduced when an ounce of just prevention would have been worth a pound of military cure in humanitarian crises. If motivated by altruism, then why are nations like the United States and the United Kingdom so slow to act and so inconsistent? Whether they take the short, intermediate, or long view of the causes of the Balkan wars, critics believe that the United States and its NATO allies had opportunities to ease the conflict; NATO's claim to be acting simply as rescuer in a situation of last resort rings hollow. In 1998 and 1999, instead of preparing for bombing, the United States could have kept peace negotiations going with Milosevic and not sought to demonize him. In 1995, when the Dayton Peace Accords were being negotiated, Kosovo could have been brought into the process, as Ibrahim Rugova, the respected Kosovar Albanian leader, asked. Yet his plea fell on uninterested ears.[32]

Defenders of President Clinton and Prime Minister Blair might reply, "If these leaders were not motivated by altruism, then by what? Certainly they took a lot of political heat, even from their own parties, for intervening." This defense suggests that there was no political gain in intervening, leaving altruism as the only plausible motivation. The pacifist critic would respond that, from the perspective of national leaders, military engagement often seems a realistic, self-interested choice, even if it looks politically unpopular. We know from reportage and memoirs written after wars that all sorts of dubious motives are in play when leaders decide to commit troops. Leaders often believe that military actions will make them look strong in the eyes of voters and enemy nations. Even what looks like an ethical motive may be a leader's attempt to assuage guilt for past inaction or to deflect charges of inaction. In a more cynical interpretation, some critics floated the suggestion that Clinton's pressing for the NATO intervention was meant to distract media attention from his recently concluded impeachment trial.[33]

Samantha Power notes that leaders usually "fight the last war." She argues that, in the case of Kosovo, the American administration was assuaging guilt for dilatory action on Bosnia, exhibiting extreme frustration that Milosevic was once again aggravating the West, and defending NATO's credibility in the court of international opinion.[34] To assert these motives on the part of the leaders of NATO nations is not to deny that they also had humanitarian ideals, but it is to note that altruistic concern alone rarely motivates action. If such motivations are necessary, then intervention is coming from a dangerous place in the political psyche, where pseudomoral intentions can easily slide into perverse intentions. The most obvious example of this is Vietnam;

however noble the intentions of the American leaders in support of the South Vietnamese, one of the greatest bars to their long-overdue withdrawal was their reluctance to appear weak in the eyes of the Soviet Union and China.[35] The problem is not merely the personality of individual leaders but an ingrained mentality that military answers are quick fixes and effective solutions.

In the current context, intervention that lacks official UN approval is vigilante action. This second claim depends on the first claim. Because individual nations are given to self-interest, and because major powers like the United States, Russia, and China can act in many spheres with near impunity, it is hard to believe that these individual nations intervene for largely altruistic motives. Even if they sometimes do, it is very difficult to assess the intentions of leaders and even more difficult to exert control over them. In our current international system, the best hope we have for acting toward the common good is to require nations to work with each other. Getting several nations to intervene together under the aegis of the United Nations provides a check on the self-interests of single nations. For this reason, the member nations of the UN have submitted themselves to a compact to work under UN authority when they address regional crises. Under the UN Charter, every nation reserves the right to fight without higher authorization when it is a matter of self-defense (Article 51). All other threats to international peace and security are to be assessed by the Security Council (Article 39), and member states of the UN may act militarily—individually or through regional associations—only with the authorization of the Security Council (Articles 43 and 48). Pacifists support this strict interpretation of the just war criterion of legitimate authority. In the case of Kosovo, they argued that NATO acted illegally, that is, outside the terms of the UN Charter. While Russia's threatened veto of any Security Council resolution calling for military intervention can be seen as obstinate and not motivated by the common good of the Balkans, this hindrance did not give the United States the right to circumvent the UN and assert a novel right for NATO to wage an interventionist war.

Pacifists do not deny the shortcomings of the United Nations system as currently configured. Nonetheless, the UN remains the most desirable decision-making body because it is a forum in which all nations have to negotiate and compromise. This forum tends to prevent hasty military involvement. Regarding the charge that the UN approach leads to delay as crises flair, pacifists support reforming the UN to make it more effective. Effectiveness does not mean making it easier for the Security Council to authorize force but developing the conflict resolution and nation-building programs that would avert crises in the first place. The failure of nations to agree on military action is not a failure at that moment but a failure long before to cooperate on proactive measures.

Usually the people being rescued bear the brunt of the violence. Whether it is better for them is highly dubious, as examples bear out. Hundreds of Kosovar civilians were killed by human error during NATO's bombing campaign. An investigation by Human Rights Watch a year after the intervention put the number around five hundred deaths in some ninety incidents—a troubling figure even if it is fewer than the thousands of civilian deaths estimated by the Yugoslav government and journalists during the bombing campaign.[36] In addition to these casualties, critics note that the bombing gave Serbia excuse to kill more citizens, that the bombing displaced hundreds of thousands of Kosovars, that the already weak infrastructure and civil society of Kosovo was further demolished, and that bitter seeds of enmity were sowed by the bombs. Problematic as these consequences are, NATO leaders responded that none of them were intended. However, critics further charge that violations of proportionality and discrimination were built into the NATO campaign in three ways. First, NATO's overweening desire to avoid combat casualties led the commanders to order aerial bombings from a great height, which diminished NATO's ability to avoid hurting the people they were trying to help. Second, NATO directed much of its attack against civilian centers in Serbia. The bombing of roads, bridges, downtown buildings, and the electricity supply was intended to undermine the will of Serbian citizens. Finally, NATO nations never seriously contemplated the use of ground troops, which would have been a way to exercise due care in prosecuting the war. Pacifists believe that these policies violated just war principles and undermined NATO's claims of humanitarian concern.[37]

The military approach obscures and takes the energy away from other approaches. As Duane Cady notes, "very few pacifists are passivists, wishing to do nothing in the face of evil. The problem is in making sure intervention is the best course and in finding ways to make intervention genuinely humanitarian."[38] Indeed, the pacifist critics of military intervention can find common cause with just war thinkers in taking proactive steps to prevent genocide and human rights abuses. We will search for such common ground in the debate that follows.

DEBATING THE ISSUES

Just war and pacifism diverge at several points in this debate, yet they undeniably share some common ethical motivations and cautions. We now turn to an exploration of the divergences and convergences among our two ethical frameworks as they address humanitarian crises.

Skepticism about Altruistic Motives

BES Starting with the humanitarian motive, a fundamental principle for just war doctrine is the duty to rescue the innocent neighbor. We addressed that fundamental ethical issue in chapter 2; both of our positions want to help vulnerable neighbors, though we disagree about whether deadly force is a legitimate method of helping. So I assume that when it comes to humanitarian crises, you as a pacifist would say that the cause of stopping ethnic cleansing is certainly just, but that alone doesn't justify turning to violence. Do you think that anything has changed for the just war case when it comes to this kind of war? Does the focus on rescue of neighbor and the downplaying of national interests make such military action any more palatable to the pacifist?

DLC Fighting a war to protect the vulnerable clearly demands a different moral evaluation than, for example, a war of conquest. In one case, the motivation is concern for the neighbor, in the other, selfish gain. But pacifists would be skeptical of even the former on two counts. First, the consequences of modern war for civilians are so devastating that it is very unlikely to be the best way to protect anyone. Use of the most advanced weaponry against a weak armed force in the 2003 Iraq War resulted in thousands of civilian deaths. In the Kosovo case, we noted at least five hundred civilian deaths and many other negative consequences caused by the NATO bombing. War is an exceedingly blunt instrument to attempt the protection of civilians and very often results in the death and injury of those it claims to be helping. A second ground for skepticism arises from the question of how frequently nations actually do fight wars solely to benefit third parties. Often such worthy motives are cited to justify actions that are in fact driven by national self-interest. Many pacifists, including myself, would concede that there are rare occasions where there seems no alternative to a limited use of military force. For me, the small-scale intervention of British troops in Sierra Leone to restore order in the context of violent drug-fuelled anarchy is one example. But such action should be seen in the analogy of policing in an international context, ideally through the action of international institutions such as the UN, and should be clearly separated from the war aims of individual nation-states.

BES Defenders of humanitarian intervention cannot afford to be insensitive or unrealistic about the first problem, for it would undermine the heart of their ethic. We who defend intervention—in general and in specific cases—feel quite agonized about it because it is tragic to see some innocent lives lost in the quest to protect a people. It is a cold comfort to appeal to proportionality when balancing civilian deaths in Kosovo against the repeal of the Serb army because those civilians were flesh-and-blood people who didn't want occupation but also didn't want to die. The just war position can only rely on its decision criteria to develop a prudent argument that the risk to civilian lives will be worth the ending of a larger problem. If there are less lethal ways to stop the problem, just war thinkers should embrace them; we can come back to those options later in this section.

Your second objection was skepticism about altruism. This is a valuable corrective from the pacifist side; it is tempting for just war defenders of intervention to romanticize the motives of the intervening nations. As I researched our Kosovo case study, I became less sanguine about what the NATO nations wanted to achieve and discouraged by the way that several great powers made the Balkans their political football. So the question for me is, How many mixed motives can a just war thinker accept? I expect nation-states to have some self-interested motives when intervening, but I believe that their decisions not to intervene and not even to put political and economic pressure on a genocidal government are usually selfish, too. Of course, in overcoming selfish or realist arguments for nonintervention, it may not be wise to swing all the way to military intervention. So the burden falls on all of us to find ways to get the international community involved in stopping genocide and human rights abuses. The hope for just war thinkers is to develop a process and a set of institutions that can make interventions less necessary by heading off problems before they start, and more effective and ethical when they do take place. In that eventuality, I agree that intervention will look much more like policing than war.

International Cooperation and Accountability

DLC So we're agreed that nation-states are unlikely to act altruistically. At a time when it's hard to persuade richer countries even to give adequate financial aid to poorer nations, it doesn't seem likely that there will be many volunteers for the much more costly enterprise of warring on behalf of others. I think a good analogy for the current international system is a nation without a police force. This lack of authority gives rise to private vigilante groups that act to protect their members or to enforce justice. Some groups may be well intentioned and well organized; others are ill intentioned, badly organized, or both. None can be relied on to act in the public interest because none is responsible to the public. In order to establish a reliable justice system, these private groups must be superseded by an accountable, publicly funded agency of law enforcement, at which point the private groups are disbanded and disarmed. Nation-states are the vigilantes in the current global system: some better intentioned, some worse, but none trustworthy to act in the interests of all. We can currently only count on their acting in the common interest when this overlaps with private interest.

BES That's a fair analogy to the international system. The laws of war are based on the Westphalian model of independent nation-states, and political observers are skeptical about a new and better model replacing this system anytime soon. It's been a feature of my Catholic tradition in modern times to place strong hopes in an effective international authority, and it's a hope I share because of its promise for fair conflict resolution among nations. Realists say that this is a pipe dream for a mixture of three reasons: Powerful nation-states won't give up their powers, there will always be aggressive states that need to be restrained, and international institutions, as they are now structured, are not accountable to the citizens of respective nations.[39] I believe that peoples and governments concerned to move toward a better model shouldn't give up the hope but must be satisfied with very slow progress—and humanitarian intervention may well be an area where we can start some genuine progress. If at all possible, decisions to intervene should not come down to single actors ignoring the United Nations. The NATO intervention was something of a hybrid case; it didn't involve a single nation, but it did occur without UN sanction. Even if the intervention was ethically necessary, we can't build international cooperation to resolve crises if the rule of law is not respected. A new path starts with fair criticisms of both the UN, which is often ineffectual and hampered by multiple interests, and the major powers because they have proven unwilling to cooperate in such a way that they put themselves on a par with other nations.

DLC So I have conceded that there are rare cases where international military action is necessary on the analogy of policing, and we are agreed that where military action is justified, it should be through the UN wherever possible. I agree that the structure of the UN Security Council needs reform before it can be completely relied on to approve military intervention in the right cases and not in the wrong ones. This means that there may be rare occasions in the interim when military intervention is justified, but vetoed, and multilateral groups should take action in any case (which, we have noted, is recognized by a recent UN report). The remaining point of difference between us, then, is how high we set the bar for such exceptional interventions. I have said that Operation Palliser, the U.K. intervention in Sierra Leone in 2000, was legitimate to address the violent anarchy there. I would have supported an early deployment of UN troops to defend thousands of civilians in the UN safe area of Srebrenica, Bosnia, to prevent their massacre in 1995. These are examples of limited deployments of military force to respond to a desperate situation not amenable to alternative responses. I do not consider that full-scale warfare with aerial bombardment, such as took place in Kosovo in 1999 or Iraq in 2003, is likely to be effective in realizing humanitarian ends.

BES In recognition of your concession to accept limited, emergency military interventions on the policing model, it is appropriate that I concede

that military interventions are often unnecessary if other foresighted actions are taken and that they are often ineffective in realizing their
stated purposes. Even in the starkest cases of humanitarian crisis, military intervention usually represents a failure of the major powers and
the UN to have headed off a conflict at an earlier stage. For instance, the
failure of anyone to intervene in Rwanda does not prove that military intervention was the only alternative to prevent the genocide. The UN commander in Rwanda, General Roméo Dallaire, repeatedly begged the UN
for more peacekeeping troops and more political support in the weeks
leading up to the hundred-day massacre in the summer of 1993. Because of the disinterest and self-interest of all the Security Council members, nothing happened. It must be pointed out that averting the
genocide may have required fighting, but early on, any use of force could
have been limited and effective. On the matter of ineffectiveness, the
blunt tool of war can create as many problems as it eliminates. While I
still believe that the NATO intervention in Kosovo was the least-bad option given the political conditions of late 1998 and early 1999, it has by
no means been a total success. Sadly, ethnic-Albanian Kosovars have
turned around and repressed ethnic Serb Kosovars. Ethnic Serb leaders
have held back from the negotiating process to establish a new government, and the Serb population is increasingly emigrating from the region
in hopes of better prospects elsewhere.[40] By contrast, the peacekeeping
mission in Macedonia led to a long-term peaceful outcome because the
intervention started early and featured a peace process that secured minority rights.[41]

Alternatives to Military Intervention

BES   Although we set the bar for military intervention at different
heights, we have located a good deal of common ground between us. It
is common ground that can enjoy broad assent from pacifists and just
war thinkers and has found expression in the just peacemaking movement. Pacifists and just war thinkers would do well to advertise this
common ground and to work through the media, academy, churches,
and advocacy groups to push their governments to shape foreign policies accordingly. Our common cause is simply the protection of people in
the most just and peaceful manner possible. The good news is that this

goal is usually best achieved by pursuing early alternatives to military intervention. Let's conclude by applying some of the ten just peacemaking principles to our case study and discussing whether we think they would have been a proper response to Kosovo.

DLC   As complex and contentious as the Kosovo crisis was, I think there were options for nonviolent resolution—even in 1999, so I disagree with you that military intervention was the least-bad option at that time. The third just peacemaking principle is to use cooperative conflict resolution, which should have been the short-term and long-term approach outside nations took toward the Balkans. Just peacemakers do not pretend that conflict resolution is a panacea, but they believe that its possibilities are often left unexplored. The prospects for conflict resolution throughout the Balkans crisis was a complex issue. But even when it came to Kosovo, some ideas are evident. Representatives of the Kosovars should have been included in the Dayton peace process, and the status of Kosovo should have been addressed in the Dayton Accords of 1995. The United States should have worked cooperatively with Russia to establish terms that Russia would accept in the Rambouillet Accords. Related principles are the seventh and tenth: to work with emerging cooperative forces and to encourage grassroots peacemaking groups. Various UN members were concerned about the KLA's use of force and its designs for power. Strong efforts should have been made to incorporate moderate and constructive Kosavar Albanian leaders, such as Ibrahim Rugova, at the earliest stage possible.

Taking a longer-term view, the fifth and six principles were and remain necessary: to advance democracy and human rights and to promote development. These are strategies that, by themselves, would not have averted the crisis brewing in 1998–99, but if the UN, the United States, and the European Union had previously made long-term commitments to the region, they would have encouraged more cooperative attitudes by leaders and better feelings among the populations of the Balkan republics. After the wars of the early 1990s, Milosevic certainly had a number of needs for rebuilding infrastructure and restoring the economy of Serbia. The international parties could have offered more carrot in the peace process before waving the stick.

BES I affirm the exploration of cooperative conflict resolution, and I agree that some different diplomatic choices earlier in the 1990s might have dissuaded or distracted Serbia from designs on Kosovo. I see no reason to think that Milosevic would have stayed his hand from further machinations in Balkan republics, given that working with him as a peace partner at Dayton failed to change his tune, but a strong rebuilding and investment plan for the Balkans immediately after the Dayton Accords would have been worth trying.

I would point to the eighth principle: to strengthen international efforts for cooperation. As we have agreed, diplomatic intercession, peacekeeping missions, and last-resort interventions should be pursued cooperatively among nations. Commitment of troops, whether fighting is envisioned or not, should proceed under UN authority except in exceptional circumstances. Reform of the United Nations needs to address the obstacles that have stymied timely diplomatic and peacekeeping intercession. One possibility is to develop better working relationships and formal processes for delegating responsibility to handle crises from the UN to regional associations—NATO, the Organization of American States (OAS), the Economic Community of West African States (ECOWAS), the Organization of the Islamic Conference (OIC), and others. It was a failure for all parties involved that the United States exercised NATO leadership as the alternative to the UN, rather than as a partner with the UN. NATO could have provided a strong and safe buffer between Serbia and Kosovo once a fair and agreeable peace process was worked out. Another option would be for the United Nations to develop its own genocide-intervention force.

In contrast to the current situation, military intervention forces would not be national forces with national commanders under UN sponsorship. Rather, the force would comprise recruits from many nations who are employed directly by the UN. It wouldn't make Security Council members that much quicker to commit troops in a crisis, but it would give them more political cover than they currently have. However, it is doubtful at the current time that powerful nations want to grant the UN the right to command its own troops, thus conferring the agency more power and legitimacy.

CONCLUSION

We began this chapter about humanitarian intervention by saying that it is an inherently difficult situation and that it would test the central commitments of each theory. What our investigation and debate seem to show is that both pacifism and just war tradition have to keep scrutinizing their methods and claims in order to avoid the dangers of failure to rescue (by pacifists) or failure to consider peaceful alternatives (by just war thinkers). In contrast to our starker differences on theories of Christian ethics and war in the previous chapters, on this concrete issue we were able to locate substantial common ground under the just peacemaking framework.

CHAPTER 4

The Challenge of Weapons Proliferation

P eople who are moved by the destruction caused by war have sought to limit the damage it causes in two main ways. The first is to reduce the number of wars. The pacifist position obviously focuses on attempting to reduce—to zero—the number of times war is seen as a legitimate means of resolving conflicts. Although the just war tradition recognizes that war may sometimes be necessary, its criteria for an appropriate war (jus ad bellum) seek to reduce the number of wars by ensuring that strict conditions are met, as we saw in chapter 2. The second approach is to recognize that wars will continue to be fought and to focus instead on controlling the damage caused by war. This is the second element of modern just war theory (jus in bello), stipulating that actions in warfare should be proportionate to their goal and should discriminate between combatants and noncombatants. It developed somewhat independently of the jus ad bellum criteria when theologians, who saw little likelihood of preventing the outbreak of war, concentrated instead on establishing conventions for how war should be fought.

There are many ways in which the conduct of war can be limited by agreement or convention: Warring parties may agree about how to treat prisoners of war, enemy civilians, and enemies who surrender. One key question in determining the destructiveness of a war, however, is the weapons used. Wars of swords and spears can and have resulted in massive numbers of people killed, but they cannot compare with the indiscriminate destructive power of the saturation bombing of German and Japanese cities in World War II or the long-term human and environmental devastation caused by the atomic bombs dropped on Hiroshima and Nagasaki by the United States in 1945. As nations have developed new weapon technologies and modes of conducting war, they have also feared the power of such weapons and so have often attempted to reach agreements to restrict their use. The Greek Amphictyonic League in the seventh century BC, for example, agreed that in war between its members, water supplies were inviolable.[1] We will later discuss examples ranging from the Church's prohibition of crossbow-men in the twelfth century to bans on chemical, biological, and nuclear weapons in the twentieth. Because the Christian just war tradition gave rise to the systematization of international laws of war, as described in chapter 2, just war criteria will figure in the political history traced by our four case studies. The case studies concern attempts to limit the development and use of certain weapons through appeals to just war principles. Later in the chapter, Christian pacifism and Christian realism will be called upon to challenge the success of these attempts.

The jus in bello requirements of the just war tradition relate most obviously to uses of particular weapons in particular scenarios. The Allies' destruction of Dresden using incendiary bombs in World War II, for example, was clearly indiscriminate and disproportionate, whereas using the same weapons in a focused attack on a munitions dump might well satisfy both criteria. Some weapons, however, by their nature may not satisfy the criteria in any conceivable scenario. Nuclear weapons are an obvious potential example of such a weapon. Because of their immense destructive power, the long-term impact of radiation poisoning on human health, and the long-term environmental devastation they cause, many have argued that they can never be used in a discriminate or proportionate way. On a very different scale, the 1997 Ottawa Treaty banned the production and use of antipersonnel landmines on the basis of their indiscriminate nature, as they pose dangers to noncombatants long after the end of a conflict.

Some initiatives on restricting weapons have gone beyond these criteria. The medieval concern about crossbows was not due to their breaching discrimination or proportionality. Similarly, the decision of the 1907 Hague Convention to prohibit poisoned weapons was based neither on discrimination because the intended victims were soldiers, nor on proportionality because, if poison weapons promised to be effective for an important military objective, then their use could be considered proportionate. In these cases, the motivation for agreeing to limitations seems to have been a particular distaste for the effect of the weapons and, thus, a desire to avoid being attacked with them by agreeing not to employ them.

Before we can consider any of these attempts to reach agreements on limiting weapon types, an initial issue needs to be addressed. Is it reasonable to hope that nations who are prepared to go to war with each other will mutually respect any restriction? One classic text of war strategy suggests not. In his influential book *On War*, Carl von Clausewitz (1780–1831), a Prussian general, stated that the aim of warfare is for one party to impose its will on another by force and that successful armies will use force "without compunction, undeterred by the bloodshed it involves."[2] As Michael Howard points out in discussing Clausewitz, if belligerent nations are reasonable enough to accept extraneous limitations on their conduct in war, there is a strong case that they should be reasonable enough to avoid fighting altogether.[3] But the latter does not happen, so we should doubt the former would either. Clearly, there are examples where warring states have mutually observed limitations about how war is to be fought, but these limitations are only likely to be respected when the political aims of the war are also limited. When a people are fighting for their very existence, they will seize on any means of defense that promises to be effective. The success of treaties to control the possession and use of arms, therefore, is highly dependent on prudential considerations. A state is likely to give up a particular weapon only if it this will not weaken its comparative military strength.

The position of rival nations in an arms race has been compared to the situation of the Prisoner's Dilemma in game theory. This situation pictures two prisoners suspected of carrying out a robbery together. They are held separately, unable to communicate, and are offered the following terms. If both confess to the crime, they will each serve five years in prison; if neither confesses, both go to jail for one year; if one confesses and the other does not, the one who confessed goes free and the other serves a twenty-year prison term. The oddity is that they cannot reach the best mutual outcome—both serving one year by refusing to confess—because it is too risky if the other does not cooperate. That is, if one confesses out of fear or in hope of going scot-free, the nonconfessing prisoner will get a twenty-year sentence. Therefore, by protecting their own interests and by not being able to trust each other when each does not know what the other is thinking, the prisoners arrive at the suboptimal result: both confess and both receive a five-year term. The similarity to two rival nations seeking military advantage over the other is compelling. If at a given point in time they are at parity in military strength, then each can gain an advantage over the other by spending more to build more or better weapons. If both spend more, however, they are likely to reach parity again, having each made a costly investment. The best mutual outcome is if neither spends more and the military parity remains, yet it is too risky to take this option in case the other does not cooperate. There is an important and relevant difference between the Prisoner's Dilemma and an arms race: In an arms race, the parties can communicate. If a system is set up whereby each nation can check what the other is doing, then the risk of cooperation is eliminated, and each nation can benefit from cooperating. Therefore, if arms control treaties have robust mechanisms for verifying compliance and appropriate ways of dealing with noncompliance, it may be rational for nations to agree to them.[4]

We will see these considerations play out in different ways in relation to the four different examples of attempts to limit weapons. The ongoing problem is as old as human society: Can groups agree to forgo the use and possession of heinous weapons and then abide by the promises they make? Following the historical presentation of this problem, we will consider how Christian theologians and churches have addressed it, relying upon pacifist, just war, and realist reasoning. Then we will make a frank assessment of the political and ethical challenges of weapons proliferation today before launching into our debate.

Case 1: Bows and Arrows

The medieval attempt to prohibit crossbows is an illuminating example of the difficulties of agreeing to limit the use of weapons. The medieval crossbow was a considerable technical advance on earlier weapons. By using metal to generate higher tension, a bolt could be propelled over three hundred meters and could pierce chain mail. This weapon was frightening because its lethal force could be projected over unprecedented distances, wholly disrupting the contemporary chivalric conventions of armed conflict. At a time when the noble, armored knight on horseback was the ultimate in military power, here was a weapon that could be wielded by archers not of the nobility, who could kill long before the knight's weapon was within range of the archer. The nobility had an interest in banning these weapons, and two attempts to do so are documented. In 1120, Charles the

Good sought to keep the peace in Flanders by prohibiting bows and arrows. Later, in 1139, the Catholic bishops attending the Second Lateran Council prohibited the "murderous art" of crossbowmen and archers as "hateful to God."[5]

Despite the support of the nobility, such measures were largely ineffective. James T. Johnson notes that Gratian's *Decretum*, a comprehensive and influential compilation of canon law published a decade after the Second Lateran Council, contained no reference to it. Hostiensis, writing one hundred years later, wholly set aside the ban in favor of the view that all weapons were acceptable in a just war.[6] Here is an example of important social conventions supported by powerful vested interests being overturned by the raw military effectiveness of a new weapons technology. Not even Christian combatants could resist using crossbows, which meant that everyone ended up adopting them.

Case 2: Chemical and Biological Weapons

More recent attempts to prohibit certain weapons include the Hague Conventions of 1899 and 1907 and the Geneva Convention of 1925. The 1899 Hague Convention, convened by the Russian minister of foreign affairs, primarily aimed at placing limits on the expansion of armed forces. It failed in this aim, but the parties did agree to prohibit asphyxiating gases, expanding bullets ("dumdum" bullets), and aerial bombardment from balloons. The 1907 convention also failed to gain consensus for limiting armed forces but prohibited the use of poison weapons and "arms, projectiles, or material calculated to cause unnecessary suffering."[7] Seven years later Europe was at war. In 1914 first the French and then the Germans fired artillery or mortar projectiles filled with poison. By 1915 Germany had developed a large-scale technique for the liquefaction of chlorine, which enabled the release of poison upwind of the target area. This practice caused many casualties. British forces developed the Livens Projector as a means of delivering large-caliber mortar shells filled with chemical ammunition in batteries of several dozen with the aim of surprising enemy troops before they could put gas masks on. In 1917 Germany introduced mustard gas, which caused mass casualties by assaulting the skin, eyes, and respiratory tracts of soldiers.[8]

The fear suffered by the troops who were subjected to these attacks is expressed in Wilfred Owen's poem "Dulce et Decorum Est." Owen was a soldier in the war who describes the impact of a gas attack on exhausted troops marching away from the front:

> *Gas! GAS! Quick, boys!—An ecstasy of fumbling,*
> *Fitting the clumsy helmets just in time;*
> *But someone still was yelling out and stumbling,*
> *And flound'ring like a man in fire or lime . . .*
> *Dim, through the misty panes and thick green light,*
> *As under a green sea, I saw him drowning.*
> *In all my dreams, before my helpless sight,*
> *He plunges at me, guttering, choking, drowning.*

Owen asks the reader to imagine walking with him behind the wagon carrying the solider away:

> *And watch the white eyes writhing in his face,*
> *His hanging face, like a devil's sick of sin;*
> *If you could hear, at every jolt, the blood*
> *Come gargling from the froth-corrupted lungs,*
> *Obscene as cancer, bitter as the cud*
> *Of vile, incurable sores on innocent tongues.*[9]

If people could, indeed, experience the episode, Owen concludes, they might not continue to teach children "the old lie: Dulce et Decorum est / Pro patria mori." The old lie from Horace is that "it is sweet and fitting to die for one's country," and for Owen, the horror of witnessing a gas attack is the ultimate evidence that such sentiments cannot survive the reality of modern warfare.

Thus, within a decade of agreeing not to use poisoned weapons or weapons that cause undue suffering, France, Germany, and Britain had each used chemical weapons on the battlefield with devastating effect. Again, the criterion of effectiveness in achieving military goals trumped a prior agreement on limiting weapon use. Following the war, a further attempt was made to restrict the use of chemical weapons, which led to the Geneva Convention of 1925. The signatories agreed to prohibit the "use in war of asphyxiating, poisonous or other gases, and of all analogous liquids, materials or devices." In addition, "bacteriological methods of warfare" were prohibited for the first time.[10] It was agreed that the treaty should prohibit the use rather than the development and possession of chemical and biological weapons, as the broader restricters were not realistically verifiable. This provision was subsequently interpreted by many states to mean no first use and, therefore, it has not prevented many countries from developing chemical weapons. Since 1925 Italy has used poison gas against Egypt in 1936 and 1937, and Japan has used it against China in 1941. Although Germany infamously used gas in its concentration camps, it was not used on the battlefield in Europe during World War II. The greatest use of chemical weapons since 1925 was by Iraq against Kurdish villages in northern Iraq and against Iranian soldiers in the 1980s.

In comparison with the previous tenets established by the Hague conventions, therefore, there have been few breaches of Geneva, so the convention must be judged a relative success. It is unclear, however, how much this reflects an international consensus about the importance of keeping to the convention and how much is due to military judgments of the ineffectiveness of chemical weapons. Countermeasures such as gas masks had already reduced the impact of gas attacks by the end of World War I. Today, for nations that can afford it, modern protective clothing means that chemical weapons no longer present a major threat to their ability to fight wars. Yet whatever the motivations, the 1997 Chemical Weapons Convention is a significant and welcome development of the 1925 convention. It requires signatory states both to declare their chemical weapons and production facilities and to agree to dispose of them in a safe manner before April 2007. At the beginning of 2005, 168 nations had joined the convention, and only six states are currently suspected of having undeclared chemical weapons programs: China, Egypt, Iran, Israel, North Korea, and Syria.[11]

The only use of biological weapons in modern warfare was by Japan. During the Sino-Japanese War (1937–45) and World War II, the Japanese army's Unit 731 tested biological weapons on at least three thousand prisoners of war from China, the United States, and other nations, killing at least one thousand of them.[12] Japan is also reported to have contaminated Chinese foodstuffs and water supplies, killing many thousands.[13] That the use of biological weapons is limited to this one case has not been due to lack of investment or capacity: Both the Soviet Union and the United States developed biological weapons during the cold war with the potential to destroy many food crops and perhaps all human life.

Fortunately, under President Richard Nixon, the United States unilaterally destroyed all its biological weapons in 1969 and negotiated the Biological Weapons Convention of 1975, which prohibited the development, possession, and use of biological weapons. The lack of verification mechanisms in the treaty has reduced its effectiveness, however. In 1992 Boris Yeltsin announced that the Soviet Union had continued its biological weapons program despite having signed the treaty. Russia is still suspected of retaining biological weapons along with China, Egypt, Iran, Israel, North Korea, and Syria.[14] It would seem, therefore, that the treaty is not the reason that Japan is the only nation to have used biological weapons. Other likely reasons are the technical difficulties of delivering biological agents, the limited effectiveness of biological weapons against suitably protected soldiers, and the lack of military advantage gained by deploying the weapons against civilians.

Since 1945 chemical and biological weapons have often been lumped together with nuclear weapons. For a while, the acronym "ABC weapons" (atomic, biological, and chemical) was used, followed by "NBC weapons" (replacing atomic with nuclear). Starting in 2002 the American media followed President George W. Bush in making "weapons of mass destruction" a popular referent for these three types of weapons. However, we follow many analysts in considering "weapons of mass destruction" a misleading term, as it elides the massively devastating impact of nuclear weapons with weapons (namely, chemical) that are less effective than conventional arms and weapons (namely, biological) that are in limited supply and of questionable effectiveness.[15] To be accurate in the terminology is not to downplay the dreadful nature of the latter two weapon types. The choice of term has obvious relevance to the case of the 2003 Iraq War, which we will discuss in chapter 6, because Iraq's supposed possession of weapons of mass destruction was given as the central justification for invasion. Determination of an ethical and effective response to a nation's attempt to develop or acquire weapons must be based on accurate information about the nation's activities and an impartial assessment of the risk posed by each type of weapon. Nuclear weapons require separate consideration from chemical and biological weapons, which brings us to the next case.

Case 3: Nuclear Weapons

A third example of attempts to limit the use of a particular class of weapons since 1945 concerns nuclear weapons. In August 1945, after the successful conclusion of the Manhattan Project, the United States decided to bomb Hiroshima with the objective of persuading Japan to surrender. The explosion had the force of fifteen thousand tons of TNT, completely devastated four square miles in the center of the city, killed sixty-six thousand people immediately, and injured sixty-nine thousand more. Three days later, Nagasaki was struck with a second and larger atomic bomb, killing thirty-nine thousand and injuring twenty-five thousand. The Japanese quickly surrendered. Many more civilians died of injuries and radiation poisoning before the end of the year.

The scale of civilian death and injury caused by the bombings of Hiroshima and Nagasaki was unfortunately not unique in World War II, in which the policy of strategic bombardment was employed on a large scale for the first time. At least fifty thousand were killed in the firebombing of Hamburg in July 1943, and a minimum of twenty-five thousand in the firebombing of Dresden in 1945. There were comparable numbers of civilians killed in other German cities. The firebombing of Tokyo in February and March 1945 exceeded the numbers killed by either of the atomic bombs; the official death toll was eighty-four thousand and may have been as high as one hundred thousand. The key difference in the use of atomic weapons was the scale of attack required. The bombing of Tokyo required 174 B-29 bombers on the night of February 23rd and 334 on March 9th, together dropping seventeen hundred tons of bombs. Hiroshima and Nagasaki were each destroyed by one bomb dropped from a single aircraft. Although the American supply of atomic bombs at the time was limited, the message was clear: The atomic age signaled the potential for limitless destruction, with very little possibility of defense.

After the war all nations were left to reflect on what this new weapon meant for future wars and for international relations. The United States continued its nuclear program and began to draw up plans for using atomic weapons against the Soviet Union in an "atomic blitz." But its position as the sole nuclear power was short-lived; the Soviet Union tested its own atomic bomb in 1949, years before the United States had anticipated. Thus began a new and dangerous era of relationship between the two states. Because there was no defense against a nuclear attack and little trust in the intentions of either side, the only way to dissuade the enemy from attacking was to convince it that an attack would provoke a severe retaliation. Previously, there was usually some warning of coming conflict, so nations could begin mobilizing for defense. The great fear on both sides in this new era was of a massive surprise attack, a danger that became even more evident after each side developed Inter-Continental Ballistic Missiles (ICBMs) equipped with nuclear warheads. This development led both sides to adopt a permanent mobilization for war and, in order to make their deterrents credible, to put their nuclear missiles on a hair trigger, targeted and ready to fire within fifteen minutes.

Whereas the superpowers invested heavily in the production and further development of atomic weapons in the years that followed, other nations showed their desire to acquire the new weapons. The United Kingdom tested an atomic bomb in 1952, and France did the same in 1960. The Cuban missile crisis of 1962 led to the negotiation of the Limited Test Ban Treaty. Signed in 1963 by the United States, the Soviet Union, and the United Kingdom, it banned nuclear weapons testing in the atmosphere, in outer space, and underwater, but permitted underground testing. Within a few months, the treaty was signed by over one hundred other governments but notably not by France and China. China performed its first atomic weapons test in 1964.

The original signatories to the Limited Test Ban Treaty recognized the dangers of further proliferation. These concerns led to the negotiation in 1968 of the Non-Proliferation Treaty, signed by fifty-nine other states. The treaty committed the three states with nuclear weapons not to transfer nuclear weapons to any nonnuclear weapons state or to assist them in the manufacture or acquisition of nuclear weapons. The nonnuclear weapons parties agreed not to develop or acquire such weapons. In return, they were promised assistance in the development of peaceful uses of nuclear technology. The nuclear weapons states also committed themselves to "pursue negotiations in good faith on effective measures relating to cessation of the nuclear arms race at an early date and to nuclear disarmament, and on a treaty on general and complete disarmament under strict and effective international control."[16] China and France, the other two states known to possess nuclear weapons in 1968, did not sign the treaty until 1992. Other notable nonparticipants were Israel, India, Pakistan, and South Africa. Israel almost certainly developed its own nuclear weapons during the 1960s but did so covertly; it has neither confirmed nor denied the existence of its program. India tested its first nuclear weapon in 1974 and tested another weapon in 1998 after Pakistan conducted its first test. South Africa pursued a nuclear weapons program in the 1980s, possibly with help from Israel, but discontinued the program in advance of the transition to majority rule that began in 1990; it became a signatory to the treaty in 1991.

Although the Non-Participation Treaty commits the nuclear weapons states to pursue in good faith a treaty for complete nuclear disarmament, there is no evidence of compliance with this article. The only disarmament treaties were those between the United States and the Soviet Union; most of these treaties failed to reduce the potential destructive power of their nuclear arsenals. The exceptions were the treaties negotiated between Soviet President Mikhail Gorbachev and U.S. Presidents Ronald Reagan and George H. W. Bush, notably the 1987 Elimination of Intermediate Nuclear Forces (INF) Treaty and the 1991 Strategic Arms Reduction Treaty (START).

Until 1998 the Nuclear Non-Proliferation Treaty had been largely successful in preventing the widespread acquisition of nuclear weapons. Only Israel and India had joined the original five; South Africa had given up its nuclear program; and other nations, such as Argentina and Brazil, that looked likely to develop nuclear weapons had decided against doing so. Since then, however, the situation has become more precarious. Review meetings for the Nuclear Non-Proliferation Treaty in 1995, 2000, and 2005 demonstrated considerable concern both about nonnuclear weapons states gaining nuclear weapons and about the lack of progress by the nuclear weapons states toward disarmament. North Korea announced in 2005 that it now possesses nuclear weapons, and it tested missiles that could serve as a delivery system in 2006. Also in 2006 Iran made moves to begin enriching uranium; its stated goal was peaceful nuclear power, but other states claimed this would allow Iran to produce nuclear weapons. Nonnuclear weapons states feared both the activities of these two states and the possibility that the United States might launch military attacks to prevent the proliferation.

The proliferation that has occurred in spite of the Nuclear Non-Proliferation Treaty points up its fatal flaw: It does not apply symmetrically to all signatories. Accepting the reality that the first states to develop nuclear weapons were not going to relinquish them, the treaty distinguishes between these states, who are permitted to keep their weapons, and all the other nations, who are not permitted to join them. Instead of focusing only on the character of the weapons, as the Hague and Geneva Conventions do, the Non-Proliferation Treaty makes a tacit judgment that some states are more trustworthy than others. But who determines which is trustworthy? It is up to the nuclear powers to decide who joins the club, which has been a source of rationalization and inconsistency. For example, Iraq's purported attempts to acquire fissile material were presented as one of the reasons for invasion by the United States and the United Kingdom, both of which possess nuclear weapons and have shown no intention of invading allies who have refused to be bound by the treaty, such as Pakistan, India, and Israel. To define nonproliferation as keeping weapons from rogue states, rather than from all nations or even from those nations in breach of treaty obligations, suggests that the nuclear weapons states have superior judgment. This attitude in turn generates resentment and ambitions among nonnuclear weapons states. If many other nations beyond the original five develop nuclear weapons, the rationale for nonnuclear nations to respect their treaty obligations becomes significantly weaker.

Another development increasing the risk posed by nuclear weapons is the argument that these weapons could be discriminate and proportionate if they were sufficiently small. Military strategists have attempted to identify scenarios where tactical nuclear weapons could be used against opposing forces in a limited nuclear war. When the Soviet Union had superiority in conventional weapons in Europe, for example, NATO strategists looked at the possibility of using tactical nuclear weapons (that is, small kiloton nuclear arms meant for battlefield use) against them as an early response to aggression. Yet even if the use of such weapons could be kept away from civilians, a broad consensus has emerged that breaching the nuclear threshold would make escalation to the use of larger nuclear weapons very likely. Provoking a full-scale nuclear war would obviously be disproportionate to any conceivable war aim; therefore, it seems that using nuclear weapons of any kind could not be justified in a just war context.

Case 4: Modern Conventional Weapons

Although weapons with the potential to cause death and destruction on a large scale generate the most fear among civilians, most of those who die in modern conflict are killed by small arms: revolvers, pistols, rifles, and light machine guns. The Small Arms Survey project estimates that between 60 and 90 percent of deaths in conflict result from the use of small arms. In

2001 the project estimated that small arms kill three hundred thousand people annually.[17] The vast majority of these weapons are traded legally, and the trade is big business. Sales of other conventional arms were worth around $40 billion in 2003. The major arms exporters are the United States ($14 billion in 2003), the United Kingdom ($6.9 billion), Russia ($5.5 billion), France ($4.9 billion), and Israel ($2.4 billion).[18] The trade is restricted only by international arms embargoes, multilateral agreements, and the export policies of individual nation-states. International arms embargoes are rare; in July 2005, there were only ten in operation.[19] There are many multilateral agreements aimed at restricting the proliferation of particular weapon types, but they are limited both in their aim and effectiveness.[20] Some states have restrictive controls on the export of weapons, yet in the absence of an international treaty restricting the arms trade, nations are forced to balance the potential profits from selling weapons against the desire to adopt an ethical policy concerning what should be sold to whom.

One example of a conventional weapon that has been limited by treaty is antipersonnel land mines. The widespread deployment of these mines in many wars has resulted in a large number of civilian casualties long after conflicts have ended. The International Campaign to Ban Landmines estimates that in Cambodia alone there have been thirty-five thousand amputees since conflict ended and that worldwide there are now between three hundred thousand and four hundred thousand survivors of land mine attacks, most of whom have been permanently disabled.[21] Concern about the indiscriminate impact of antipersonnel land mines and the long-term threat they represent to civilians led to a campaign to ban them, which culminated in the 1997 Ottawa Treaty prohibiting their possession and use and mandating the destruction of stockpiles. In February 2004, the treaty had been ratified by 144 countries, but among the 42 that have not signed are China, India, Russia, and the United States.

Similar concerns have been raised about cluster bombs. Because these bombs split into bomblets that are often brightly colored, those that do not explode on impact present a danger to civilians, especially to children who think they are toys. Sadly, the Ottawa Treaty does not cover these weapons, and there seems little international will to abandon their use.

There has also been little progress in limiting the use of depleted uranium weapons. Enriching uranium for use in nuclear reactors and nuclear weapons creates depleted uranium as a waste product, so states with nuclear programs have significant stockpiles of the fissile material. Highly dense, it is valuable both in armor-piercing missiles and in armor plating. However, it is radioactive and toxic, so its use in weapons pollutes the air and the immediate environment. For this reason, the UN Human Rights Commission voted in 1996 and 1997 to ban depleted uranium weapons. Yet these weapons remain in use in many armed forces, including all the permanent members of the UN Security Council.

THEOLOGICAL RESPONSES TO WEAPONS

The ethical witness of the Christian tradition through these historical moments has been largely, but not exclusively, voiced through the just war tradition. Pacifism has often been criticized by just war thinkers as having nothing constructive to add to decisions over what weapons to use and what weapons to develop or refrain from developing. However, in the nuclear age, pacifism has enjoyed renewed respect for its witness against the folly of the "mutually assured destruction" theory on which nuclear deterrence is based. In contrast, the other Christian voice that has been important in the twentieth and twenty-first centuries is that of Christian realism, which asserts that we cannot live in a world without force and that responsible leaders sometimes have no choice but to violate the rules of war.

Let us first step back and look briefly at what Christian thinkers were saying during the eras of these four case studies. The motive for the Catholic Church's medieval attempts to restrain crossbows was a twofold fear: fear of the destructive potential of these weapons to the belligerents themselves and, especially, fear that their use would enlarge the wars in which they were used. Moral concern about noncombatant civilians had not been fully articulated in just war tradition at this point. Still, recognition of the effects of uncontrolled war on women, children, and nonfighting men formed part of the motivation for bans on weapons and restrictions on certain times for fighting. For instance, the Second Lateran Council's ban on crossbows and its expansion of the Truce of God does not mention the general populace, but its condemnation of arson does, and its denunciation of jousts refers both to the deaths of the participants and the effect on public morals.[22]

Late medieval theologians, particularly Vitoria and Suarez, developed and systematized the just war criteria, providing guidance on a range of problems concerning conduct in war. Recognizing problems of doubt as to just cause and the possibility that each party to a war might be partly just and partly unjust in its cause, Vitoria and Suarez gave the jus in bello criteria greater prominence than jus ad bellum criteria.[23] James Turner Johnson comments that "at this stage in its development the jus in bello is almost entirely a statement in regard to noncombatants—who they are, and the rights belligerents possess toward them and their property."[24] Yet Vitoria's and Saurez's treatment of proportionality was such that it "open[ed] the way for the erosion of restraints in the name of military necessity."[25] Just war tradition was in a period of transition at this time, and it was left to later thinkers, such as the Puritan theologian William Ames and Dutch lawyer Hugo Grotius, to strengthen noncombatant immunity.

Restrictions on certain weapons did not figure much in the work of these thinkers or even in the works of secular just war theorists and international lawyers until the late-nineteenth-century treaties and conventions mentioned in case 2 above. Therefore, locating explicit theological commentary or Church documents relating to special categories of modern weapons before the advent of the nuclear arms race is difficult. The development and use of the bomb shocked the whole world into awareness, the Christian community included. Pacifists and, for the most part, just war thinkers asserted that it was immoral to use such a destructive weapon on an entire city of noncombatant civilians. A representative statement from the time is that of G. E. M. (Elizabeth) Anscombe, a British philosopher who worked in the Catholic natural law tradition: "For men to choose to kill the innocent as a means to their ends is always murder, and murder is one of the worst of human actions. . . . With Hiroshima and Nagasaki we are not confronted with a borderline case. In the bombing of these cities it was certainly decided to kill the innocent as a means to an end."[26] Anscombe conceded that the bombings saved many more American and Japanese lives than would have been lost from an invasion of Japan, yet she disputed that invasion was the only option. The Allies sought only Japan's unconditional surrender, and they ignored Japanese offers to sue for peace. Given those facts, the Allies could not claim extreme necessity. Even if the facts were otherwise, there are some things human beings should never do—murder being foremost among them. The atomic bombings were murder.

Against the just war view, the Protestant theologian Reinhold Niebuhr's qualified support for the atomic bombings reflects the ad hoc and flexible approach of Christian realists to a moral limit: They express the importance of the moral limit; recognize that in this imperfect and sinful world, holding to the limit can have bad consequences; violate the limit with a mournful attitude if the consequences seem important enough; and then describe how the moral limit still retains its value as an ideal. We see this pattern in Niebuhr's seemingly ambiguous reaction to the atomic bombings. We read him a few months after the bombings: "Critics have rightly pointed out that we reached the level of Nazi morality in justifying the use of the bomb on the grounds that it shortened the war."[27] However, when the president of Harvard asked him to clarify his signature on a statement of Christian leaders criticizing the bombings, he wrote, "I myself took the position that failing in achieving a Japanese surrender, the bomb would have had to be used to save the lives of thousands of American soldiers who would otherwise have perished on the beaches of Japan."[28] What keeps these statements from being fully contradictory in Niebuhr's mind is that he, unlike Anscombe, thought that circumstances matter a great deal. He accepted the necessity for the United States to develop the bomb in the context of the atomic race with Nazi Germany; he accepted the tragic necessity of the bomb's use on Japan in the context of Japan's refusal to surrender. But he also thought that the Allies could have managed circumstances to give Japan the option to avoid the bomb's use:

> We can criticize the statesmen, however, for lack of imagination in impressing the enemy with the power of the bomb without the wholesale loss of life that attended our demonstration of its power. Suppose we had announced the perfection of the bomb to the enemy, threatened its ultimate use, and given some vivid demonstrations of its power in places where the loss of life would have been minimal. The moral advantage of such imagination would have been tremendous. As matters stand now, we have completely lost our moral position . . . without recognizing how difficult we have made repentance for a vanquished foe who feels that he was defeated by the use of an illegitimate form of destructiveness.[29]

However, Niebuhr neglects the United States demands for unconditional surrender and the Japanese overtures cited by Anscombe. He can, therefore, be charged with a lack of imagination of his own.

As we can see, Niebuhr wanted to avoid a direct violation of the discrimination principle, but he did not think this was possible—or rather, it was not ethically and politically responsible—in a world of conflict. "Once bombing has been developed as an instrument of warfare, it is not possible to disavow its use without capitulating to the foe who refuses to disavow it. No man has the moral freedom to escape from these hard and cruel necessities of history."[30] This attitude may seem unchristian, but Niebuhr thought it was the only sensible position for Christians who acknowledge that God offers forgiveness "to the contrite sinner who realizes it is not possible to live a sinless life on earth."[31]

Another of the hard and cruel responsibilities of world leaders who entered the atomic age was to address the risk of massive human death and environmental devastation from the use of nuclear weapons. For Christian realists, America's cold war arms race with the Soviet Union was a tragic necessity, because the Communist dictatorship could not be trusted not to use nuclear weapons against the West unless it faced an equal risk of annihilation. A number of Christian just war thinkers who were influenced by Niebuhr and impressed by the threat of the Soviet arsenal argued that nuclear deterrence could find support within the just war system, despite the policy's implied threat of massive civilian deaths. Methodist ethicist Paul Ramsey, for example, painstakingly developed a system of "graduated deterrence" that did not necessarily depend upon "seriously threatening the indiscriminate destruction of populations."[32] The nuclear deterrent should not be counterpopulation; it should rather be primarily counterforce (targeted at the Soviets' nuclear arsenals) and possibly countercombatant (targeted at its military instillations and personnel).[33] Graduated deterrence would, indeed, threaten a destruction that could be disproportionate, but Ramsey thought that such a threat was not unique to nuclear weapons and that it could be distinguished from indiscriminate threats.[34]

Other Christian thinkers were not impressed by such attempts to justify the arms race. Even granting the need for protection against the Soviet Union, they saw no end to the practice of the United States and the USSR constantly one-upping each other's strategic stockpiles, which was exactly what was happening. Thus, Church leaders found it necessary to assert a moral imperative for nuclear arms reduction. An early, striking claim came from Pope John XXIII in 1963:

Everyone, however, must realize that, unless this process of disarmament be thoroughgoing and complete, and reach men's very souls, it is impossible to stop the arms race, or to reduce armaments, or—and this is the main thing—ultimately to abolish them entirely. Everyone must sincerely cooperate in the effort to banish fear and the anxious expectation of war from men's minds. But this requires that the fundamental principles upon which peace is based in today's world be replaced by an altogether different one, namely, the realization that true and lasting peace among nations cannot consist in the possession of an equal supply of armaments but only in mutual trust.[35]

From the 1960s through the 1980s many Christian denominations—both individually and through ecumenical organizations such as the World Council of Churches—promulgated statements of concern about nuclear proliferation, educated their members about these concerns, and lobbied governments to negotiate arms reductions. Parallel efforts occurred in many of the major religions (often the liberal wings), and Christian groups increasingly made common cause with these efforts. In 1983, the National Conference of Catholic Bishops of the United States issued a controversial and widely debated pastoral letter, *The Challenge of Peace*. In addition to explicating the just war tradition and encouraging Christians to work for peace, they addressed the morality of American nuclear deterrent policies. Naturally, they categorically rejected counterpopulation use of nuclear weapons. They also declared a first-strike policy immoral, doubted that there could be any moral use of tactical nuclear weapons on a limited basis, and allowed the possession of nuclear weapons as a deterrent—but only provisionally as a step toward deep cuts in strategic arms to be negotiated with the Soviet Union.[36] A few years later, in 1986, the United Methodist Council of Bishops of the United States went a little further in their letter, *In Defense of Creation*. Although not taking an officially pacifist stance, their analysis of the issues and their vision for Christian behavior flowed more directly from an ideal of Christian nonviolence and peacefulness than from the just war tradition. On the deterrence controversy, they wrote, "Deterrence must no longer receive the churches' blessing, even as a temporary warrant for the maintenance of nuclear weapons."[37] However, they did not depart from the Catholic bishops in their judgment that it would take some time for American leaders to reduce nuclear stockpiles through negotiation; they recognized that the United States could not immediately and unilaterally disarm.

Having expressed these principles, the churches could celebrate the cuts in strategic arms negotiated between the United States and the USSR in the mid- to late-1980s, and the further deep reductions that followed the breakup of the USSR in 1989. But as described in this chapter, the détente between the United States and Russia hardly removes all the threats to the world community.

Christian ethicists, ministers, and church leaders continue to challenge several assumptions concerning modern weaponry that often go unquestioned in political and media discussions. There is the assumption of the necessity of nuclear weapons. Not only do the superpowers retain nuclear weapons, but more and more nations want to join the nuclear club. There is the assumption of the indispensability of weapons research. Christian commentators remain concerned that several nations are continuing to develop and could launch such weapons or sell them to terrorist groups. There is the assumption of the legitimacy of the arms trade. The U.S. Catholic Bishops wrote a letter in 1995 that began "The arms trade is a scandal. That weapons of war are bought and sold almost as if they were simply another commodity like appliances or industrial machinery is a serious moral disorder in today's world." Although the desire to maintain the nation's economic strength from defense spending is understandable, "jobs at home cannot justify exporting the means of war abroad."[38] There is the assumption of the moral superiority of high-tech weapons. Precision-guided munitions (PGMs) were used to dramatic effect in the Gulf War; a higher percentage of PGMs has been used in each American military operation since 1991. The ability of a computer-guided missile to hit a specific target within a matter of inches has led many to assume that war can be waged with virtually no risk to civilians. But that is a dangerous assumption because PGMs are only as accurate as the intelligence by which they are guided. Mistakes are always made and civilian targets hit. For instance, the massive amount of ordnance rained down on Iraq in both 1991 and 2003 caused a great many civilian deaths, both directly and indirectly. Finally, there is the assumption of the adequacy of short-term and isolated thinking. Against analyses of decisions to go to war based largely on discrete military objectives, Christian thinkers want to press concerns about the long-term effects of war on human health, the environment, local and global economies, and the fabric of society.

To conclude, what does this history of Christian reflection on the ethics of weaponry reveal about the three ethical positions? Just war's descriptive understanding of and normative proposals for arms limitation are challenged by the two other Christian ethical perspectives. Against just war thinkers' description that the community of nations has made moral progress in banning indiscriminate weapons and limiting proliferation, both pacifists and realists read history to reveal that just about every weapon that can be developed has been developed and used. Both groups believe that bald political considerations rather than ethical beliefs drive arms treaties. Normatively, pacifism takes this situation to mean that, although it is important to place whatever limitations on arms that can be politically agreed, genuine security from total war cannot be achieved when some nations consider themselves more enlightened than other nations and thus exempt themselves from rules against the possession and use of indiscriminate weapons. In addition, pacifists believe that the other two positions insufficiently acknowledge the ways that military preparations and social injustices fuel the spiral of violence that eventually results in wars.

Christian realists are likewise critical of just war thinkers' description of the success of ethical appeals in politics. In the context of international power relations, moral principles such as love, peace, and forgiveness are valuable as ideals, but they cannot operate as political guidelines. (Realists believe that pacifists are also often guilty of this confusion.) In their normative ethics of war, then, Christian realists allow for "tragic" violations of the traditional rules in urgent situations. Christian realists have no objection to the goal of arms reductions treaties, but they think that liberal democratic nations—namely, the United States and European states—should not treat totalitarian regimes as moral equals. The democracies may need to assert power even in violation of agreements in order to preserve their strength against brutal regimes. In the end, despite their differing views of political morality, all three ethical positions are realistic enough to agree that arms treaties will only work when fair and effective mechanisms for verification are put in place. But can we realistically hope that the nations of the world will be wise enough to work for the international common good?

NONPROLIFERATION: MORAL DEMAND
OR MILITARY STRATEGY?

In this chapter we have tried to give a realistic account of the success of past attempts at limiting the use of particular weapons. The moral is sobering: The successes of arms limitation have been few and far between, usually when the strategic value of the weapons prohibited is small. In the Prisoner's Dilemma, discussed at the beginning of the chapter, the optimal win–win result is achieved when both parties cooperate. In the case of arms control, the winning result would be to reduce the danger of being attacked by indiscriminate weapons and to avoid devoting scarce economic resources to new weapon systems. It is easy to forget that most neighboring nations benefit from this win–win scenario. Britain and France no longer maintain large armed forces to protect themselves from attack from each other. Similarly, the United States and Canada benefit from not having to maintain defenses or deter aggression across their long mutual border.

A more recent example of nations building a positive relationship is Argentina and Brazil. In the 1970s there were grave fears that the rivalry between the two states would lead to each developing nuclear weapons. Then, in 1985, the new civilian government in Argentina approached the Brazilian authorities in the expectation that a reasonable and mutually beneficial agreement could be reached. Because Brazil shared these hopes, this result was quickly achieved. Neither country currently possesses nuclear weapons. Similarly, in a brief period in the bilateral relationship between the superpowers in the late 1980s and early 1990s, Presidents Gorbachev and Reagan succeeded in negotiating a series of agreements that led to reductions in conventional and nuclear forces in Europe. The agreements we have surveyed that control chemical and biological arms are also examples of many states appreciating that their interests are best served by prohibiting particular types of weapons.

However, given the history we have surveyed in this chapter, it is hard to avoid the conclusion that agreements to limit weapons usually fail when the need for them is greatest. The greatest threat to global security is nuclear weapons, yet the provisions of the Non-Proliferation Treaty have been broken both on the side of the nuclear states (which have not pursued disarmament and have been remiss in their responsibility to prevent the transfer of nuclear weapons technology to other states) and on the side of nonnuclear states (where it is likely that others will follow North Korea in reneging on their treaty obligations). The 1996 Chemical Weapons Convention was welcome, but it concerned weapons that most states did not consider major strategic assets because they are difficult to deploy, ineffective against suitably equipped troops, and not a significant deterrent in the age of nuclear weapons. Arguably, the few states that did consider them to be of military value were those who continue to retain or develop them despite the convention. The lose–lose result in the Prisoner's Dilemma is for both parties to conclude that they cannot trust the other and, therefore, that they must act on the expectation that the other will not cooperate. This mindset has been the major operative strategy toward weapons control at the most critical times. As a result, the world is now subject to the dangers of weapons of awesome destructive potential, nuclear weapons foremost among them. Unless there is a rapid change in international relations, the restraints on nuclear proliferation will likely be weakened, and the group of states possessing nuclear weapons will steadily increase.

Following this stark appraisal of the prospects for weapons control, the key ethical question is whether and how nation states might be influenced toward policies that promise an alternative to the lose–lose result. Clearly, an urgent peacemaking task at the beginning of the twenty-first century is to build up institutions with the potential to foster trust among nations, in turn enabling states to reach weapons control agreements that reliably provide for both verification and responses to breaches. It is critical, then, that strategies for nonproliferation (preventing the spread of particular weapon types) and counterproliferation (responding to occasions when nonproliferation has been unsuccessful) are crafted so that they are in the interests of all states. Otherwise, these strategies will rightly be seen merely as attempts by the states that are currently powerful to retain their military superiority.

Restricting the proliferation of both conventional arms and nuclear, chemical, and biological weapons is clearly a crucial task to which just war theorists and pacifists should be jointly committed; it is one of the practices of the "Just Peacemaking" project we discussed in chapter 2. This chapter has shown that success in arms limitation is heavily dependent on trust established through other practices, such as the development of international institutions. Part of maintaining this trust in arms negotiations is establishing inspection regimes that can be relied on to discover treaty breaches. The discussion of this chapter has also shown that only treaties formulated to bring benefit to all parties in the long term stand any chance of enduring success.

Debating the Issues

DLC At the beginning of the chapter we noted that there was a divergence in the just war tradition between those who sought to reduce the incidence of war by making the jus ad bellum criteria more restrictive and those who thought it more realistic to attempt to make war less destructive by developing the jus in bello criteria. The pacifist perspective is clearly closer to the first approach, but it is interested in arms limitation for three key reasons. First, money spent on arms is not available for more creative uses. Many of these uses, such as providing aid to the social and economic development of poorer nations, have a direct impact on global security, apart from other beneficial effects. Second, the development of weapons makes war more likely. Possessing weapons creates opportunities to use force as an instrument of national policy that would not otherwise be available. It is true that the developing of weapons by other nations curtails these opportunities, but that merely creates an expensive and more unstable status quo, which brings us back to the first point. Third, when wars are fought, advanced weapons make them more destructive. Pacifists are not so idealistic as to let their hopes of preventing war override their concern to reduce the bad effects when it does. They are interested, therefore, in efforts to place limits on the deployment of particular weapons, especially when those weapons cannot be used without killing and injuring civilians on a large scale.

BES Agreeing with your three points, I would add that there is a difference between the Christian and philosophical expressions of just war tradition, on the one hand, and the legal codification of just war, on the other. Christian and philosophical just war thinkers have tried to tamp down the recourse to war with jus ad bellum criteria and the destructiveness of war with jus in bello criteria. Generally speaking, this just war tradition agrees with pacifists in putting more emphasis on ad bellum and getting the use of those criteria right. But the legal codification of just war doctrine from the end of the Middle Ages through the modern arms conventions has focused on in bello limitations. The reasoning has been threefold: Politically, it was often difficult to assess comparative claims of justice (ironically, because neither side was being very just!); legally, there was no higher authority to adjudicate the competing claims; and pragmatically, for nations to agree to put aside certain destructive methods promised to protect all parties from total war. The practical argument has ethical warrants as well: protecting civilians and preserving some measure of civilized cooperation among nations. From the Christian just war perspective, I hope that nations will get leverage from the pragmatic arguments for arms limitation to make ethical progress. I am not overly optimistic about what this can achieve, but, as you suggest, some limitation is better than none. The just war perspective, especially in its Christian form, fully shares the three cautions you just raised about the negative consequences of arms proliferation. Arms control is one of the areas in which our two traditions can make great common cause.

Conventional Weapons Trade

DLC So pacifism and the just war tradition share some common ground, especially in relation to those realist perspectives that would be dubious about any attempts to place moral constraints on weapons. But there are important points of difference between us, too. Because you believe that war is a legitimate action for nation-states in particular circumstances, you are committed to the manufacture, trade, and use of many kinds of weapons in an international context. We may be able to agree that nuclear, chemical, and biological weapons should not be used, but as we have seen, most people who die in conflicts do so from small arms: rifles, pistols, and light machine guns. The United States and the United Kingdom are leading manufacturers and marketers of these weapons. From a pacifist point of view, there would be great gain in prohibiting trade in any kind of weapons; certainly any other trade that resulted in hundreds of thousands of deaths each year would be prohibited. Too much focus on particular kinds of weapons risks missing the larger problem.

BES We can both heartily commend the voices that the Christian churches have raised against the arms trade; just war and pacifism share this common cause. As a U.S. citizen I am especially concerned that my country take moral accountability for its role as the leading producer and exporter of arms. Our heavy exports—often to corrupt, militarist leaders in developing nations—divert those countries' economies from productive investment and create stockpiles of arms that are misused by armies and rebels. All of this is unfair to the ordinary people of developing countries. In recent years it is also clear that this arms trade is harmful for us in the exporting countries. The buildup of small arms in many trouble spots of the world has exacerbated civil wars that have entangled the United States and Europe, such as the Balkan Wars. These arms can be and have been sold on the black market, finding their way to criminal, rebel, and terrorist groups. The former Soviet Union, for instance, left 2.5 million tons of conventional munitions in the former Ukraine, where they have been hard to secure and thus keep off the black market.[39] Unfortunately, it has been difficult for churches, peace groups, and development organizations to get the developed countries to focus on this routine arms trade, though they have had some success with weapon categories such as landmines. The economies of the industrial nations—especially the United States—place more weight than they should on defense spending; that needs to be changed. Industrial nations need to reinvest smartly so as to cause as little dislocation to their workers as possible. Maintaining domestic defense jobs at the cost of dumping arms, missiles, and military vehicles on the developing world is wrong and dangerous.

Nuclear Weapons and Deterrence

DLC   We can agree, then, that there's a moral problem in the manufacture and trade of conventional weapons as such—even apart from the controversial ones such as landmines or those manufactured from depleted uranium. There are obviously additional moral concerns, however, when we consider weapons that cannot be used discriminately or proportionately. The clearest case of this is nuclear weapons. Let's start with the American use of atomic weapons in Hiroshima and Nagasaki. Can we agree that these were extreme violations of the jus in bello criterion of discrimination and, therefore, were illegitimate?

BES   Absolutely. If the principle of discrimination means anything, it has to mean that those bombings were immoral. They were tragic on their own terms and, even sadder, they were not exceptional because the intentional bombing of civilians became standard practice by all sides in World War II. As the sixtieth anniversary of the American bombings of these cities just passed, the world has been taking stock of the historical and political context of the decision as well as of the consequences. The most interesting question, in my opinion, sits at the intersection of ethics and history: Did the United States really have a better option? The historical consensus for many decades was that the bombings were not necessary to get the Japanese to end the war on ne-gotiated terms. Other historians have challenged that without the shock of the bombs—both bombs—the Japanese would not have ended the war, and many thousands more lives on both sides would have been lost in protracted fighting on the Japanese mainland. Even if the later histor-ical arguments are stronger, I think we can't condone the atomic bomb-ings. History clearly shows that the Truman administration didn't seriously consider alternatives to using the bomb, such as a test demonstration or a negotiated peace. Perhaps the Japanese war council would not have re-sponded to these initiatives, but it would have made some moral differ-ence to have pursued them.[40]

DLC This is a clear case where the just war tradition shows its affinity with one aspect of pacifism: Neither is prepared to reduce judgments about warfare to an evaluation of their consequences. I'm not convinced that the results of not using atomic weapons against the Japanese would have been worse than the devastation they caused; worse, per-haps, for some U.S. servicemen, but the overall cost of their use is incal-culable. For both the pacifist and just war traditions, it could be the case that the consequences of not using atomic bombs would have been worse, and yet it would still be illegitimate to use them. That's the coun-terintuitive judgment they both have to defend against the realist posi-tion, as we noted in chapter 2. We've mentioned the argument that smaller nuclear weapons could be used morally, but concur that the sig-nificance of going over the nuclear threshold again makes this unsus-tainable. So if we agree that use of nuclear weapons is illegitimate from both pacifist and just war perspectives, can we also agree that their pos-session and threatened use as deterrent is also illegitimate?

BES Yes, again, that judgment should be agreed by both positions against the realist position, but with the qualification (for just war thinkers) that holding nuclear arms as a deterrent to another nuclear power is sometimes a necessary evil. Nuclear deterrence operates on the notion, "if you are so crazy as to start devastating our country, you can expect we will devastate yours." Thus, the strategy depends on an implied threat to kill civilians on a massive scale. I would say that the threatened use of strategic nuclear weapons is illegitimate and that any possession of nuclear weapons is a morally compromised situation that needs to be changed as quickly as is feasible through mutual, verifiable arms control agreements.

DLC Your position looks dangerously close to the realist one when you talk about "necessary evil." Isn't the just war tradition based on the idea that it is right and good to wage war for the right reasons in the right way, as compared to the realist position that you sometimes have to do bad things to bring about the best result? Threatening the wholesale destruction of civilian society is antithetical to just war thinking; surely, this is a case where the national policies of the states possessing nuclear weapons are flatly opposed to the just war tradition. To justify maintaining a deterrent, even in the short term (and who thinks it will be short term on current policies?), looks to me like an abandonment of the principled just war position in favor of realist consequentialism.

BES Just war thinkers shouldn't give up the stance that it is wrong to threaten wholesale destruction. To clarify, what just war doctrine strictly forbids is the indiscriminate and disproportionate use of a weapon. The development or possession of an inherently indiscriminate weapon is derivatively wrong but doesn't rise to the level of the moral scandal at Hiroshima. We can imagine a country holding the position that it will possess nuclear weapons but never use them. Of course, no nuclear nation ever said that, and deterrence couldn't work that way. Still, it suggests there are differences to be drawn in the ethical evaluation of a nation's policies based on how many and what kind of weapons it has, how it targets them, and what it is doing to reduce the risk of their use. We have suggested more than once in this book that we have to do ethical evaluation from where we are and not from a counterfactual location. So I think the American Catholic bishops were correct in the 1980s to argue that the U.S. nuclear deterrent was only provisionally tolerable as a temporary policy on the path to negotiated reductions. It was morally tolerable as a lesser evil. Their reasoning on this point was consequentialist; just war theory can't do without some consequentialism, but it can resist giving it pride of place.

DLC Possession without demonstrable intent to use is no deterrent and, therefore, pointless, is it not? It says something about the international environment engendered by nuclear weapons that even the reasonable provisional positions you espouse, such as statements of "no first use" or "no intention to use," are not policies to which nuclear states commit themselves. The nuclear environment is one built on mistrust and hidden intentions.

The Urgency of Nonproliferation

BES The question that follows is, what about now—what is the point of our nations holding any nuclear weapons today? We agree that nonproliferation is an urgent task. For any of the nuclear nations to possess such weapons constitutes a continuing indiscriminate threat, as we've just discussed; it also creates risks of accidental use, of transfer to or theft by terrorist groups, and of proliferating nuclear weapons to new states. However, I imagine we are both discouraged by recent trends.

DLC My take on this is that we are in very dangerous times. The Non-Proliferation Treaty was a deal on the basis of action on two sides: refusal to seek weapons by nonnuclear states and disarmament by nuclear states. Both parts have been reneged on. It is shocking that the United States and the UN Security Council don't seem concerned about proliferation except in Iraq, Iran, and North Korea. What about India and Pakistan? What about Israel? Just because India and Israel are allies of the United States and the United Kingdom, and Pakistan is the United States' partner in the war on terror, we cannot give them or any nation including ourselves a pass. A policy based on who our friends are is deeply flawed.

BES It is, indeed, time to end the double standards. What will it take to do that? One new challenge is for every nation to put itself on equal terms regarding open verification. Unless we all play by the same rules, we can't expect the newer nuclear states and nuclear-jealous states to join the game. None of the nuclear states want to open themselves to scrutiny. Yet it would create a lot of good will and establish a moral highground for the United States to be open about its programs and to be inspected on the same terms as other nations. It's very troubling that, in August 2004, the United States backed out of a ten-year effort to create a treaty for nuclear weapon inspection and verification, complaining of cost and intrusiveness. Without American and other major power leadership on such initiatives, they completely collapse.

DLC Getting inspections straight would be a start, but it doesn't take us much further; we already know pretty well what nuclear weapons the nuclear powers have. The problem is that there's no intent to disarm; too often, as we have seen in this chapter, nonproliferation is a strategy for some nations to retain military dominance over others. The United States, for example, as the nation-state with significant global dominance in military power—spending half of the global total of military expenditure in 2004[41]—seeks to be able to project this power wherever necessary in order to secure its own global interests. This aim goes far beyond defending its own territory. A major interest, for example, is securing access to oil supplies from the Persian Gulf. Because the United States (together with its ally Israel) remains the only military power operating in the region with nuclear weapons, it enjoys considerable freedom of action. To protect this freedom, it has an interest in preventing other states from becoming similarly equipped. For Iraq to have obtained nuclear weapons, for example, would have significantly constrained the ability of the United States to impose its will on the region. The development of nuclear weapons by Iran is similarly of major concern to America's regional interests. Obviously, the United States is not unique in seeking to advance its own interests in this way, though it is currently unique in its ability to do so. There is, therefore, a nonproliferation or counterproliferation agenda that is aimed not at making the world a safer place for all states but at maintaining the military superiority of some states, and this is part of what frustrates attempts to prevent the proliferation of weapons, nuclear and otherwise. International progress will only be made if, following the Prisoner's Dilemma, all parties believe they stand to gain by maintaining their treaty obligations.

BES The common good of the international community would be well served by nonproliferation. It's only reasonable that all nations have a stake in reducing the risks of nuclear war. But there are two perversions to the Prisoner's Dilemma. I will apply them to the United States, but the first pertains to any of the great powers and nuclear states, and the second can apply to every nation in some measure. First, nations stand in unequal power relationships. Therefore, the United States has less incentive to cooperate—that is, if it thinks about the benefits in the short term and from the perspectives of its military and economic policies, as opposed to thinking about long-term benefits to its environmental and counterterrorist policies. The second perversion is ideology. No nation and no leader come at things without some fundamental assumptions about the world. The assumptions I have just mentioned are weaknesses in the American view of the world—and they are endemic to both Republican and Democratic administrations, if exaggerated in the former—that I want to see changed. As should be evident by the positions I have taken in our debates, I am a sympathetic critic of my nation. I believe that my nation wants to do a lot of good in the world, has done much good, and will continue to do so. But it needs to exert greater leadership as a moral leader among equals.

DLC The issue of weapon proliferation is bigger than the United States, obviously. I don't underestimate the role of the United Kingdom as a major supplier of arms and want to play my part in challenging it. At the moment, however, the United States is uniquely able to influence international events for better or worse. It has the power to facilitate the transition to an international order in which all nations have a stake in the maintenance of peace and justice. My hope is that it can escape a preoccupation with securing its own position long enough to see that even the security of a global hyperpower is dependent on a just global order for all. Success in nonproliferation strategies demands that nuclear states like yours and mine demonstrate a new willingness to take the concerns of other nations seriously.

BES Perhaps an example would help us here. Iran is widely suspected of having a clandestine nuclear weapons program, and it possesses missiles that could deliver warheads out of the country. For several years now, Iran has been itching to resume processing of nuclear materials in power plants; it says it needs to do so for its energy needs. The United States and several other nations are very suspicious that Iran will make nuclear weapons, so Europe has taken the lead in trying to get Iran to give up its nuclear refining program in exchange for technical and economic incentives, such as other types of power plants. But Iran's conservative Islamic ideology as well as its strong national pride make it hard for its leaders to see themselves in a common good with the rest of the world, especially the West. It is very difficult for external nations to get a sovereign state to do something it doesn't want to do. So the question for you is, If we grant that major powers like the United States and the United Kingdom have to sacrifice their exceptionalist attitudes, won't it still be the case that Iran may do what it wants and not cooperate? Reason, good will, and incentives may still be ineffective—then what?

DLC I read your question as, If we have unsuccessfully tried everything else to get Iran to give up ambitions to nuclear weapons, should we invade? I think that question is unhelpful and even dangerous because it shifts the focus away from the responsibilities of the nuclear states belonging to the Nuclear Non-Proliferation Treaty. To put it bluntly, given the current state of the treaty, I think Iran has good reason to wish to develop nuclear weapons. To use military means to prevent it from doing so would be the most blatant example of promoting narrow national interests under the guise of nonproliferation. Before we face the question of what we do if all else fails, we need to look seriously at the "all else." What would make a difference to Iran's position would be if there were a serious prospect of the nuclear disarmament that Russia, the United Kingdom, the United States, China, and France signed up to, with other nuclear states—especially Israel—following suit. This would remove two motivations for Iran's nuclear program: the perceived need for a deterrent and the sense of being an inferior world power because of not having nuclear weapons.

BES My question suggested not the desire to threatenc but an honest frustration about the nuclear designs of nondemocratic nations. I concede, though, that the proposal for a military attack on Iran should be strongly resisted, not the least because it would be incredibly dangerous and leave the global community less safe. It would also violate just war principles—unless, at minimum, Iran posed a clear and imminent danger of deploying nuclear weapons in violation of international agreements. I agree with a professor at the U.S. National War College who recently wrote: "Engaging an autocratic regime in order to buy a tentative cap on its nuclear ambitions and hoping that political reforms will outpace bomb-making are hardly neat and tidy solutions or ones likely to warm the hearts of those who crave bold statements of U.S. global supremacy. But we Americans are always seeing the world as a series of problems to be solved rather than challenges to be managed. Impatience with Iran is likely to become self-defeating; patience, meanwhile, offers no guarantee of success. It remains, however, the best option we have."[42] I want the world to get to the place you just described, but that is going to take a while. Some first steps forward would be not forbidding the development of nuclear power to states that want it, risky though that may be, and requiring all nations to submit to the same inspections regime.

CONCLUSION

Because just war tradition places the inviolability of civilians from attack at the heart of its guidelines for conduct and because pacifism is deeply troubled by the human toll of warfare, we found in this discussion significant common ground for criticizing unfettered trade in conventional arms, any use of nuclear weapons, and policies that encourage nuclear proliferation. However, we located differences in strategy and urgency when it comes to nuclear deterrence and nonproliferation. From a pacifist stance, Clough says unequivocally that nuclear deterrence and possession are immoral. Underneath all of his politically engaged debate, the element of Christian witness to peace should not be missed. Stiltner sees just war theory's political prudence as recommending a measured approach to a similar goal, yet he believes this requires him to give a qualified moral support to nuclear possession by Western nations. Many critics, both pacifist and realist, feel that the just war thinker holds a contradictory position. The point that might be most debatable was introduced here but awaits full exploration in chapter 6: Is it right to go to war to prevent another nation from becoming a threat?

CHAPTER 5

Political and Holy Terrorism: Frameworks for Analysis and Action

Consideration of terrorism is essential to this book's investigation because terrorist groups often think of themselves as belligerents in a just war or a just revolution, and governments often respond to terrorism with military actions. Indeed, many international terrorist groups arise and operate in the context of civil wars and separatist struggles. Other international groups see themselves as locked in a protracted war with one or more foreign governments or societies, or even against an entire culture or religion. Groups commit *international terrorism* when one or more of three features are present: the perpetrators cross international political boundaries to commit their acts; they are sponsored by foreign governments; or they create an international incident by striking at military, political, or international transportation targets.[1] Most of the acts that spring to the reader's mind are likely to be international acts. Examples include airplane hijackings by Palestinian groups in the 1970s; most of the bombings related to the Northern Ireland conflict; the suicide bombings and settler violence in Israel's occupied territories; and al Qaeda bombings since 1998 in New York, Washington, DC, Kenya, Tanzania, Saudi Arabia, Madrid, and London.

Other terrorist acts are classified as *domestic terrorism,* in which citizens of a nation attack an internal target without the involvement of external nations or international groups. Examples are animal rights groups that bomb a university lab and abortion clinic bombers in the United States. A government's response to the domestic version of terrorism relies on criminal investigation and police arrests much more than on military action; nonetheless, the same questions of justice that are raised in regard to military force must be asked of the government's police response.

Terrorism is undoubtedly a significant problem of violence, even though it does not cause the same level of devastation as war itself. In the year 2000, there were forty-three deaths from international terrorism and 735 from domestic terrorism, and an estimated 300,000 people perished from combat or war-related causes.[2] Terrorism is, nevertheless, an urgent moral problem because it can pave the way to overt wars and can rise from the ashes of war as a toxic aftereffect. Fundamentally, it is a moral problem because it harms humans and ruptures the fabric of societies. Consider these troubling statistics drawn from the National Memorial Institute for the Prevention of Terrorism (MIPT) Terrorism Knowledge Database, which comprehensively catalogs international terrorist incidents committed since 1968 and domestic incidents worldwide since 1998.[3]

- International terrorists have caused more than 14,000 deaths and more than 14,000 injuries worldwide since 1968.
- Since 1998, domestic acts of terrorism worldwide account for more than 21,000 deaths and more than 50,000 injuries.
- International terrorism has grown more destructive. There were 1,788 deaths from international incidents in the 1970s, 4,096 in the 1980s, 2,990 in the 1990s, and already 5,578 in the half-decade between 2000 and 2005. Likewise, the number of injuries rises with each decade.
- The 1990s saw a decline in the number of international incidents—from a peak of 420 incidents in 1991 to a low of 104 incidents in 2000. However, international terrorist incidents have been sharply on the rise since 2000.
- The Middle East has been by far the most deadly region since 2000. Before 2000, roughly one-quarter of deaths from terrorism worldwide occurred in that region, but since 2000, over half of all deaths from terrorism have occurred there. The driving factor has been the insurgency and civil war in Iraq: at least 13,000 deaths attributable to terrorism have occurred in Iraq since 2003. Israel and its occupied territories are the site of the next largest collection of deaths, over 1,900 deaths in the last half-decade.

Who is committing these acts and causing these deaths? The MIPT Terrorism Knowledge Database tracks more than 240 terrorist groups in Western

Europe, 70 in North America, 120 in Latin America, 200 in the Middle East, 100 in South Asia, 70 in Africa, and dozens in other regions of the world. (Of course, some of these numbers represent the same group operating in more than one region, and not all the groups are currently active.) The greatest portion of these groups, 30 percent, are classified as nationalist or separatist in their aims whereas 18 percent are religious; 17 percent, communist or socialist; 10 percent, leftist; 5 percent, right-wing or racist; 5 percent, anarchist; 4 percent, environmentalist or antiglobalization; and 10 percent, other.[4] Another perspective is to notice which groups cause greatest concern to governments. The United States government currently classifies 41 groups as "designated foreign terrorist organizations"; it puts the greatest financial and political pressure on these groups and any of their state sponsors.[5] The British government currently proscribes 25 international terrorist organizations under the Terrorism Act 2000, as well as 14 Irish groups under previous emergency legislation.[6] Excluding the United Kingdom's additional list of Irish groups, the majority of organizations on both the United Kingdom's and United States' lists are jihadist and Palestinian groups. Still, it is important to note that most ideologies and most regions of the globe are represented on the lists.

This chapter's purpose is to analyze the responses to terrorism offered by pacifism and just war theory. Because we are approaching this topic as theologians, we will be aware throughout of the problematic relationship that religion has with terrorism, especially in the last several decades. In several of our cases, terrorists have been nurtured by radical strains of Christianity or Islam. Although this fact does not impugn these religions as a whole, it must be appreciated that religious motivation is a causative factor of some terrorism if the threat of terrorism is to be adequately addressed. Furthermore, ethical responses made from the standpoint of religious commitment—in our case, Christian commitment—must take great care not to fall into a symbolic dynamic that moves from belief in God to indiscriminate violence in the name of God.

CASE STUDIES OF TERRORISM

Can societies threatened with terrorism eradicate the threat? In the last part of this chapter, we will explore three model answers: the military, law enforcement, and peacemaking approaches. However, to determine which of these approaches—singly or in combination—will be both effective and ethical, we need to understand the problem. We will present an overview of the characteristics, causes, and varieties of terrorism through several examples. Four of these examples are the following case studies that will be cited frequently throughout the chapter to draw comparisons and contrasts among terrorist groups.

Case 1: Timothy McVeigh and the Oklahoma City Bombing

On April 19, 1995, McVeigh and a small group of conspirators bombed the Murrah Federal Building in Oklahoma City in the American heartland. A rental truck packed with a fertilizer-based explosive ripped the side off the nine-story building, killing 168 adults and children, and wounding more than 500. McVeigh was a disillusioned veteran of the Gulf War who identified with a militant subculture called Christian Identity. Christian Identity is a reactionary, apocalyptic movement whose members await a cataclysmic battle between forces of light and darkness that will restore America to its Christian roots and libertarian polity. Christian Identity sees as an enemy just about everything non-Christian and associated with modern, pluralistic culture: Jews and other non-Christians, practitioners of abortion and what they consider sexual immorality, supporters of gun-control laws, the United Nations, foreign governments, and the U.S. government.[7] McVeigh, with the help of Terry Nichols and Michael Fortier, modeled the bombing on a scene in the novel *The Turner Diaries*, a highly inspirational piece of literature in the movement. They thought the attack would spark an all-out revolution of fellow-minded militants against the U.S. government. After the attack, it did not take long to arrest McVeigh and the others. Nichols was sentenced to life in prison and McVeigh was executed in 2001.

Case 2: The Bombing of Pan Am Flight 103 by Palestinian Terrorists

On December 21, 1998, Pan Am flight 103 was bombed en route from London to New York, killing all 259 passengers on board as well as 11 people on the ground in Lockerbie, Scotland.[8] A number of organizations concerned with Middle Eastern politics were involved. Although the immediate perpetrators were four Palestinian political terrorists (the key figure in the attack was thought to be Hafez Kassem Dalkimoni, a forty-three-year-old Palestinian from the Popular Front for the Liberation of Palestine–General Command, or PFLP-CG), two governments were sponsors—one an Islamist state, the other a Pan-Arabic dictatorship. The former sponsor, Iran's Revolutionary Guards, was a military force created by Iran's clerics to defend its revolutionary government from external and internal threats. More influential support was provided by the Libyan government of Colonel Muammar Qaddafi. In 1991 the head of security for Libyan Arab Airlines and his assistant were indicted in relation to the attack. For many years, Qaddafi stonewalled the investigation, but then he began to cooperate with a view toward getting economic sanctions against Libya lifted. In April 1999 he handed over the two accused suspects to London's Scotland Yard. The trial in The Netherlands reached a verdict in January 2001, sentencing the senior official to life imprisonment and finding the other not guilty. The following year Libya agreed to pay compensation to the victims of the attack, and in 2003 it formally accepted responsibility for the bombing. These developments led the UN to lift its sanctions against Libya in September 2003.

Case 3: Republican and Loyalist Violence in Northern Ireland

Since the 1800s British rule over Ireland and then Northern Ireland has been the occasion of guerilla war, rioting, police crackdowns, torture, and terrorism. The Irish Republican Army (IRA) took shape in 1919, seeking the independence of Ireland from the United Kingdom by means of a guerilla war against British forces between 1919 and 1921. Its associated political party, Sinn Fein, signed a controversial treaty with the United Kingdom in 1921, accepting full independence for the twenty-six lower counties of Ireland but not for the six of the north, which were to remain in the Kingdom. The IRA took up the nationalist cause of separation, casting itself as a police force for the protection of Catholic citizens (though it also engaged in sporadic guerilla/terrorist attacks), and the Sinn Fein and other parties continued to work politically for independence. In 1969 violent riots broke out between Catholic and Protestant citizens in the North. This gave birth to the Provisional IRA. These "Provos" stepped up a campaign of terrorism and in short order became the default IRA, as the more moderate group faded away in influence. The Irish/Catholic nationalist cause is termed "republican," suggesting identity with the Irish Republic. However, its goals are not homogenous; some republicans seek reunification with Ireland and others seek political and economic reforms that are not necessarily premised on separation from the United Kingdom.

Protestant citizens, who are of British ancestry, have opposed this cause. The political leadership is loyalist, that is, committed to remaining part of the United Kingdom and loyal to its government. Several loyalist paramilitary groups have responded to the republican cause and IRA terrorism with intimidation, revenge killings, and terrorism of their own. These groups include the Ulster Defence Association, the Ulster Volunteer Force, and the South Londonderry Volunteers. Similar to the republicans, the loyalists constitute a diffuse movement. Some politicians, social leaders, and groups are extreme; others have sought a peaceful resolution to this protracted conflict known as "the Troubles." Both movements are driven by official leaders and organized groups and parties and are sustained by the sympathies and long-standing traditions of the Catholic and Protestant populations. The Northern Irish struggle is often popularly spoken of as a Catholic–Protestant religious war. We disagree. We adopt the view that it is primarily a political struggle that has been exacerbated by the religious and cultural differences between the two populations. The paramilitary and terrorist groups often claim the mantle of religion to stir up the support of their constituents.

Since 1969 terrorism has been a primary vehicle of fighting for the cause on both sides. The MIPT Terrorism Knowledge Database lists thirteen terrorist groups that have operated in Northern Ireland since 1969. Five republican groups have committed 153 acts of terrorism, and six loyalist groups have committed 89 acts of terrorism (one other loyalist group has committed no reported acts, and one terrorist group is not related to the Troubles). These numbers are only a part of the violent picture, for there are forms of violence (such as riots and beatings) that have not been defined as terrorism; some acts go unreported or are never credited to a known group; and some of these groups sustain themselves with other criminal activities such as extortion, bank robberies, and drug trafficking. Terrorist acts have abated, though not disappeared, since a peace process began with the Good Friday Accords in 1998. Hopes for the peace process have been, by turns, robust and dire. One major obstacle was the IRA's unwillingness to disarm its militias, but a very promising moment came on July 28, 2005, when the Provisional IRA announced that it was disarming immediately and asked all related IRA groups to submit to verifiable disarmament.

Case 4: Al Qaeda's Jihadist Terrorism

Al Qaeda, whose name is Arabic for "The Base," is an extensive and loose jihadist terrorist network that intersects and cooperates with many other terrorist groups inspired by extremist interpretations of Islam.[9] Many groups share al Qaeda's ideology of jihad, or holy war, against the United States, Israel, and their allies. Jihadists derive inspiration from Islam, although their interpretation of the Qur'an is rejected by all mainstream Muslim leaders and theologians, for whom jihad is both a spiritual struggle and a doctrine of just war not unlike that found in the Western/Christian tradition. However, jihadists' criticisms of the international policies of the United States and the United Kingdom and their disillusion with certain Western values are widely shared; speeches, media, websites, and polls from the Muslim world have revealed significant sympathy among Muslims regarding the grievances of jihadist groups, some agreement with their aims, and minor support for their methods.

Al Qaeda came into existence in the late 1980s and burst to worldwide notoriety with the September 11, 2001, attacks on U.S. targets.[10] Previously, however, its operatives had been involved in several notorious terrorist attacks. Al Qaeda has not claimed responsibility for all the attacks attributed to it, but its money, its network of operatives, or its example may have helped bring plans to fruition. Its earliest terrorist attack may have been three bombings targeted at U.S. troops in Yemen in December 1992. Since then the organization has been linked to the failed bombing of the World Trade Center in 1993, bombings in Saudi Arabia from 1995 onward, attacks on U.S. embassies in Kenya and Tanzania in 1998 (killing more than 200 people), and the bombing of the USS *Cole* off the coast of Yemen in 2000 (killing 17 American sailors).[11] Since 2001 al Qaeda has claimed responsibility for a number of incidents—especially in Saudi Arabia, but also in Iraq, Turkey, Indonesia, and Kenya. When the Abu Hafs al-Masri Brigade bombed four commuter trains in Madrid on March 11, 2003, killing 191 and injuring 600, it claimed responsibility on behalf of al Qaeda. The same group claimed responsibility for the bombing of three trains and a bus in London on July 7, 2005, killing 56 commuters. The

Brigade may be an active al Qaeda cell in Europe, or it may simply be a name that disparate jihadist groups and individuals have claimed to make themselves appear more connected to each other and to Osama bin Laden than they really are.[12]

Osama bin Laden is the founder of al Qaeda. The wealthy son of a prominent Saudi family, he traveled to Afghanistan in the late 1970s to fight with the mujahideen—Muslim rebels resisting Soviet occupation. Bin Laden and thousands of "Afghan Arabs," as they came to be called, came from Middle Eastern countries to support their Afghan coreligionists. But these foreigners were more ideologically driven than the Afghan tribal leaders. The U.S. government, with the assistance of Pakistan, Saudi Arabia, and even China, helped finance, arm, and train the mujahideen in the 1970s and 1980s. U.S. president Ronald Reagan called them "freedom fighters . . . defending principles of independence and freedom that form the basis of global security and stability."[13] U.S. support was, therefore, one of the many factors that facilitated bin Laden's ascendance.[14] As so often happens, the United States operated on the principle that "the enemy of my enemy is my friend" without reflecting on the long-term consequences of arming this subnational group. A significant policy flaw was leaving the mujahideen in Afghanistan with their weapons and without support or direction after the Soviets withdrew.[15] After the Soviets left, the mujahideen turned their attention to other ideological struggles in the Muslim world. Bin Laden and the Afghan Arabs were able to remain operative in the country despite the misgivings of some local leaders. Bin Laden used his experience against the Soviets and his family fortune to support several local struggles and eventually to create al Qaeda.

Over the next several years, bin Laden's base of operations shifted from Afghanistan to Saudi Arabia, to the Sudan, and then back to Afghanistan. All these nations gave some form of sponsorship to al Qaeda—at the very least, a space in which to plan, train, and recruit. Afghanistan became al Qaeda's main base because a reactionary Islamist government under the Taliban took power there in 1996. The Taliban allowed al Qaeda to establish terrorist training camps in remote mountain regions. After the African embassy bombings in 1998, President Clinton launched air strikes against some of these training camps, but it is not clear that these attacks did much to disrupt the group. Al Qaeda has proven to be adaptable and can relocate its operations quickly. President Bush's invasion of Afghanistan to oust the Taliban and round up al Qaeda members dried up some of its state sponsorship. However, bin Laden eluded capture, and al Qaeda's terrorist attacks have continued.

CHARACTERISTICS OF TERRORISM

The saying "one person's terrorist is another person's freedom fighter" reflects the disparate assumptions that people bring to the job of moral evaluation. It is often assumed that terrorism is, therefore, difficult to define objectively; indeed, the tendency in the news media, at least before September 11, 2001, was to shy away from the use of the term.[16] For good reasons, defining terrorism is perplexing. The label is often put to emotional and partisan uses. The term is highly pejorative, thus few terrorist organizations claim it for themselves.[17] The methods of terrorism change over time and according to social context. Terrorism looks somewhat like war and somewhat like crime, so which of these two phenomena to use when defining it is debatable. Despite these concerns, the analytical literature on terrorism reflects a good deal of agreement about what terrorists do and why.[18] To start with a representative definition from that literature might be helpful. "Terrorism is a synthesis of war and theatre, a dramatization of the most proscribed kind of violence—that which is perpetrated on innocent victims—played before an audience in the hope of creating a mood of fear, for political purposes."[19] This definition by Cynthia C. Combs appropriately focuses our attention on the four most common characteristics of terrorism:

1. Using and/or threatening violence as the primary tactic.
2. Intending to terrorize, that is, to instill fear in a broad population through dramatic acts of violence.
3. Seeking political, social, and cultural changes—however lofty—instead of mere private gain.
4. Attacking civilians indiscriminately and/or intentionally.

Any definition of terrorism that refers to these four characteristics is likely to be reasonable. Let us look further at each one.

The Use and Threat of Violence

Terrorists are infamous for their use of violence and threats of violence as the primary tactic for instilling popular fear in the hopes of instigating political and social change. "These terrorists *are* what they do. And what they do is murder," says Stephen P. Cohen, a Middle East specialist.[20] His statement was made about al Qaeda and allied groups, but it applies to the acts or wishes of virtually every terrorist group. The statistics given earlier suggest how deadly terrorism is. We focused on human deaths and injuries, but terrorism is also known for violence against buildings, transportation systems, and public infrastructure. Some terrorists avoid targeting persons but still use violence against property as their tactic. For instance, fringe animal rights groups have bombed or burned research labs. In the primacy they give to violence, terrorist groups differ from popular reform movements and political parties. Terrorist groups are often connected to a political movement, but they leave it to other organizations to seek political change—for example, Sinn Fein's role as the political arm of the Irish Republican Army (IRA). Other groups have vague political wishes but make no efforts to engage either in politics or popular organizing, which was true of the small group around McVeigh as well as the extensive and highly disciplined al Qaeda network. Although both groups had generalized political and social grievances, neither made specific demands before their spectacular attacks, and neither previously engaged in nonviolent options to effect change. This preference for violence has several reasons. Most notably, terrorists almost always regard themselves as soldiers in a war against a powerful government and/or society. When a war is on, the strategy is to attack. In addition, terrorists are often small in number compared with their adversary, so they find that clandestine violence, especially bombings, are a more effective use of their limited resources than open fighting with the army or police. Additional factors lead to the tactic of violence, including the next characteristic.

The Dramatic Quality of Violence

Terrorism is "the language of being noticed," wrote the novelist Don DiLillo.[21] Terrorists seek to terrorize a populace, to "create a mood of fear," according to our representative definition by Combs. In fact, "fear" is too limiting a word; terrorists seek to create emotions such as anger, exasperation, and sympathy among several publics. In this regard, acts of terrorism have a quality that has been described as dramatic, theatrical, or performative. The sociologist Mark Juergensmeyer describes acts of terrorism—particularly religious terrorism—as "performance violence." He explains:

> In speaking of terrorism as "performance," I am not suggesting that such acts are undertaken lightly or capriciously. Rather, like religious ritual or street theater, they are dramas designed to have an impact on the several audiences that they affect. Those who witness the violence—even at a distance, via the news media—are therefore a part of what occurs. Moreover, like other forms of public ritual, the symbolic significance of such events is multifaceted; they mean different things to different observers.[22]

Is terrorism about ideology or strategy? In fact, it is typically about both. The dramatic quality described by Juergensmeyer helps us put together these two ways of looking at terrorism. He imagines a spectrum running from a strategic/political pole to an ideological/symbolic pole, with terrorist acts or groups plotted in between the two poles.[23] The drama of a terrorist attack serves both the ideological and strategic goals of the terrorist group, in whatever combination they exist. On the strategic side of the spectrum, terrorism against the agents of unpopular rule can benefit recruitment to the movement. Dramatic uses of violence can publicize a local conflict abroad, perhaps impelling foreign governments and international bodies to put pressure on the ruling government. The publicity may also lead foreign governments or private organizations to funnel aid to the group. On the ideological side of the spectrum are cases of religious terrorism. Because religions are inherently symbolic, terrorist groups that are religiously motivated are prone to interpret their grievances, their enemy, and themselves in symbolic terms. Terrorist groups in Christianity (such as Christian Identity and similar separatist militants in the United States) and Islam (such as Hamas, Hezbollah, and al Qaeda) have invoked their respective religion's apocalyptic scriptures and traditions to cast their fight against society as cosmic battles in which they are the warriors of God arrayed against the forces of evil. The uncompromising Jewish partisans in the Israeli–Palestinian conflict have included notorious examples such as Baruch Goldstein (who shot and killed twenty-nine Palestinian worshippers at a mosque in Hebron), Yoel Lerner (who assassinated Prime Minister Yitzak Rabin for supporting a peace process), and Rabbi Meir Kahane (founder of the extremist group Kahane Chai, or Kach, in Israel's West Bank). In all of these instances of religious violence, the symbolic elements express the terrorists' conviction that they are players in a sacred drama and warriors in a cosmic holy war. However ineffectual the act may seem from a strategic standpoint, the terrorists succeed in communicating their vision of the world. They feel that their otherworldly values have been honored and that, somehow, they have assisted God's plan. But do these terrorists always have worldly political goals as well?

The Motive of Political, Social, and Cultural Change

Our representative definition of terrorism states that terrorists have political goals. Bruce Hoffman goes so far as to say that the political characteristic "is absolutely paramount to understanding [terrorism's] aims, motivations and purposes and critical in distinguishing it from other types of violence."[24] Clearly, most terrorist groups operate in the context of a political struggle and assert political goals, such as the overthrow of a government perceived as oppressive or independence from the majority society. Even so, terrorist attacks usually stiffen the resolve of the targeted government and populace. Thus, terrorism seems a politically unwise tactic. In addition, religious terrorists do not seem to think pragmatically; initially, what political benefit could redound to the perpetrators of such attacks as the September 11 hijackings, the Oklahoma City bombing, and the gunning down of Muslim worshippers is difficult to understand.

If "political purposes" in Combs's definition is rendered as "long-term political, social, and cultural changes," it becomes clear that religious terrorists do seek to reorder power relationships in society. Their attacks may not look politically smart if politics is limited to altered policies, invitations to the negotiating table, and success at the ballot box. But our examples do show that religious terrorists such as al Qaeda, Timothy McVeigh, and Baruch Goldstein want governments to change policies, voters to shift allegiances, and their own religious vision to sway politics. They firmly believe that the political powers they despise will eventually withdraw, be replaced, or be drawn into a losing fight. They firmly believe that more and more of their coreligionists will join their ranks as the battle is cast into sharp relief. Some terrorists are deluded about public opinions. McVeigh was one, for he thought his bombing of the federal building would spark a broad-based revolution of Christian patriots against the U.S. government. But others, such as al Qaeda leader Osama bin Laden, are rather astute in manipulating the emotions of multiple publics, both the sympathetic audience and the enemy audience. McVeigh, then, aimed at a short-term political goal but in a strategically reckless manner. Bin Laden aims at longer-term political goals such as the withdrawal of American troops from Saudi Arabia and a socioreligious ascendancy of radical Islam throughout the Arab world. These results are not impossible to imagine.

There is a specific link between the tactic of dramatically terrorizing a populace with violence (the first two characteristics) and terrorists' political/social goals. Military historian Caleb Carr argues that the purpose behind all terrorism is to destroy the populace's "will to support either leaders or policies that the agents of such violence find objectionable."[25] We see this dynamic operating through many examples, regardless of historical, political, or religious context. Through much of the nineteenth and twentieth centuries and even today, a great deal of terrorism has been practiced by ethnonationalist liberation movements and directed mostly against military installations, army troops, police officers, and organs of political control. Such guerilla tactics, even when they do not affect civilians directly, aim to make the ruling powers and their political constituents so worried, or at least exasperated, that continuing the objectionable policy is no longer worth the trouble.

Despite the categorical denials of many political leaders, the uncomfortable truth is that terrorism works. It communicates a message widely, generates sympathies among some publics, and causes fear, anger, and/or pain among other publics. In many cases, terrorists have achieved their political goals, or a portion of them—sometimes in the short run, more often in the long run. Unfortunately, the propensity for terrorism to work is enhanced when governments reward terrorism. American law professor Alan Derschowtiz argues that all too many nations do exactly that—not only do many sponsor terrorism overtly, but most others, including the United States and the United Kingdom, have selectively applied their stated principle that "terrorists should never be rewarded." Of course, determining what counts as a reward provokes controversy. For instance, Derschowitz believes that the Palestinian terrorist groups have been placated far too often by the UN, European nations, church bodies, and even the United

States. On the other hand, for the targeted government to dig in its heels and never respond to terrorists or their stated grievances can lead to an intractable cycle of violence. For the Northern Ireland and the Israeli–Palestinian peace processes to have gotten underway, parties that fought and used terrorism against each other had to open lines of communication.

Targeting Civilians

This final characteristic can be treated briefly because it has been evident throughout the foregoing discussion. Terrorists, we have seen, either intentionally target civilians or attack military and political sites in an indiscriminate manner. Terrorists of all stripes hijack passenger aircraft, bomb subways, blast nightclubs, and kidnap civilians for the dramatic, emotional impact. When terrorists do not attack civilians directly, they typically give little or no regard to civilian bystanders. They usually do not warn the public before an attack, and they use methods such as car bombs, arson, and chemical agents whose deadly effects cannot be narrowly focused.

Caleb Carr portrays the targeting of civilians in a historical context that makes clear the ethical responsibilities of nations:

> What has to date been viewed and treated as a uniquely modern phenomenon is in fact the current stage in a violent evolution whose origins extend as far back as does human conflict itself: terrorism is, in other words, simply the contemporary name given to, and the modern permutation of, warfare deliberately waged against civilians with the purpose of destroying their will to support either leaders or policies that the agents of such violence find objectionable.[26]

Carr is clear that, as a matter of intention, terrorism is quite distinct from accidental civilian deaths in warfare. Yet not only do nations and citizens bear some political responsibility for not responding early and in the most effective manner to terrorism, but very often nations are morally culpable for responding in kind. Carr's bottom-line recommendation is that nations must not adopt the same kinds of tactics used by terrorists. Nations must not target civilians. This is both a political and military imperative.

Unfortunately, in both war and counterterrorism, nations generally are guilty of engaging in indiscriminate military acts. These range from intentional attacks in war (such as the United States' nuclear bombing of Hiroshima and Nagasaki) to mistaken actions (such as British police gunning down an innocent man soon after the July 2005 terrorist bombings because they thought he was about to detonate a bomb). As we argued in chapter 2, the intentional targeting of civilians is never moral; moreover, under the principle of double effect, simply ensuring that an attack is aimed at a military target does not absolve a government from responsibility for civilian causalities if it fails to take due care regarding the proportionality of the action. If a government is insensitive to how its actions are perceived, even accidental deaths of civilians can undermine the cause of counterterrorism. The perverse brilliance of terrorism is that it can draw the besieged government into looking like, or even becoming, the evil party.

RETHINKING THE WAR VERSUS CRIME PARADIGM

With these four characteristics, we have tried to present an account of terrorism that is not emotional and partisan but objective and informative. Such an account does not exhaust the definitional controversies surrounding the topic. The question that seems to generate the most controversy deserves a section of its own because the answer to this question directly influences the methods chosen for combating terrorism: Are terrorist attacks crimes or acts of war? As we will see in this section, terrorism does not fit neatly on the grids established by international laws of war and domestic criminal laws. Both grids provide guidance for analyzing and responding to terrorism. However, some terrorist movements operate in the murky middle ground between war and crime, partaking of the characteristics of both. In fact, we believe that "acts of war" and "crimes" are inadequate terms with which to approach the problem. More illuminating is to consider the constitution of terrorist groups.

Civilians, Groups, and States

According to many definitions, only nonstate actors can count as terrorists. Nation-states, their official agents (soldiers and police), and uniformed belligerents are not terrorists although they can commit war crimes. For instance, the U.S. government's official, legal definition of terrorism is "premeditated violence, perpetrated against noncombatant targets by subnational groups or clandestine agents, usually intended to influence an audience."[27] So what are we to make of examples such as the United States bombing Japanese cities? It appears to satisfy all four characteristics of terrorism. In the realm of counterterrorist policy, Israel's retaliatory bulldozing of the homes of suicide bombers, although it does not kill civilians, is a violent act against civilian property. Its dramatic purpose is to deter future terrorist attacks by causing potential suicide bombers to fear that their families will be harmed in retaliation. Is this destruction of homes a form of terrorism?

The answer turns on the difference between a legal and an ethical account of terrorism. Legally speaking, terrorist groups are subnational or transnational organizations; they are nonstate actors. States are not terrorist organizations as a matter of law. If they intentionally target civilians in war, they can be charged with war crimes; if they do so outside of war, they can be charged with crimes against humanity. (In principle this is so, but the victors in war are rarely, if ever, charged with crimes.) States can act as sponsors of terrorism; they can supply funds, arms, and/or training to terrorist groups. For doing so, they may face UN sanctions and even military reprisals, though the basis in international law for military consequences remains a murky, contested, and undeveloped matter. But ethically speaking, individuals, groups, and states can adopt the terrorist method of using dramatic violence against civilians to instill fear in the hopes of causing social change. Indeed, the word "terrorism" and the modern concept of it derive from a state's use of violence: The French Revolutionary Tribunal in 1793–94 executed thousands of citizens and exerted control through fear under its *régime de la terreur*.

To address these complexities, we propose that a table with two scales can characterize diverse types of terrorism better than the binary categories of war and crime. In table 5.1 the first scale shows what kind of agent is involved: states, civilians, or terrorist groups.

In fact, terrorist groups overlap with states and civilians: Some groups are heavily state sponsored; others are private groups that constitute a domestic threat. The second scale shows the characteristics of terrorist acts. Moving toward the states side, we cross from terrorism into just or unjust acts of war through the gray area of military terrorism. Toward the civilian side, we cross from terrorism into ordinary crimes through the gray area of terrorizing crime.

TABLE 5.1

A Map of Terrorist Agents and Acts

Scale 1 Agents	Aggressions of states							
				Aggressions of civilians				
			Aggressions of terrorist groups					
Scale 2	Acts of war	Military terrorism	All four characteristics of terrorism				Terrorizing crime	Violent crime
Acts	A	B	C	D	E	F G	H	I

The letters in the second scale correspond to examples in table 5.2. The letters sort out a range of terrorist acts that reflect our analytical characteristics, as well as acts that begin to shade away from terrorism in some regards. Regions B and H are the transitional regions where some but not all of the characteristics hold or where the charge of terrorism is contested. For us, region B acts count as military terrorism in light of ethical evaluation based on the four characteristics. Likewise, region C acts count as terrorism practiced by a state against its own citizens. Because these are state actors, the acts described have not fallen under international laws of terrorism but rather under rules of war in region B and under crimes against humanity in region C. Even if they are not prosecutable, acts in regions A to C are still wrong if they harm civilians intentionally. Region H is mostly a type of domestic crime, but it retains the quality of using violence to instill fear in an enemy.

Our four case studies appear in regions D to G. Moving away from a simple war-versus-crime paradigm is useful for understanding all four cases. The bombing of Pan Am flight 103 falls in region D. As we have seen, Libya accepted responsibility for this attack, so it falls within the state-aggression category, but it was nonmilitary and conducted by a terrorist group and so beyond regions A to C. The response to the attack recognizes both aspects: Libya was penalized as a state through economic sanctions—ultimately leading it to acknowledge its responsibility and pay compensation—but there was also a criminal trial to prosecute two of the individuals responsible.

The al Qaeda bombing campaigns since 1998 falls in region E; al Qaeda is a loose, transnational network operating with indirect support from some states. However, it is differentiated from region D in not being a representative

TABLE 5.2

Examples of Terrorist Agents and Acts

Type of aggression	*Examples*
A. Acts of war: attacks by militaries against each other in wartime	■ D-Day landing by the Allies in Normandy (December 1944): just according to jus in bello ■ U.S. firing on Iraqi soldiers retreating from Kuwait (February 1991): unjust according to jus in bello
B. Military terrorism: intentional or indiscriminate attacks by militaries on civilians in wartime	■ Axis and Allied bombing raids on enemy cities during WWII ■ U.S. atomic bombings of Japan (August 1945) ■ U.S. army massacre of approximately 350–500 civilians in My Lai, Vietnam (March 1968)
C. State terrorism against its own citizens	■ Stalin's purges, killing tens of millions of Soviet citizens ■ Operations of the "death squads" of many Central American countries (1980s)
D. Terrorist attacks sponsored and directed by states, or committed by state agencies	■ Massacre of over 750 villagers in El Mazote, El Salvador, by paramilitaries controlled by the El Salvadoran military and indirectly supported by U.S. funding (December 1981) ■ Bombing of Pan Am flight 103 over Lockerbie, Scotland, by persons acting with the sanction and support of Libya, killing 270 people (December 1988)
E. Terrorist attacks by transnational organizations with multiple and/or indirect state sponsors	■ Saudi Hezbollah guerillas' bombing of the Khobar Towers in Dhahran, Saudi Arabia, with support of Iran, killing 19 U.S. military personnel (June 1996) ■ al Qaeda bombings/attacks on African embassies, New York, Washington, Madrid, and elsewhere (1998 to present)
F. Terrorist attacks by sub-national political, guerilla, or religious groups	■ Irish Republican Army bombings in Northern Ireland and Great Britain and Loyalist counterattacks ■ Sarin gas attack in Tokyo subway by the Aum Shinrikyo cult (March 1995) ■ Palestinian suicide bombings in Israel

(continued)

TABLE 5.2 *(continued)*

Examples of Terrorist Agents and Acts

Type of aggression	*Examples*
G. Terrorist attacks by individuals, small groups, and unorganized mobs	■ Oklahoma City bombing by Terry McVeigh and co-conspirators (April 1995) ■ U.S. anarchist Theodore Kaczynski, "the Unabomber," mailing letter bombs over 18 years, killing three people and wounding 29 (arrested April 1996)
H. Terrorizing crime: Assaults by criminal organizations/ groups to instill fear in enemies or for extortion and control	■ Mafia "hits" on other crime-family members ■ Gang violence against other gangs
I. Violent crime	■ Felonious murder and manslaughter

of any one state and from region F in its international character. Its position in the center of our schematic illustrates the challenge of responding effectively to it. The U.S. war on Afghanistan that began in October 2001 was an attempt to deny the network a state-sponsored safe haven as well as to catch the organization's leaders, but the eventual ousting of the Taliban went well beyond these counterterrorist aims. Although the 2003 Iraq War was also linked to the campaign against al Qaeda, there is no plausible evidence of any links between al Qaeda and Iraq before the war, though the war itself allowed a relationship to take hold. Because al Qaeda's attacks were not those of an enemy nation, however, these military responses have arguably been both disproportionate and counterproductive. Other strategies have included attempts to deny the network access to economic and material support and to intercept and prosecute individuals involved in planning or carrying out attacks.

The IRA terrorist campaign against the British presence in Northern Ireland is an example of region F of our scale because the IRA is a highly organized group and is differentiated from the smaller scale of groups in region G. However, its attacks are directed only against Great Britain, rather than having the international dimension of regions D and E. The British government has used the army extensively to preserve order in Northern Ireland and has occasionally resorted to direct attacks, such as the 1988 killing of IRA suspects in Gibraltar. Its overall strategy is best understood, however, as using the army primarily in a policing rather than military role; it has been a law enforcement strategy, albeit one in which many civil liberties were suspended, especially when the army interned suspected group members in the early 1970s. At this point on our scale, there is no alternative but to take a law enforcement approach, as no state sponsor is involved.

The April 1995 Oklahoma City bombing belongs to region G of the scale because this was propagated by a conspiracy of a few individuals rather than by an organized terrorist group. However, it was a terrorist attack rather than a terrorizing crime done for profit (region H). The appropriate response at this point on the scale is clearly to treat the conspirators as criminals.

Implications for How to Respond to Terrorism

A proper understanding of the nature of particular terrorist groups must guide the authorities' responses to them, as the comments in the preceding section make clear. Military responses are more plausible at the left end of the scale, and law enforcement strategies are clearly appropriate at the right end. A third strategy that has the potential to apply across the scale is that of attempting to resolve conflicts by different forms of peacemaking. Before we debate the issues raised in this chapter, it is helpful briefly to survey these three options.[28]

Military responses. If terrorism is interpreted as a warlike attack on a nation-state, the obvious response is a military one. Those who attack civilians must be attacked in return, both to punish their aggression and to reduce or eliminate their capacity to conduct further attacks. Attempts may be made to kill extrajudicially those who have carried out terrorist attacks or assassinate the leaders of organizations thought to be responsible (as Israel has done against Hamas and Islamic Jihad leaders), to destroy resources supporting terrorism (such as the destruction of al Qaeda training camps in Afghanistan by the United States in 2001), or to attack directly nations suspected of supporting terrorism (such as the U.S. attacks on Libya in 1986).

The first and obvious difficulty in responding to most terrorist attacks with military means is finding a target. If terrorist groups are operating secretly, their identities, whereabouts, and sources of support may be unknown. Without intelligence, a military response is impossible. If the accuracy of the intelligence is dubious, a military response risks causing significant damage and casualties without doing any harm to the terrorists. The U.S. destruction of a pharmaceutical factory in the Sudan in 1998 is one example of such a mistake. Even when a terrorist group is known to be residing in a nation, a military attack on the nation may do more disproportionate harm and cause a civil breakdown that makes terrorism more likely to take root. Think of Israel's war on southern Lebanon in the summer of 2006. This ill-considered war, though directed against strongholds of the Hezbollah terrorist group, had the effect of turning international opinion more strongly against Israel than it had been before. The Lebanese government dropped whatever interest it had in restraining Hezbollah because now it had more reason to be angry at Israel. The war caused over a thousands deaths, massive destruction, and a refugee problem, and yet left Hezbollah in a strengthened position. A similar mistake has been made by the United States in Iraq. An additional difficulty occurs when the location of terrorist suspects is known, but they are in the midst of other populations and cannot be attacked without hurting innocent civilians. Israeli attacks on Palestinian refugee camps have frequently been the cause of civilian deaths for this reason. Clearly, a military response is a very blunt instrument, unsuited for accurately targeting small groups of individuals. Terrorists often choose their mode of operations precisely to make themselves as invulnerable as possible from military attack.

These challenges in finding an effective means of military intervention must be considered alongside a wider point: The use of military means in response to terrorism has a strong potential to be counterproductive. Even when attacks are well targeted, but especially when they are not, the use of military means may be successful only in increasing support for the terrorist group. As we have seen, terrorists seek an audience, and attacks on them or on civilians allow them to portray themselves as rightfully seeking revenge for unjust aggression. For this reason, provoking a violent response from the state attacked may, indeed, be a key aim of a terrorist attack. Consequently, a military response actually functions as a reward for terrorism.

Law enforcement responses. If terrorism is understood primarily as the transgression of laws by individuals or groups, the obvious response is to attempt to apprehend and prosecute those responsible and to use intelligence to anticipate and prevent further breaches of the law. Law enforcement approaches, therefore, include policing and intelligence, restricting the freedom of terrorists by banning organizations, freezing sources of funding, and detaining individuals. As we have seen, these approaches are most clearly appropriate at the right side of our terrorism table, but given the development of institutions such as the International Criminal Court and the potential for soldiers and their leaders to be prosecuted for war crimes, these approaches can potentially extend across the range of terrorist attacks.

Law enforcement in relation to terrorism is not straightforward. Catching those who plan and perpetrate terrorist attacks is challenging in the context of well-organized groups acting as secretively as possible. Preventing attacks is a great deal harder and is heavily dependent on excellent intelligence. Obtaining or making public the evidence that would justify a criminal prosecution may be impossible. This difficulty puts pressure on governments to allow detention without trial, as was done by the British government against the IRA in 1971. Alongside the United States, the British government has also extended the period of detention without charge for terrorist offenses in the wake of the September 11 attacks. This practice clearly presents a dilemma for states that espouse freedom as a core value: To improve the potential to prevent attacks, civil liberties must be curtailed, but being forced to restrict civil liberties suggests the terrorists have been successful in their attempt to disrupt the life of the society. Zealous changes to the law with the aim of making it easier to prevent terrorism may therefore be seen as a victory to terrorists in the same way that aggressive military responses may.

Peacemaking responses. Where the military response treats terrorists as enemies, and the law enforcement response treats them as criminals, the peacemaking response treats them as potential dialogue partners. Responses under this heading focus on examining the complaints of terrorists and being alert to legitimate concerns and ways to address them. A primary response is to attempt dialogue with those who are threatening or who have carried out attacks and to look at ways of resolving the conflicts identified in the dialogue by other means. Other strategies include nonviolent opposition to the terrorists in the form of marches, such as the one that followed the bombing in Madrid in 2003, or more directly, as when the family of Robert McCartney (murdered in Northern Ireland in 2005) stood up to the IRA and campaigned for his killer to be brought to justice. Advocates of the peacemaking approach regard it as proactive, seeking fair treatment for all minority groups in a nation and, therefore, reducing the risk that individuals become violently disaffected. This is the only approach of the three we have surveyed that offers the potential to resolve conflicts that give rise to terrorist attacks rather than simply respond to their effects. It is the strategy that pointed the way to a possible end to the terrorist campaign of the IRA in Northern Ireland and the British mainland. In 1989 British government representatives met with the IRA in secret after the group contacted them to say that the conflict was over. Although progress since that time has been uneven, the talks led to a peace process that looks to have the potential to bring peace after a long conflict.

From the perspective of the other approaches, this one initially seems highly suspect, if not treasonous. If the other approaches are in danger of rewarding terrorism indirectly, this approach seems to be in danger of rewarding it directly: responding to the demands of terrorists risks encouraging other groups to use terrorist tactics. Many in Northern Ireland, for example, objected to conciliatory moves by the British government towards the IRA, such as the release of prisoners convicted of terrorist attacks. Although the principle of not giving in to terrorism is important, it should not be absolute. To make it absolute would lock terrorist groups and governments in irreconcilable conflict because governments would be unable to respond to legitimate concerns of terrorist groups, who in turn would feel they have no recourse but to continue attacking. Although peacemaking could rarely be used as a response to terrorism apart from law enforcement strategies, neither military nor law enforcement responses are likely to bring an end to terrorist campaigns without some peacemaking element.

Debating the Issues

DLC The analysis of terrorism we've presented in this chapter provokes the sharp question, In what way do our respective positions provide an ethical framework for responding to terrorism? One crucial preliminary, however, is how we understand the causes of terrorism. Of course, one position many favor is that terrorism is irrational and without coherent motive—the actions of psychopaths. This leads immediately to the conclusion that the only effective response is to hunt down and kill or imprison those planning attacks and those supporting them. I think there are some terrorist groups for which this account is close to the truth, but that it's an inadequate understanding of the terrorist organizations that present major threats today. For recruitment and material support, these groups depend on a clearly developed rationale that is plausible and effective in motivating their constituencies. The leaders of these groups, and those they recruit, are fundamentally misguided that terrorism is a legitimate means, but I believe they are not irrational.

Obviously, intelligence work and policing activities in order to prevent them from carrying out attacks—and punishing those who plan or carry out attacks—are crucial. Because terrorists are not irrational, however, it is also important to examine the causes of their disaffection and to address any legitimate injustices that fuel it. Ideally, of course, these injustices should be addressed before they drive individuals to terrorism. Far from rewarding terrorism, a government's action on issues where the grievances are justified is actually likely to weaken support for the terrorists among the publics that identify with their cause.

BES   We agree on the vital importance of understanding the motivations, assumptions, and goals of terrorist groups. They are not irrational, as explained by our third characteristic of terrorism. One finds a large gulf on this point between specialists on terrorism (despite the variety of disciplines and political perspectives among them) and political leaders who undertake counterterrorist programs. All too often, the latter speak as if terrorists are completely irrational, evil, and driven by ideology to such an extent that they have no viable goals for political and social change. Their reasons for talking in this way make sense on one level: Leaders don't want to admit that any of their policies may have provoked terrorists into action. It may also serve the ambitions of a leader to whip up citizens' fears of a shadowy, inexplicable threat. But citizens are ill served when this happens because counterterrorism programs cannot be effective if we don't try to understand how particular terrorists think.

Now, your final sentence is the really controversial point: Should understanding the rationale of terrorists be geared to policies to address their grievances, or does this amount to rewarding the terrorists? Partisans in the current debate over terrorism see this as an either/or option, but it really has to be taken case by case. I think governments should be careful not to reward terrorism in obvious ways. One example was that the West German government allowed some of the Palestinian kidnappers at the 1972 Munich Olympics to go free so as to get a few captured

German citizens released. But in general, I think our nations can't avoid taking a hard, honest look at policies that may be giving motivation to terrorists.

Evaluating the War on Terror and the Military Model

DLC   We definitely have to consider grievances when we debate possible responses to terrorism. It is also important to understand the historical background, sociopolitical context, and religious or cultural character of each terrorist threat. We did so in our four case studies, brief as they were. It would make no sense for the governments involved to approach all of these cases in the same way. To use the rhetoric that we are engaged in a "war on terror" is to make the problems we face so generic, emotional, and symbolic that they are not amenable to clear-headed analysis. Clear analysis has been all the harder to achieve when the focus has been on a religion and an extremist movement that is not well understood in the West. Of course, to understand the religious ideology of al Qaeda and related groups is important, as we presented in the case study, but this understanding should complement rather than substitute for the other components of understanding. One conclusion to which appreciation of the religious dimensions of jihadist terrorism would lead is that a militaristic response is even less effective than against more overtly political groups, don't you think?

BES   Yes, appreciation of the religious dimension of terrorism should lead our societies to a multipronged strategy in which military tactics are much less prominent than has been the case in the war on terror. We need to avoid exacerbating the threat of religiously inspired terrorism by not putting religious people under such pressure that they feel their very existence is threatened, and by not contributing to the symbolism on which extreme groups thrive. To be specific, I believe that the U.S. policy of waging a war on terror has unnecessarily inflamed Muslim opinion around the world—not so much for its pursuit by military special forces of al Qaeda in Afghanistan as for its military aggression in Iraq coupled with torture scandals and eviscerations of prisoners' rights. These practices and ill-considered domestic security measures make most Muslims—even U.S. citizens—feel insecure. The small number of extremists see all this as confirmation of what they believed all along: that the West wants to attack Islam. The military pursuit of al Qaeda is morally plausible (but still debatable) to just war theorists as a response to the September 11 attacks, but the predominately military tenor of the U.S. policy has undone much goodwill in the Muslim world and emboldened terrorist groups.

DLC The language "war on terror" slips nastily between metaphor and literalism. Predecessor terms, such as the "war on drugs," were clearly intended as metaphors, but in this case the weight of the language has been allowed to slide into justifying two very real wars—in Afghanistan and Iraq. There's an unpleasant irony in the other half of the phrase too. Far from seeking to defeat terror, policies falling under this heading have depended for their support on maintaining and exacerbating the fears of citizens. Language matters.

BES Now, for me, to challenge the primacy of military response is not to deny that most organized terrorist groups think of themselves as fighting a war, and that we should take them at their word. I am challenged by Caleb Carr's claim: "There has always been a central problem with insisting that terrorists are criminals rather than soldiers: this generally limits to reactive and defensive measures the range of responses that the American and other governments can justifiably employ. . . . In truth, terrorism *is*, as its perpetrators so often insist, a form of warfare, and only when we recognize it as such will we be able to formulate a comprehensive and meaningful response to its threat."[29] Characterizing al Qaeda and other groups as criminals or belligerents makes a great deal of difference to the strategies nations will take in response. I think it is not an either/or option, but has to be both/and. When the nineteen hijackers perpetrated the September 11 attacks, their acts were domestic crimes but also a military aggression by al Qaeda. Given that al Qaeda isn't a state, the United States couldn't declare war against the group, but it was and is appropriate for the United States to use military operations as part of its response, especially when al Qaeda was already responsible for several other attacks on American military and political installations around the world. When perpetrators and conspirators were apprehended after the London bombings of July 2005, domestic police work against them as criminals was the necessary response in order to stop immediate threats and to find out exactly who these attackers were. But the British government cannot afford to think of the threat only as one of police work, because that won't head off attacks and won't address any external sources of support for the perpetrators.

DLC   In the long term, what will head off attacks are better relationships between Western and Arab nations, aimed at finding a way to resolve the Israel–Palestine conflict. In the short term, what will head off attacks is continued, focused attention on intelligence gathering and policing, aimed at arresting those preparing to attack or at least preventing the attacks from being successful. Where available, intelligence can also be used to isolate groups from their supporters. The military mode of response in Afghanistan and Iraq has unquestionably increased the threat of jihadist extremist terrorism, tripling the number of attacks from the record level of 175 attacks in 2003 to 655 in 2004, according to the U.S. National Counterterrorism Center.[30] The only alternative interpretation is that the number of attacks would have been as high if there had not been wars in Afghanistan and Iraq, which is wildly implausible. This empirical evidence supports the obvious truth that, at least where there is no known state sponsor of terrorism, responding to terrorism as warfare is nonsensical. The attacks in Afghanistan could be defended on the grounds of attempting to locate those responsible for the attacks of September 11, 2001, though they were conspicuously unsuccessful in this aim. Surely we can agree that the 2003 Iraq War had nothing to do with responding to terrorism and has precipitated a rise in terrorist attacks. The injustice of using terrorism as an excuse for invading Iraq was not lost on potential terrorist recruits. Do you have an example of a successful use of military action against terrorism?

BES   Misguided and mishandled military responses to terrorism are very likely to embitter the people we are trying to win over in the battle of ideas. Whatever you think of Carr's military model for characterizing and responding to terrorism, we can agree that he's absolutely correct that targeting civilians or causing any more than very minimal and genuinely accidental harm to them is a strategy destined to fail (his book *The Lessons of Terror* is replete with historical examples). That practical principle alone casts the Iraq War in the category of failures before we even get to ethical matters. But do military responses to terrorism work? Are there examples, as you ask? The attacks on Libyan leader Qaddafi in the mid-1980s are often mentioned as a success, but the facts suggest a dubious legacy. Terrorist incidents linked to Libya, including the Lockerbie bombing, rose for the two years after the U.S. aerial strike on Qaddafi in 1986. After that, Libya-linked attacks dropped off sharply. I think it is likely that the total economic and political pressure on Libya made more of a difference than military strikes. Qaddafi was keen to have the economic sanctions lifted in later years. Another set of mixed examples are Israeli responses to Palestinian terrorism. Even though some claim that the attack on the Jenin refugee camp, for example, was both tailored and effective, the perception by the Palestinian public and international community only fueled the cycle of violence. What I see as effective and necessary is a strategy to keep terrorist groups on the run from any state-sponsored safe havens. I don't agree that the Afghanistan operation was conspicuously unsuccessful, but I think the United States erred in making it a matter of regime change and nation-building rather than a very swift and decisive Special Forces military operation. Our need to collaborate with dubious warlords in the Northern Alliance delayed our operation, and the removal of the Taliban government bogged us down in nation-building. It is still early to assess the long-term success of Afghanistan, but on the positive side of the ledger I would place the fact that it removed al Qaeda's existing base of operations. The problem is that the United States lacked a tailored and consistent strategy; al Qaeda members that survived and eluded capture likely moved over to Pakistan, an autocratic regime with whom we have an ambiguous relationship.

DLC It's obviously a good idea to reduce the opportunities for terrorists to plan attacks, so putting pressure on any states that support them is an important policy goal. The support offered can clearly range widely, however. It could be giving terrorist groups freedom to meet, recruit, and plan, such as many have accused the United Kingdom of doing in London. It could be citizens of a state providing financial backing to terrorists, as in the case of individuals in the United States who supported the IRA over a long period. It could be state funding of terrorist activities, such as the U.S. funding of the mujahideen in Afghanistan. Or it could be more direct involvement, such as Libya's involvement in the Lockerbie bombing. Each case of support for terrorism needs its own careful response, aimed at making it harder for terrorist groups to operate. The final goal must be establishing a strong international consensus that terrorism is unacceptable as a means to any goal. But this seems a long way off, particularly as many American and British citizens continue to believe the indiscriminate attacks on German and Japanese citizens during World War II were justified. Are we not guilty of objecting to terrorism only when we're on the receiving end of it?

BES It's essential that the international community with a common voice condemn all terrorism and all intentional attacks on civilians. Lip service is paid to that principle, but governments are quick to undermine it if doing so appears to be in their national interest, and citizens are tempted to forgo the principle if they feel they have to beat the terrorists at their own game. Sinking to the tactics of terror is a response that terrorism is designed to bring out, so citizens and leaders must show strong character and resist the lure. In the examples you mention, I think American and British citizens are not guilty of condoning terrorism for the most part, yet it is their responsibility to know about the policies of their nations, to speak up against immoral acts of their governments and militaries, and to choose ethical leaders. Of course, there is a wide variety among citizens in their support for policies and leaders; moreover, citizens and politicians do challenge their governments, as many Americans have in response to the revelations of torture in Iraq, or as so many British citizens and members of parliament did against the Iraq War. Terrorists err in holding citizens and bystanders fully responsible for everything a government does.

Evaluating the Law Enforcement Model

DLC On the matter of strategy, I still worry that military reprisals and preemptive attacks undermine these principles. I'm not convinced by the arguments you've offered for military attacks against terrorists. But you've admitted that the military approach can't be the primary strategy. So wouldn't whatever tactics of force you think need to be used be best handled under a law enforcement paradigm? This could include pursuing actual perpetrators, but also tracking terrorist groups, constricting funding, and so on. Whatever law enforcement and intelligence strategies the United States uses against domestic terrorist groups such as right-wing paramilitaries, can be used against groups like al Qaeda, although with additional or different agencies because that group operates transnationally. I think the United Kingdom to date has operated an effective law enforcement model, for the most part; where the United Kingdom has deviated from it, it has been the least effective (the disastrous Bloody Sunday shootings in Northern Ireland in 1972 spring to mind). This does not mean that my country has been successful in preventing all attacks, but we have acknowledged that military approaches seem significantly less effective. Certainly in Northern Ireland, giving a greater role to the army would have precipitated further resistance from republicans. For me, law enforcement and peacemaking strategies are complementary, but a military response to terrorism is almost guaranteed to be counterproductive.

BES The law enforcement model of response fits more comfortably with just war theory than a military model of response. I affirm proactive law enforcement as the primary strategy for governments to deal with terrorism, complemented by a thoughtful collaboration with other groups in society for a just peacemaking response. I agree with you that military re sponses only make sense when the direct involvement of another government is clear. Even then, military responses must be judiciously used. As presented in chapter 2, just war tradition doesn't think of policing and war as completely different types of actions; they are judged by the same principles. That means if I support policing responses to terrorism, I could support military responses if they meet the just war criteria and are the most prudent course. Likewise, policing involves force, and any decisions to use force should be ethically guided.

In addition to the techniques you mention, there are a number of important protective measures that the current American administration—for all its passion about winning the war on terror—has bizarrely failed to pursue. Namely, American ports are vulnerable to the shipment of bombs or deadly weapons, as only a very small percentage of foreign cargos are searched upon arrival. American nuclear power plants are vulnerable to attack. *Time* magazine hypothesized a scenario in which a relatively small band of terrorists could overcome a plant's light defenses and cause a reactor meltdown within minutes.[31] Nor has the government looked carefully enough at the vulnerability of the commercial food supply. The government has focused a great deal on airline security but has not thought creatively and proactively about the potential next attack, which won't be a replay of September 11. One reason for these gaps is a failure of political nerve to force changes on industries that lobby against new spending for security. Another major reason is that we have sunk too much money in the military response—that is, Iraq—and thus failed to invest in these protective measures.

DLC   Of course, adopting a law enforcement model is not the end of the debate. In many countries, including our own, there have been significant restrictions of civil liberties following the al Qaeda attacks on the United States in 2001. We mentioned in this chapter the different ways terrorism can be rewarded; for me, provoking nations to more repressive laws—such as expanding detention without trial—goes some way to realizing the aims of terrorist attacks. If our nations want to nurture peaceful subcommunities, if they are concerned to undermine factors that foster religious extremism, then domestic security measures that make the Muslim community feel targeted are not going to help.

BES   I agree about the perils of more repressive laws. On this matter, the sensible counsel is that each nation has to find the right balancing point between civil liberties and public security. The USA Patriot Act, passed by the U.S. Congress just weeks after the September 2001 attacks, has some useful and some problematic points. Certain improvements in the way that intelligence work is coordinated among agencies of the U.S. government made a lot of sense. Unfortunately, the American political culture at the current time is such that the problematic points are not being challenged by enough politicians.[32] It is interesting that in the United States, the major controversy surrounds civil liberties and not so much the rights and protections of minority groups. The concerns expressed reflect America's strong tradition of free speech. But why hasn't there been as much controversy over minority rights? The situation probably reflects a restrained response to airport security as well as American demographics. There was a lot of concern about the possibility of ethnic profiling of Arabs and Arab Americans (or those who simply look darker skinned) in the months after September 11, but there were only a few early excesses. Security at airports settled into a system of comprehensive screening complemented by additional random searches rather than searches based on ethnic profiles. I think that's for the best; not only is it ethically sound, but an ethnic-profiling method would actually be a clumsy tool and a public relations mess. Demographically, there are reasons to believe the Muslim community is better integrated into the United States than into several European countries. Many in the American Muslim community are African American converts; not many are recent immigrants from politically volatile Middle Eastern countries, as tends to be the case in various pockets of Europe. So the United States may simply be lucky that social integration of Muslim community has worked out well so far. But all Western nations need to give concerted attention in the future to political, economic, and educational policies that will integrate ethnic and religious minorities. Alienation of minority groups—whether domestic or immigrant, whether religious or ethnic— can be a precursor to terrorism.

Developing Peacemaking Strategies

DLC Those comments bridge our discussion from law enforcement to the peacemaking strategies we've highlighted: establishing dialogue between embittered parties to discover grievances, addressing grievances through changes of action, and negotiating long-term policy reforms. It is crucial that governments confronting terrorism take these strategies seriously. I appreciate the risk of seeming soft on terrorism by seeking to understand the grievances that provoke it or by seeking dialogue with the perpetrators. I also appreciate that there are some moments in conflicts where dialogue is impossible. But it's the only approach that promises the end to a conflict, rather than just the amelioration of it. I don't mean that governments should be pressurized by terrorist threats to do things that are unjust. But a reasonable response to a threat or attack is to ask what is motivating that aggression and to seek ways of addressing what motivates it. Where terrorists are expressing legitimate concerns—obviously in a wholly illegitimate way—governments should consider whether there are appropriate actions that would respond to those concerns. In the context of the current al Qaeda campaign, for example, it is obviously essential that law enforcement strategies are followed for pursuing and prosecuting those who have been involved in attacks as well as seeking intelligence to prevent further attacks wherever possible. But I also think it would be timely to give a great deal of international attention to further steps in the peace process between Israel and Palestine. The "never give in to a terrorist demand" rule would suggest we shouldn't make any new moves in that context for fear of being seen to reward the attackers, but from my point of view, making further attempts to resolve that conflict is something that should have been done in any case, and the need to abate a grievance leading to terrorism is just an additional motivation to make progress.

BES Indeed, continued strong support from the United States, United Kingdom, and the community of nations on the Israel–Palestinian peace process is vital. We are both committed—as are our governments—to the goal of an autonomous Palestinian state coexisting with a secure Israel. The unresolved political and social relationship of those two nations makes the region a major site of terrorism and militarism and provides a symbolic fuel to jihadist terrorism elsewhere. In the end, Israelis and Palestinians will have to come to a point where they trust each other enough, and the dialogue necessary for this can't take place without the efforts of civic groups, such as religious bodies, peace groups, advocacy groups, and educational institutions. Peace processes don't come out of nowhere; they are preceded and, in many ways, carried to fulfillment by the witness, outreach, and service of ordinary citizens through such institutions.

DLC South Africa is a good example of the process you are talking about. It was not because the African National Congress and other liberation groups engaged in occasional (and minor, compared to the violence of apartheid) acts of terrorism and political violence that South Africa changed. It was the steady and largely peaceful witness of black South Africans under leaders such as Bishop Desmond Tutu. When ANC leader Nelson Mandela was released from jail in 1990, he renounced the ANC's earlier adoption of violence and added his moral power to nonviolent reform movement, supported by the disinvestment campaign of groups in the developed world. Black South Africans finally won through peaceful protest and the ballot box. Importantly, the leaders of this movement continued in a peacemaking mode by preferring truth and reconciliation (hence, the commission by that name) over vengeance and punishment. There are likewise both Israeli and Palestinian peace groups; there are ordinary citizens who have been striving to reach beyond the impasse and communicate their desire to live together peaceably.

BES Our examples serve as a reminder that religion can play a constructive as well as a destructive role in the area of terrorism. We clearly agree—and want our fellow citizens and fellow church members to recognize—that religious extremism is not the only kind of terrorism; that religion can be an aggravating source of terrorism but never its only cause; and that no religion, including Christianity, is immune from misinterpretations that justify terrorism. We join in urging religious groups to claim their important role in the peacemaking approach to terrorism. It is up to the leaders and the ordinary members of each religion to talk about and put into action the loving and peaceful essence of their faiths. Many commentators have said in the past few years that Islam is fundamentally a religion of peace and that its great majority is nonviolent but that more Muslims need to speak out in condemnation of terrorism committed by Muslims. Those statements are true, but Christians cannot mandate how Muslims speak. We can put our efforts into doing the same as it applies to ourselves, our denominations, and the societies in which we are in the majority. These attitudes and reforms are taking root in faith communities, as seen in the growing efforts at Christian-Jewish-Muslim dialogue. Such building up of relationships is the only effective long-term answer to terrorism.

CONCLUSION

We have assessed three strategies for responding to terrorism. Stiltner's just war position locates some limited value in military responses but places greater stress on the combination of law enforcement and peacemaking strategies. Clough's pacifism is similar but would put the greatest effort into the peacemaking model because that model addresses the root causes of terrorism and does not aggress on human life. He does not deny the government's role in apprehending criminals and taking various sensible steps to avert attacks, yet he would have us be vigilant that law enforcement powers are carefully monitored and guided by justice, lest they slide into the errors of militarism. Both of us find a number of benefits in the peacemaking model although we do not pretend that this approach is politically popular or that it can be pursued without risks and sacrifices. We joined in finding many flaws in the military model, a model that remains attractive to superpowers seeking a resolute response to terrorism. The 2003 war on Iraq was partly justified as a military response to terrorism; we examine this case study in the next chapter.

CHAPTER 6

Spreading Democracy or Asserting National Interests? The Case of the Wars on Iraq

We have just finished analyzing and debating three contemporary issues of warfare—military intervention in humanitarian crises, weapons proliferation, and terrorism. All three of these issues are implicated in our final applied topic, which concerns the rights and wrongs of the great powers waging war to remake the governments of other nations. We have in mind the role that the United States and the United Kingdom are playing in the Middle East, specifically in Iraq. The 2003 Iraq War, its precursor events, and its aftermath constitute our case study in this chapter.[1] The case that the Bush and Blair administrations made for invasion of Iraq invokes arguments we have seen in the previous chapters. The war was promoted primarily as a necessary response to the imminent threat posed by Iraq's suspected nuclear and chemical weapons programs. Secondarily, the Bush administration presented the war as an important front in the war on terror. American advocates for the war played on residual anxieties from September 2001 and the fear of another 9/11–style attack. Some advocates took care not to claim a direct connection between al Qaeda and Saddam Hussein, but many did argue that Saddam would supply weapons of mass destruction to terrorists if given the chance.[2]

A third argument—of inferior importance for the administrations but primary for some Christian and some liberal supporters—was that the war amounted to a humanitarian intervention because Saddam was a brutal dictator who had gassed the Kurdish population in 1988, had violently suppressed the Shia Muslims after the Gulf War, and had arrested and executed thousands of dissenters. A fourth argument was less clearly stated but significant: Deposing a despotic leader and replacing his regime with a democratic government was in the interest of the United States, the United Kingdom, and the "community of free nations." This remaking of Iraq would begin to spread democracy in the Middle East, leading to greater regional security, reduced terrorism, and more humane self-governance.

In a sense, then, the Iraq War could have been studied in any of the three prior chapters. But the confluence of these four arguments makes it an illuminating example to consider in detail: a case of military intervention to change a sovereign regime for a combined purpose of international security and internal democratic reform. In just war language, the war has been considered by both advocates and critics alike as an instance of "preventive war"—not one that preempts an imminent attack but one that aims to forestall a future threat from developing. Preventive war is not unknown in the history of nations, but it has been given special prominence by supporters of the war on terror. Under that rubric, the fourfold justification was first invoked for the invasion of Afghanistan in 2001. The United States ousted the Taliban government on the argument that it was providing a safe haven to the terrorist al Qaeda organization, therefore, harming and destabilizing many other countries. The United States also argued that the Taliban's human rights violations created an ethical reason to remove it from power. In the future, similar arguments could be invoked to justify other preventive wars by major powers. Thus, to test the arguments carefully is particularly important. The analysis in this chapter will contribute to a deeper ethical understanding of the Iraq War and address new challenges that will shape international relations in the twenty-first century. A fundamental ethical question in this chapter will be whether preventive war represents a new and acceptable category of just war, or whether it is simply a new way to dress up the assertion of national self-interests.

BACKGROUND: IRAQ AND THE WEST, 1917-2003

Here we will survey relevant background information about Iraq's history with the West and the decision-making context that led to the invasion before surveying, in the next main section, the arguments and the troubling challenges raised by war and its aftermath.

From British Colony to Ba'athist Regime

When British troops invaded Iraq via Basra in 2003, those with sufficiently long memories must have recognized history repeating itself because Britain had invaded through the same port twice in the twentieth century.[3] In October 1914 the Ottoman Empire declared itself on the side of Germany and Austria-Hungary in their war against France, Russia, and Britain. Britain immediately landed at Basra and by the end of 1918 had occupied the provinces of Basra, Mosul, and Baghdad. The Ottoman Empire withdrew from the area, and the British occupation of these three provinces was the origin of the Iraqi state. Owing to widespread resistance to its rule, Britain agreed to establish a kingdom. It conducted a bogus referendum to choose the first king and granted Iraq independence in 1932.

Self-rule did not create political stability; coups d'etat occurred in 1936 and 1941 as relations with Britain worsened. Iraq tried to get closer to the Axis powers during World War II, prompting Britain to invade to ensure its access to its airbase at Basra. The British military intervention ended the cycle of military coups for a while, yet a further coup in July 1958 overthrew the monarchy and instituted a republic. Once again Iraq's relationship with Britain deteriorated, and this time Iraq turned to the Soviet Union for support. In 1961, the Iraqi prime minister made a claim to Kuwait immediately after its independence, citing in support that it was previously part of the Ottoman province of Basra. At the request of Kuwait, Britain sent troops to defend it, which were later replaced by an Arab League force.

The political instability continued in the years that followed. The Ba'ath Party carried out a coup in 1963, but the new leaders were ousted by a further coup in the same year. Five years later, in July 1968, the Ba'ath party and others instigated a coup that resulted in a lasting change in Iraq's political leadership. The Ba'ath party is a secular, pan-Arabist movement founded in Damascus, Syria, in 1944. In Iraq, it was thoroughly dominated by Sunni Muslims, an ethnoreligious branch who were the minority. The Ba'ath party suppressed the political power of Kurds and Shiites and expressed a pan-Arab nationalism hostile to Israel, Britain, and other Western nations.[4]

Iraq took full control of the Iraqi Petroleum Company from foreign investors in 1972, which meant that the government accrued an astonishing degree of wealth with the steep rise in oil prices of 1973. Tensions rose with

Iran during this period, but neither side wanted full-scale war, so in 1975 they announced that their differences had been resolved. At the end of that year, Iraq was earning $8 billion annually from oil and spending 40 percent of this revenue on arms. The newfound affluence led to improved relations with western states. Saddam Hussein had come into a position of power with the Ba'ath takeover in 1968; he became vice-chairman of the Iraqi Revolutionary Command Council and vice president of Iraq. Over the course of the 1970s, he took control of Iraq's oil policy, which put him in a position of considerable power. When Hasan al-Bakr, Iraq's elderly president, resigned in 1979, Saddam, having already ruled de facto for some years, was sworn in as his successor within hours. He acted immediately against his political opponents, executing as many as five hundred senior party figures.

Saddam thought the relative position of Iraq could be improved by challenging Iran, so he began instigating trouble with the neighboring nation in 1980. He publicly renounced the 1975 treaty, calculating that this would force Iran to disengage from border clashes. On September 17, 1980, he declared disputed parts of Iran to be part of Iraq and then launched an invasion on September 22. This turned out to be a catastrophic error; the Iranian people, though surprised by the invasion, quickly rallied and resisted the invasion by volunteering in massive numbers. An Iranian counterattack in 1982 led to heavy casualties and created over forty thousand Iraqi prisoners of war. The war began to take a heavy toll on Iraq's economy. Oil revenues fell from $26 billion in 1980 to $9 billion in 1982 after the destruction of oil terminals; by 1983, Iraq had $25 billion of foreign debt. Some Ba'ath party members realized the disastrous consequences of the war and sought a settlement with Iran, but Iran showed no interest. Saddam Hussein likewise rebuffed such overtures; instead, he sought cash from other Arab governments in order to step up the war effort.

The United States aimed to maintain a balance of power that favored neither nation decisively. Yet the United States favored Iraq because it more greatly feared the ascendancy of Iran as a radical Muslim power. Furthermore, the United States despised the regime that connived with Iranian students to hold sixty-six Americans hostage for fifteen months in 1979–80.[5] The decisive factor in the ending of the war in 1988 was the intervention of U.S. naval forces in the Gulf, together with support for Iraq in other forms, such as the provision of detailed satellite information. A ceasefire agreement left both nations where they had been eight years earlier but with hundreds

of thousands of causalities and wrecked economies on both sides. Iran suffered greater losses, with perhaps three hundred thousand fatalities, compared with one hundred thousand Iraqi deaths.[6] Overall, the war cost more
than one trillion dollars and left Iraq with 60 to 80 billion dollars of foreign
debt. Sixty thousand Iraqi prisoners of war needed to be repatriated, and
one million were still in the armed forces.

Iraq's human losses included a massive number of intentional deaths. In
1987–88, during the period of improving relations between Iraq and the
United States, Iraq intensified its campaign against the Kurds in the north of
the country to suppress any hopes of Kurdish autonomy. Saddam's forces
killed close to one hundred thousand Kurdish citizens through a combination of chemical weapons, conventional attacks, and abductions of people
who were never heard from again.[7] This gross violation of human rights constituted genocide—a systematic attempt to destroy a population identified by
a shared ethnicity.[8] That Saddam gassed his own citizens in addition to Iranian soldiers is a sad but undisputable fact. It is also a sad but indisputable fact
that the United States and the international community knew about Saddam's genocide of the Kurds for several months before it leveled any official
complaint. Scattered media reports began to corroborate the attacks in the fall
of 1987; the March 1988 chemical attack on the town of Halabja—which
killed five thousand, making it the deadliest of the chemical attacks—was
well covered by the media.[9] Samantha Power's Pulitzer-prize-winning book,
"A Problem from Hell": America and the Age of Genocide, tells a sobering tale
of the United States' moral equivocation in the face of this evil.

> Although intelligence and press reports of Iraqi brutality against the
> Kurds surfaced almost immediately, U.S. policymakers and Western jour-
> nalists treated the Iraqi violence as if it were an understandable attempt to
> suppress rebellion or a grisly collateral consequence of the Iran–Iraq war.
> Since the United States had chosen to back Iraq in the war, it refrained
> from protest, denied it had conclusive proof of Iraqi chemical weapon
> use, and insisted that Saddam Hussein would eventually come around.[10]

After the Kurdish issue was covered up by the Reagan administration, relations with Iraq seemed to be at a tolerable status quo, and the baton of American power passed to George H. W. Bush.[11] But Saddam was faced with a
desperate domestic situation. When the Arab nations refused his request

that they forgive $40 billion in loans and increase the price of oil, he began to consider whether further military action would provide oil revenue and make regional leaders more compliant to his will. Thus, Saddam began complaining about Kuwait, the nation to Iraq's southwest.

The Persian Gulf War

Kuwait is an oil-rich nation governed under a constitutional monarchy. The disputes between the two nations over territory went back some years (recall Iraq's claim over Kuwait and Britain's intervention in 1961). Saddam's specific grievances concerned the location of the border between them, claims that Kuwait was drilling into Iraq's territory for oil, and the ownership of an island in the Persian Gulf.[12] Kuwait held a lot of wealth in oil resources but had no significant military and could never hold up in a war with Iraq.

At an April 1990 meeting with President Hussein, U.S. Ambassador April Glaspie is reported to have told the Iraqi leader that the United States considered his border dispute with Kuwait a regional matter on which the United States took no position. In hindsight, critics of the war claimed that this incident displayed impure motives on part of the Bush administration because it gave Iraq permission to invade Kuwait. It hardly seems likely that the United States wanted Iraq to invade Kuwait. President Bush immediately condemned Iraq when it did invade a few months later and initiated the process that would eventually repel the invasion.[13] Whatever one makes of the United States' diplomatic fault in this incident, observers agree that it did not give Iraq the moral or legal right to invade Kuwait. The error of the United States and the community of nations as a whole is that they wanted to maintain the status quo and were unwilling to get involved in regional disputes—even at the price of treating an aggressive dictator solicitously.

On the morning of August 2, 1990, after making public assurances to other nations that it would not invade Kuwait, Iraq did just that.[14] The Kuwaiti army was quickly overwhelmed, but it was able to fight long enough to allow both its air force and the royal family to escape the country. Soon, some one hundred thousand Iraqi troops occupied the country, taking control of the media, installing a new governor, and holding thousands of Western visitors hostage. Within a few days, the UN Security Council passed resolutions requiring Iraq to withdraw and placing economic sanctions on Iraq.[15] The Arab League likewise passed a resolution condemning the invasion. Iraq refused to withdraw, restating its claims that much of Kuwait constituted the nineteenth province of Iraq. The United States quickly sent troops to the Gulf to defend the northern border of Saudi Arabia because Saddam had also expressed grievances against the Saudi regime. Occupying Kuwait gave Saddam two advantages: a strong position for invading Saudi Arabia and the ability to disrupt other nations' economies by controlling Kuwait's oil supply in addition to Iraq's own.

Whether Saddam meant to act on either of these advantages is not clear; he probably wanted to exploit the fears of his future mischief as a bargaining chip that would allow him to hold on to some of Kuwait. Iraq looked for a negotiated path to this goal, but Bush held a coalition of nations together that flatly required Iraq to withdraw. It took five months for these diplomatic efforts to transpire, as well as for a massive military force to be amassed in the Persian Gulf. UN Security Council Resolution 678, passed on November 29, 1990, set a deadline of January 15, 1991, for Iraq to withdraw and authorized member nations to use "all necessary means to uphold and implement" the Security Council's will. A final attempt at diplomacy was made in early January 1991 when Secretary of State James A. Baker visited Iraqi Foreign Minister Tariq Aziz in Geneva. The six-hour meeting revealed no conciliation by Iraq, so talk turned to the United States' willingness to fight and Iraq's willingness to withstand that fight.[16] Bush made good on his threat. The coalition, led by American commanders, commenced air strikes on Baghdad on the night of January 17, 1991. On February 24, after a little more than a month of aerial bombing all over Iraq and Kuwait, the coalition launched a ground offensive that pushed the Iraqi army out of Kuwait in just one hundred hours. After checking with his advisors, Bush called a ceasefire on February 27 because the Iraqi army had withdrawn from Kuwait.

An impressive number of nations supported the UN Security Council resolutions, even several Arab nations. Over thirty-five nations supplied military resources or financial aid to the attack on Iraq, including several, such as Canada, that are not typically militarist in orientation. Nevertheless, the Gulf War was ethically controversial among Western publics, political commentators, and theologians and ethicists. As in most public debates over prospective wars, just war criteria framed the public debate in the Western societies. Table 6.1 summarizes the main claims made on each side of the debate.

TABLE 6.1

Ethical Arguments For and Against the Gulf War

Just War Principles	In Support of the Gulf War	Against the Gulf War
Just cause	▪ War would reverse the invasion of Kuwait, based on the principle of national sovereignty. ▪ War would deter an attack on Saudi Arabia. ▪ War was necessary to defend the rights and welfare of Kuwaitis.	▪ The price of oil was not a just cause. ▪ Some claims of human rights abuses were falsified.
Right intention	▪ Coalition nations acted so as to achieve the stated cause. ▪ They expressed no desire to occupy Iraq, to control Iraq's oil, or to abuse the Iraqi people.	▪ Too many conflicting rationales were offered. ▪ Economic considerations appeared to be the true motivation. ▪ Western nations had supported Saddam previously.
Legitimate authority	▪ UN Security Council Resolution 678 provided for military force.	▪ The U.S.'s diplomatic leverage pressured other nations to go along. ▪ Methods of individual nations for deciding to commit troops can be challenged.
Last resort	▪ Saddam gave no indication that he was willing to comply with UN resolutions, so the invasion of Kuwait would become permanent. ▪ Iraqi citizens would suffer from prolonged economic deprivations.	▪ In view of the risks, economic sanctions and diplomacy should have been given more time to work.
Proportionality of expected results	▪ The stated causes were morally worth the risks. ▪ Reversing the invasion would also constrain Saddam from invading Saudi Arabia.	▪ Thousands of troops might die, as well as tens of thousands of Iraqi soldiers and civilians. ▪ Saddam might use the war as an excuse to attack Israel and Saudi Arabia, to cause

TABLE 6.1 *(continued)*

Just War Principles	*In Support of the Gulf War*	*Against the Gulf War*
		environmental damage, to use chemical and biological weapons, and to kill hostages.
Reasonable hope of success	■ The coalition clearly possessed overwhelming power.	■ (Conceded to pro-war side.)
Discrimination	■ Coalition forces held to the principle by using precision-guided munitions.	■ Aerial bombing was unnecessarily massive and prolonged. ■ Civilian infrastructure was intentionally targeted.
Proportionality in conduct	■ Just causes were achieved. ■ Stability was restored (for a while). ■ UN was able to inspect and destroy Iraq's illegal weapons.	■ 1,500–56,000 Iraqi soldiers died. ■ 1,000–3,500 civilians died. ■ Up to 100,000 Kurds and Shiites died in Saddam's postwar repression. ■ As many as 110,000 deaths may be attributed to the devastation of Iraq. ■ Thousands of U.S. veterans suffer from Gulf War Syndrome.

The proponents of attacking Iraq found their strongest arguments in just cause and legitimate authority. The stated causes comported with just war tradition and international law. The legality of the war was backed by an explicit UN Security Council resolution. Indeed, this was the first time—and so far the only time—that a broad coalition of nations started a war with explicit UN approval. The antiwar argument placed great stress on the weak and conflicting intentions stated for the war. Because administration officials cited the price of oil and its ramification on the American economy as one of their rationales, serious doubt was cast on the other stated causes and intentions. The two sides differently assessed the likely destruction and other risks. The pro-war side did not talk about the possibility of hundreds of thousands of deaths; the critics' assessment of the human cost showed better foresight. So should economic sanctions have been given more time to work? The pro-war side was probably right that sanctions alone would not have forced Saddam out of Kuwait, but the antiwar side was correct in saying that the sanctions and diplomatic pressure would not have been nearly as deadly as the war turned out to be.

Both just war thinkers and pacifists were troubled by three departures from the just conduct criteria of discrimination and proportionality. First, precision-guided munitions—the smart bombs so celebrated in the media at the time—still relied on human decision making, so civilians died by mistake. The moral fault is not so much that accidents occurred as that military leaders spoke as if mistakes almost never occur, thus shielding the public from the human costs of the war. Second, the aerial bombing campaign was so massive and went on for so long that civilians were certain to die. Much of this campaign targeted the civilian infrastructure, such as bridges and the electricity supply. The effects of this destruction caused indirect deaths when, for instance, hospitals could no longer function and water was rendered unclean. A few thousand civilians died from the war itself, but many thousands more died from the aftereffects, as table 6.1 notes.[17] Third, U.S. forces fired on the retreating Iraqi army in the last few days of the ground war, even after President Bush called a ceasefire. The road from Kuwait City back into Iraq became known as the "Highway of Death" because retreating soldiers died as they fled.[18] The potential legal and ethical violations were not fully investigated, and no one was held to account.[19]

Based on this analysis, some just war thinkers supported going to war; others thought it would be unethical and imprudent. The actual conduct of the war did not tend to change either side's overall assessment, though supporters wished that some military decisions had been handled differently. Pacifists not only joined these criticisms but they also believed that the results revealed the common conduct of war—conduct that is repeated in every war and thus provides a strong reason against going to war in the first place. We will explain our own opinions in the debate section.

The Continuing Struggle with Saddam

The world's—and specifically the United States'—military struggle with Iraq did not end with the Iraqi army's retreat from Kuwait. The first decision faced by the coalition was whether to intervene in the army's attacks on Kurds and Shiites and, therefore, to reopen the war. The senior Bush came under special criticism because he made statements that seemed to encourage these two groups to rise up against Saddam's rule, only to abandon them when they did. Secretary of State Baker maintained that the United States did not have the moral or legal right to carry the war to Baghdad and oust Saddam. "We owed it to our troops, our officers, their families, and American taxpayers, we believed, to get in, perform a clearly defined mission, and get out."[20] Many just war thinkers agreed with Baker but on the basis of the war's legally defined just cause. Some just war thinkers and realists argued at the time, or in retrospect, that taking the war to Baghdad and removing Saddam from power in 1991 would have been sensible. Pacifists claimed that the humanitarian crisis never would have happened had the war not been waged in the first place. The United States did eventually intervene to create safe havens for Kurdish refugees and eventually a status quo returned—with Saddam fully in power as before.

Soon after the war, the UN Security Council passed resolutions requiring Iraq to forsake all offensive weapons programs. Three tools were used to force Iraq's compliance. The first was that Iraq submit to inspections to ensure that all its nuclear, biological, and chemical (NBC) weapons and development programs were thoroughly dismantled. In the early 1990s, inspectors discovered that Iraq had secretly enriched uranium, and they found plans for an Iraqi nuclear weapons program. The inspections regime succeeded in ensuring that this program was fully documented and then eradicated.[21] However, Saddam tried the patience and the nerve of the United Nations as the decade wore on; he became increasingly emboldened to frustrate the UN Special Commission (UNSCOM) inspectors and the International Atomic Energy Agency (IAEA) inspectors. At no point did he fully cooperate and honestly disclose all his munitions. This tension came to a head in late 1998 when Iraq refused to cooperate with U.S. nationals working for UNSCOM. With the support of the United Kingdom, President Bill Clinton responded with a four-day aerial bombing campaign of Iraq on December 17–20. In the midst of a sexual scandal and impeachment proceedings, however, he had neither political leverage nor popular support to push the matter further. So from 1998 until the fall of 2002, there were no UNSCOM or IAEA inspectors in Iraq.

The second tool was military: The U.S. Air Force policed no-fly zones over northern and southern Iraq. The purpose of this operation was to constrain Saddam's ambitions to suppress Kurdish autonomy in the north and Shiite Muslim activism in the south. Iraqi ground batteries tracked coalition planes by radar—a threatening precursor to launching missile attacks—and Iraqi fighters occasionally challenged coalition forces and strayed over the limits of the no-fly zones. U.S. planes shot down at least one Iraqi fighter and attacked surface-to-air missile systems and command-and-control facilities.[22] These incidents show that the fighting of the Gulf War, in a sense, didn't really end, but entered a low-intensity phase.

A third tool the international community used was economic sanctions. Nations were forbidden from doing business with Iraq in a number of ways; they were especially forbidden from selling Iraq military supplies and dual-use technologies (technologies such as radar and communications that are meant for civilian purposes but could be diverted to military use). Iraq was also constrained in its ability to sell oil, which generated much of its national income. Given that Iraq's people were already hurting from the effects of war, economic sanctions risked further harming the innocent by denying them food, medicine, and jobs. The UN, therefore, put in place the oil-for-food program, which allowed Iraq to sell a certain amount of oil on an ongoing basis (not at its full capacity), the proceeds from which could only be spent on food and medicine under UN supervision. Even with this program, the sanctions had a devastating impact on the health of the Iraqi population. One credible survey estimates that, from 1991 to 1998, there were between 100,000 and 227,000 deaths of children under five years old beyond the expected mortality rate. About one-quarter of these deaths were related to the war itself; the rest were due to sanctions.[23] The moral responsibility for this suffering must be shared between the nations that imposed the sanctions and Saddam Hussein, who diverted much money for his own purposes and refused to make the political changes that would have led to the sanctions being eased.

The effectiveness and proportional value of these strategies are difficult to assess. Through the 1990s, critics of American policies argued that the only impact of sanctions was the suffering inflicted on the Iraqi population, and they challenged the low-intensity conflict of the no-fly zones. Although constraining Saddam Hussein's ambitions, the policies did not affect his obstinacy. The international community was in a difficult position. Should it continue with economic pressure that was not effecting the desired changes in the Iraqi regime but was contributing to the suffering of innocent people?

Or should these nations end the sanctions, which would bring economic relief to Iraq and its people but would also send a message that Saddam could
act with impunity and would give him room to rebuild an arsenal? The situation was further complicated by the mixed motives of many nations; as a result, the central players on the Security Council were unable or unwilling to
think of ways they could move beyond the status quo of economic sanctions.[24] In retrospect, the combination of the three strategies apparently did
work to prevent Saddam from building or rebuilding nuclear, biological, and
chemical weapons, but that economic sanctions played a significant role in
this success is doubtful.

The United States and Iraq after September 11

The unresolved nature of the Gulf War and the struggle with Saddam
through the 1990s paved the way to the second war. Many of the arguments
for the first war remained applicable. However, many issues changed in the
twelve years between the two wars. George W. Bush, son of the first President
Bush, succeeded Bill Clinton as president, taking the oath of office on January
20, 2001. Eight months later, al Qaeda launched the attacks of September 11.
Bush quickly found a new direction for his foreign policy and much of his domestic policy: what he called the "war on terror." Bush was receptive to this
direction in part because it mingled with his "crusading liberal" worldview.[25]

This long-standing American worldview weaves together a passion for
freedom and democracy with an eschatology that pits forces of good against
evil. Crusading liberalism believes that America has a unique, God-given
mission to bring freedom and democracy to the world. President Bush's
post–September 11 speeches are suffused with the language of crusading
liberalism. The broad acceptance of these values among citizens showed
them to be a ready audience for his war on terror message. Perhaps also because of Bush's strongly evangelical Christian faith, he was primed to lead
this charge against terrorism and religious extremism after September 11;
the strategies of his advisers provided the specific path for implementing
this grand but hazy vision.

As the first overt action in this war, the United States invaded Afghanistan
on October 7, 2001, less than one month after the September 11 attacks.
Before President Bush had seen this nation-building project to completion
or admitted the true nature of the effort, he turned his attention to Iraq.

WHY ATTACK IRAQ? ETHICAL ARGUMENTS
AND THEIR RAMIFICATIONS

The Iraq War could be analyzed in a pro-versus-con format according to just war criteria, but we think it is more illuminating to cluster the arguments according to the type of cause that is highlighted. We describe the four most widely employed arguments for just cause together with the corresponding counterarguments.[26] This apparent virtue—that there were several legitimate causes for war—also complicated the debate and allowed politicians to amend their rationales as the first argument proved unfounded. We will present some of this political complexity as space allows, but we will be mostly concerned to show how Christian pacifists, just war thinkers, and realists aligned with these arguments.

An important distinction in just war doctrine is relevant to the following pro-war arguments. The just war tradition has long allowed preemptive attacks on the basis of self-defense, but not preventive wars to preclude a future threat from emerging.[27] According to Michael Walzer, a preemptive defensive attack is allowed when a nation faces "sufficient threat" of an imminent offensive attack. Imminence is a "necessarily vague" standard, but it is not without content. Walzer specifies it to mean

- manifest intent to injure
- a degree of active preparation that makes that intent a positive danger
- a general situation in which waiting, or doing anything other than fighting, greatly magnifies the risk[28]

Such case-by-case judgments that the enemy is preparing and intends to attack could be flawed, but they still have to be based on evidence that is interpreted with right intent. A preventive (also called "preventative") war would be based on evidence that a threat is growing, even though it is not yet imminent. The pragmatic argument for preventive action is that eventually the threat will come to the point that preemptive action would be justified, so it is better to act earlier, taking military advantage of the element of surprise and creating, in theory, a less destructive and shorter military engagement.[29] In the context of an ethic based on consequences, this pragmatic argument is also a principled argument for creating more benefits with less harm.

The Catholic bishops of Germany stated in January 2003, "A security strategy, which professes to be based on the idea of a preventative war, contravenes Catholic teachings and international law." They said that a preventative war was an aggressive act and could not be defined as an act of self-defense.[30] This statement of principle—with which the authors of this book agree—enjoys broad agreement among pacifists and just war thinkers. A judgment as to whether the invasion of Iraq qualified as preemption or prevention depends both on keeping the conceptual distinction straight and getting the facts right. In the arguments that follow, determining whether America's and Britain's assessment of a given threat reasonably satisfies Walzer's criteria will be important.

The WMD Argument—The Case for War

The most often cited cause for war against Iraq was that the international community faced a severe threat from Iraq's clandestine weapons programs. Iraq was charged with having weapons of mass destruction (WMD), a phrase that was meant to convey a sense of urgency and fear of annihilation far beyond Iraq's borders. The WMD argument had evidentiary, ethical, and legal bases. As evidence, advocates noted Iraq had used chemical weapons in its war against Iran and against Kurdish minorities in its own country, killing tens of thousands of people. Weapons inspectors cataloged Iraq's holdings of chemical and biological agents in the 1990s, and much of this weapons material—thousands of liters of anthrax, for instance—could not be accounted for in the inspections of 2002–3. American and British intelligence claimed that they had evidence that Iraq tried to procure the means to develop nuclear weapons. Iraq continually failed to cooperate fully with weapons inspectors. U.S. Secretary of State Colin Powell presented a list of these particulars to the United Nations, purportedly showing an extensive, well-concealed WMD program.[31]

Ethically, in just war theory, a threat of imminent attack would constitute just cause for a preemptive attack. Although there was no evidence that Iraq was preparing weapons for delivery or threatening any country, Iraq's uncounted past programs and uncooperativeness in weapons inspections were taken to be seriously risky. Prime Minister Blair went so far as to warn that Iraq could have a nuclear weapon ready in forty-five minutes, yet this turned out to be an embarrassing exaggeration.[32] The ethical debate on this point relied greatly on the evidence and how to interpret it. Critics of the war said that the advocates were not calling for preemptive war but preventive war, completely dismissing just war theory's caution, sobriety, and presumption against violence. Advocates of the war on these grounds saw the evidence as providing enough risk to justify preemption; later, when the threat turned out to be grossly overstated, some said the war was not justified after all, and others shifted their emphasis to another argument.

Legally, based on this evidence, the United States, the United Kingdom, and their allies held that Iraq's undisclosed programs stood in violation of international law. Security Council Resolution 1441, passed unanimously on November 8, 2002, reminded Iraq that it already stood in material breach of numerous previous resolutions dating back to 1991.[33] It called upon Iraq to come into full compliance with these resolutions immediately, or to face "serious consequences." This threat prompted Iraq to allow weapons inspectors back into the country and ostensibly to cooperate with the process, even as it stymied the inspectors. Hans Blix reported to the UN Security Council on February 14, 2003, that Iraq was still not effectively cooperating with the inspections process, though later, close to the start of war, he believed that Iraq's behavior was improving and that inspections should be given more time.[34] The legal debate during this period focused on how cooperative Iraq had to be to avoid "serious consequences" and what those consequences were. The United States claimed that a military attack was already included in the meaning of Resolution 1441, but several Security Council members disagreed. The United States–United Kingdom attempt to get a second resolution, one that clearly spelled out military attack as the consequence, faced defeat, so the draft resolution was withdrawn.

Those making the WMD argument for war relied on the premise that the community of nations would not hold Iraq accountable for its violations. Over the previous twelve years, Iraq had shown no intention of disarming. Saddam was very effective at eluding the inspectors and then cooperating just enough to avoid retaliation. Advocates for war predicted that, as happened in 1998 when there was no effective Security Council response to Iraq's expulsion of inspectors, the will of the Security Council to hold Iraq to terms would erode a few years after the crisis of 2002–3 abated. Given the history of the inspections regime and the lack of consequences for Iraq's noncompliance, war advocates believed it simply would not prove possible to contain Iraq from developing NBC weapons eventually.

The WMD Argument—The Case against War

In the prelude to the war, the critics conceded that Saddam probably possessed some chemical and biological weapons and that he certainly had ambitions to develop nuclear weapons. However, they maintained that war was not necessary to keep Saddam in check. Once weapons inspectors were readmitted to Iraq under UN auspices, a monitoring system was in place; so even if Iraq failed to be fully cooperative, it would have found it very difficult to amass a significant number of weapons and place them in an offensive position. As noted in chapter 4, biological weapons have proven ineffective and hard to produce, and neither biological nor chemical weapons can easily be deployed long range. The only type of truly mass destruction weapon is nuclear—a technology that requires a good deal of money and sophistication and thus is not easy to hide.

Between November 2002 and March 2003, weapons inspectors were picking up the trail of the inspections that ended in 1998, cataloging what material Iraq may have had and searching suspected sites, including ones recommended by American and British intelligence. Although Hans Blix, the lead weapons inspector, and Mohammad el-Barradai, director of the IAEA, reported some frustration with Iraq's cooperation, both men felt that their inspections were yielding results. They both asserted that they needed, at the very least, more time to complete their work as it became evident that the coalition was about to launch war. The subsequent failure to find any stockpiled weapons or material (beyond some very degraded, very small caches) or to prove that an effective research program was in place demonstrates how misguided it was to wage war before the inspectors had completed a comprehensive investigation. To be sure, the presence of an inspections regime in Iraq would have needed to stay in place probably as long as Saddam remained in power, but such a scenario, although frustrating, was manageable. The supposed threat, if reasonably assessed, gave no reason for waging war out of frustration.

So what went wrong and what has that revealed about the motivations for this war? These heavily researched and extensively debated questions are more complex than we can treat here. Briefly, we note three options for describing the failure of the argument. The first is that the intelligence was flawed through honest mistakes, misinterpretation, and Saddam's duplicity. The United States and the United Kingdom acted on the best evidence they had, and it was better for them to err on the side of disarming Iraq. The Bush administration and its most ardent supporters have maintained this line; Tony Blair has taken responsibility for a flawed intelligence system but still states that he acted responsibly on the evidence before him. The mainstream of political opinion in the United States has moved to a second account: that there were not only innocent mistakes but also systematic flaws in the gathering and interpretation of intelligence. The political leaders were at fault for not having remedied weaknesses in the intelligence system and for not moving more cautiously in face of flaws that were known—or could have been known—about specific intelligence claims. Some taking this position only charge Bush and Blair with poor decision making and leadership; others charge that the two leaders put pressure on the intelligence community to get the interpretations they wanted and that they presented skewed evidence to the public.

The more one sees intentional meddling and misrepresentation, the more the second position shades into a third: that the two administrations knew that evidence of Iraqi weapons was very weak from early on. Furthermore, this position suggests that they trumped up the evidence in order to gain domestic and international support for a war they desired for the sake of democratization or more sinister goals. Paul Wolfowitz, U.S. undersecretary of defense and a leading architect of the war, admitted in an interview a few months after the invasion, "For bureaucratic reasons we settled on one issue, weapons of mass destruction, because it was the one reason everyone could agree on."[35] British officials were aware of this deception and went along with it. The infamous "Downing Street Memo" of July 23, 2002, reports on a meeting between Blair and key British officials. The foreign policy aide who authored the memo summarizes what Sir Richard Dearlove, head of Britain's foreign intelligence service (the MI6), reported on his recent talks in Washington:

> There was a perceptible shift in attitude. Military action was now seen as inevitable. Bush wanted to remove Saddam, through military action, justified by the conjunction of terrorism and WMD. *But the intelligence and facts were being fixed around the policy.* The NSC [National Security Council] had no patience with the UN route, and no enthusiasm for publishing material on the Iraqi regime's record. There was little discussion in Washington of the aftermath after military action.[36]

This and other memos were unearthed by British journalist Michael Smith. Extensive investigative reporting on both sides of the Atlantic yields the impression that both governments were duplicitous about their true motives. Hence, the leaders did not exhibit right intention. We will take up this matter in the debate section, but it is clear to us that it is ludicrous to maintain that there were only honest mistakes in the intelligence process. However duplicitous the two administrations were, they are clearly culpable for acting contrary to intelligence assessments suggesting that the inspections process was yielding effective results.

The Humanitarian Argument—The Case for War

Humanitarian concern ran through many arguments for war, and it was likewise expressed by critics of the war. Hardly anyone in the West defended Saddam Hussein as a leader or as a person. Rather, Saddam was broadly acknowledged to be a dictator who encouraged a cult of his personality; wasted the resources of his country on lavish palaces for himself; had his political enemies arrested and killed; brutally repressed his citizens, especially Kurds, Shiites, and anyone suspected of disloyalty to the Ba'ath party; developed and used chemical weapons against Kurds and Iranians; and started wars against Iran and Kuwait. His sons Uday and Qusay stood in line to succeed him, and in the positions of power that they already held, they had proven to be just as brutal as their father. Human rights groups have documented the violations of the regime. Here is a summary from a well-respected human rights activist:

> Along with Cambodia's Pol Pot, Saddam Hussein's regime was one of the two most cruel and inhumane regimes in the second half of the twentieth century. Using the definition of genocide specified in the 1948 Genocide Convention, Iraq's Baath regime can be charged with planning and executing two genocides—one against the Kurdish population in the late 1980s and another against the Marsh Arabs in the 1990s. . . . Genocide is only part of Saddam Hussein's murderous legacy. Tens of thousands perished in purges from 1979 on, and as many as 300,000 Shiites were killed in the six months following the collapse of the March 1991 Shiite uprising. One mass grave near Hilla may contain as many as 30,000 bodies.[37]

Given what was known about Saddam, did outside nations have the moral responsibility to wage a war to save the Iraqi people from this brutality? Furthermore, did they have the legal right?

An argument for invasion of Iraq on humanitarian grounds would fit the same pattern of arguments made in favor of NATO's intervention in Kosovo, including the right of smaller coalitions of nations to act as rescuers in an urgent and extreme crisis if the United Nations fails to act. Advocates for a humanitarian war believed that the ethical criteria had been met. Norman Gervas, for instance, argued that facts listed earlier crossed a threshold: "This was one of the *very worst* of regimes in recent decades. Consequently, the overriding of the principle of national sovereignty was justified, if it was, not because Saddam Hussein was a dictator but because his regime fell on the wrong side of a moral threshold of extreme inhumanity. That should have delegitimized it as an acceptable member of the community of nations."[38] Although Saddam's most dramatic violations of human rights took place some years in the past, the humanitarian advocates pointed to the ongoing human rights violations and the prospect of no future relief from the Hussein family and the Ba'ath party. A war on humanitarian grounds would be both a matter of legal justice to remedy past abuses and a prevention of future abuses.

The Humanitarian Argument—The Case against War

Ending Saddam's rule because of his treatment of his citizens was an appealing humanitarian motive, but it did not provide a sufficient ethical rational for war for two reasons. First, the criterion of just cause cannot be stretched to justify a preventive war when there is no evidence that a humanitarian crisis is looming. Otherwise, the doctrines of self-defense and defense of the innocent become meaningless. Paul Savoy, a former law school dean and former public prosecutor in the United States, argues:

> The doctrine of humanitarian intervention cannot be applied retroactively to morally justify war as a means of punishing a political leader for past atrocities, such as Saddam's killing of more than 100,000 Kurds in the Anfal campaign, which occurred almost fifteen years before the invasion. Because it is essentially a principle that permits the defense of others, the doctrine of humanitarian intervention, like the concept of self-defense,

requires actually occurring or imminent large-scale killing to justify the use of military force.[39]

Such critics are not condoning Saddam Hussein's past crimes. They believe that he should have been brought to justice but through a process of declaring him a war criminal, marginalizing him in the international community, and waiting for the appropriate moment when internal political changes would make apprehension by internal or external actors possible.

The second problem is that a war on Iraq—or any nation—will be destructive to the very people the attackers say they want to help. It is disproportionate to kill thousands of civilians when the war is not going to save civilians from imminent death. As Savoy puts it, "What would we think of a police chief whose war against crime resulted in killing thousands of innocent bystanders in the course of apprehending a criminal suspect, even a criminal as despicable as Saddam? The officer who breaks the law, who becomes a law unto himself . . . is more dangerous than the criminal."[40] Savoy applies this description not only to military personnel who abused Iraqi prisoners but also to President Bush as the "police chief" of this war.

Christian critics of the Iraq War, both pacifists and just war thinkers, believed that the human cost of war just was not going to be worth it. A variety of religious leaders said in a public letter that the humanitarian mission was to preserve life, not take it.

> Tens of thousands of innocent civilians could lose their lives. This alone makes such a military attack morally unacceptable. In addition, the people of Iraq continue to suffer severely from the effects of the Gulf War, the resulting decade of sanctions, and the neglect and oppression of a brutal dictator. Rather than inflicting further suffering on them through a costly war, we should assist in rebuilding their country and alleviating their suffering.[41]

In short, the humanitarian argument for war struck critics as well intentioned but naïve at best, a cynical ploy at worst.

The Terrorist-Connection Argument—The Case for War

This argument is controversial and, indeed, convoluted because there is no evidence that Iraq had any role in the attacks of September 11. Indeed, only a few prominent advocates of the war drew this connection.[42] What many advocates for the Iraq War believed, instead, was that a proper response to September 11 required nations to start taking seriously the threats being prepared by jihadist groups and rogue states such as North Korea and Iraq. The first level of connection between terrorism and Iraq is simply this realization of the need to be proactive. The second connection is that an Iraq armed with nuclear, biological, or chemical weapons would present a serious threat to many countries because of its ability to supply terrorists. It does not matter that the conservative Islam of al Qaeda is not shared by Saddam; rogue leaders are willing to adopt any strategy to cause trouble for their enemies. Third, there were some proven connections between Iraq and Arab terrorism; for instance, Saddam encouraged suicide bombings in Israel through monetary rewards to the families of dead bombers. To the extent that advocates for war made the threat of future terrorism a central part of their case, they were arguing for a preventive war. As noted above, such an argument is hard to square with the just war tradition. For just war thinkers, the proper use of the terrorist-connection argument was to justify Bush's and Blair's concern to put Iraq's possible weapons programs at the top of the international agenda and to get inspectors back in the country. This argument, therefore, points to the WMD argument as the most clearly justified cause for war. But for some advocates, jihadist terrorism leads to the fourth argument of democratizing the Middle East.

The Terrorist-Connection Argument—The Case against War

That a connection could be established between Iraq and the September 11 terrorist attacks was implausible from the beginning. Common sense suggested that Osama bin Laden, whose dream is to institute Islamic theocracy throughout the Arab world, had little love for the secular dictator Saddam Hussein, and vice versa. Bin Laden thought that Saddam was the same kind of selfish, haughty ruler as the Saudi monarchs, whom bin Laden despised. What Saddam's regime and al Qaeda shared (in common with a wide range of Arab political groups) was anti-Semitism, anti-Israel policies, and a wish to expel American influence from the Middle East. Was this enough for the two groups to form a common cause?

American intelligence agencies were aware of communications between Iraq and al Qaeda in the 1990s. At different times, each side investigated whether it could get support from the other, but nothing developed on this front. The independent and bipartisan 9/11 Commission concluded in its July 2004 final report: "The [intelligence] reports describe friendly contacts and indicate some common themes in both sides' hatred of the United States. But to date we have seen no evidence that these or the earlier contacts ever developed into a collaborative operational relationship. Nor have we seen evidence indicating that Iraq cooperated with al Qaeda in developing or carrying out any attacks against the United States."[43]

Despite the weak evidence, a perceived connection between the events of September 11 and Saddam Hussein was influential in gaining support for the war from Americans. Many Americans felt the connection on an emotional level, owing to their fear of future terrorist attacks. President Bush's naming of Iraq as a "front in the war on terror" in post–September 11 speeches linked the two threats in the public's mind. Therefore, it is not surprising that four months before the start of the war, a survey found that 66 percent of Americans believed Saddam Hussein provided assistance to the men who planned the September 11 attacks. Although this belief was weakening slightly before the war, two-thirds of Americans supporting the war believed in the direct connection between Saddam and September 11.[44] Critics believe that Bush's rhetorical strategy was inappropriate; along with the WMD arguments, the terrorist-connection rhetoric constituted a deceptive strategy to sell the war to the American public. Although there was no link between Iraq and international terrorism before war, the aftermath of the war made Iraq a major site of terrorism and, ironically, succeeded in establishing the link it was supposed to break.

The Democratizing of the Middle East Argument—The Case for War

Most advocates for war thought that all three of the foregoing arguments had merit; most pro-war arguments rolled these arguments together into a cumulative case, even while holding out one of the arguments as primary or as the legal justification. It was natural to seek a link among the arguments, and democracy suggests itself as the most logical connection. Dictatorial governments threaten neighboring governments, spend resources on militarism, and harm their citizens. Democratic regimes are more likely to be at peace with their neighbors, spend on development, and treat their citizens fairly. By this way of thinking, the long-term problems presented by Iraq could best be remedied by following through with the United States' official policy (since 1998) of "regime change" and allowing a democratic government to take root in Iraq. Political commentator Andrew Sullivan offers an example of this argument, which he says holds true, despite the failure to find weapons in Iraq. His starting point was jihadist terrorism.

> The reality of 9/11 was a terrifying one. It was that we faced a fanatical enemy determined to kill any civilization or people who objected to the restoration of a medieval, theocratic dictatorship in the Middle East (and, eventually, as with all such ideologies, elsewhere). We'd ignored or appeased them for years. . . . The fundamental cause of this new, totalitarian ideology—forged in the Egypt of the 1960s—was Arab autocracy and dictatorship. . . . Only democracy could allow these forces to exhaust themselves sufficiently to remove the underlying threat. . . . Where better to build an opportunity for a more democratic future than in the cradle of civilization, Iraq?[45]

For Sullivan, the purpose of war on Iraq was not retribution for al Qaeda's attacks but, first, to prevent Saddam from supporting terrorists and gaining destructive weapons in the future and, second, to turn around the totalitarian and anti-Western political culture of the Middle East, which transformation would erode the appeal of Islamist extremism among future generations. The argument for democratization is squarely a preventive argument, one that relies on a long chain of speculation about cultural developments after the war. The postwar reality has brought the unhappy developments of an insurgency and a brewing civil war. Despite this, Sullivan believes that events are vindicating the argument:

> Iraqis have freedoms today they haven't had in decades; the January [2005] elections were arguably an earthquake in democratic governance that is still producing after-shocks in Lebanon, Libya, Jordan, and even Iran. Although physical security is still dismally remote, there are many places in Iraq where reconstruction is beginning, where democratic norms are being instilled, where free people exchange ideas, where the kind of police-state terror we in the West cannot really understand no longer exists. . . . In the long run, we may well look back and see that it was

this leveraging of a tiny democratic space in the heart of the Arab world that saved us from cataclysm.[46]

It appeared that the goal of democratization was an afterthought because the Bush and Blair administrations put the WMD threat in the foreground. But democratization rhetoric pervaded speeches by President Bush and Prime Minister Blair in the year before the war. Once again, leaders and advocates varied in the stress they placed on the rationales. From their point of view, if they offered several causes for war and at least one of them "stuck," then there was a just cause. The democratization argument is more effective than any of the other arguments alone because it can embrace each of them, but it is also more problematic because it drifts further away from the traditional criteria for preemptive attack.

The Democratizing of the Middle East Argument—
The Case against War

Many critics find the first three arguments so implausible that they believe the Bush and Blair administrations could only have had a plan for remaking the Middle East in mind from the start. Indeed, suggestions of such a plan were in view before 2001; we have mentioned that "regime change" was official U.S. policy since 1998 and that the rhetoric of democratizing Iraq was woven through Bush's prewar speeches. Critics charge that both Bush and Blair put the burden on the falsified threat of WMD and never presented the democratization argument forthrightly so that it could be discussed in political and public forums. That they were not frank opens the door to a more cynical reading of the entire war. For the sharpest critics, the goal of regime change in Iraq was driven by American and British national interests—such as support for Israel, access to affordable oil, and leverage against other Middle East leaders—and by various personal and political motivations of Bush and Blair.

Advocates reply that Bush and Blair were sincere in wanting to prompt democratic change in Iraq and the region. Critics raise several objections to this reply. First, for the United States and the United Kingdom to assume they know what is best for Iraq, or that they can forge an improved country, is extremely arrogant. Second, it is illegal under international law to invade a nation for such an aim. Wars of genuine self-defense do not require UN authorization, and humanitarian interventions might not require UN authorization if the crisis is truly urgent. However, preventive/democratizing wars—if they may happen at all—could only be legal under the aegis of the UN. Third, war unleashes unknowable consequences. The transition has not been smooth, many more have died than expected, and the country totters on the brink of all-out civil war.

Finally, the very goal of democratization must be questioned. Is democracy a cure-all for Iraq's ills? Fareed Zakaria's provocative book, *The Future of Freedom*, suggests not.[47] He argues that democracy is not an unmitigated good and, by itself, is not a path to stability and freedom. Democracy can easily give power to demagogic and theocratic movements. The Iranian revolution was a populist movement that ousted an authoritarian leader, but it gave power to radical Shiite clerics who are illiberal and anti-Western. This is hardly the model wanted for Iraq, yet radical Shiite clerics in southern Iraq now wield great power owing to the vast numbers of Shiite Muslim Iraqis who vote for the parties approved by the clerics. Zakaria points out that liberal political institutions, such as civil rights and a free market, are needed alongside—or even prior to—democratic institutions such as the ballot. Otherwise, liberal institutions often fail to develop after an abrupt shift to democratic rule.

An interesting point is that Zakaria actually supported an invasion of Iraq, but he wanted it to be done with international cooperation through the United Nations and with a clear plan for rebuilding the nation afterward.[48] The most curious fact about the democratization argument is that the theorists and leaders of this war wanted to create the conditions for a free, democratic, liberal Iraq, and to generate political reforms for the region. However, as the Downing Street Memo quoted above reveals, "There was little discussion in Washington of the aftermath after military action." The abject failure to plan, along with many diplomatic errors, doomed this perhaps high-minded goal to failure.

Since the Invasion: A Country in Crisis

As with all wars, ethical analysis must also be directed to the fighting phase of the war and the postwar actions of the parties. We will only cover a few of the many important developments since the end of the combat phase in order to give a sense of how the jus in bello criteria analyze the still unfolding aftermath. The most important factor in such analysis is human deaths: how many, how they were caused, and whether they could have been avoided. Sadly, even as we write, the dying continues in Iraq, and the toll has been high. In the three-year period following the beginning of the war (March 20, 2003–March 19, 2006), more than thirty-six thousand Iraqi civilians, over two thousand American military personnel, and over one hundred personnel belonging to other countries (chiefly the United Kingdom) have been killed.[49] In addition, hundreds of foreign journalists and reconstruction workers have been kidnapped and killed. Thousands of Iraqi soldiers were killed in the major combat phase, and unknown numbers of insurgents have been killed.

Not captured in this calculation are the deaths caused by the war's damage to infrastructure and the effects on civilian health. A study by the medical journal *The Lancet* estimated that the overall risk of death for an average Iraqi is 2.5 times higher now than before the invasion, and the risk of death from violence is 58 times higher.[50] Although the large number of deaths caused by the insurgency were generally not expected by advocates or critics, the critics say that no one should be surprised that overall casualties would rival the first war. No one should be surprised that an open-ended invasion into a nation, many of whose citizens did not want to be invaded, has led to such a result.

The number of deaths is therefore related to one of the notable results of the war: a political vacuum that allowed a violent insurgency movement to take root. The first expression of the political vacuum was widespread looting that occurred immediately after the end of the major combat operations. Not only were stores looted—which is, at times, a necessary act for people to provide for their needs—but also government offices, museums, and even military sites were looted as well. Coalition troops seemed unprepared, and their commanders unwilling, to control the looting. The problem is that such a breakdown in social order has led many Iraqis to distrust the occupation forces, building discontent that has funneled some people into the insurgency. Many observers argue that the United States sent in too few troops to secure the country adequately. General Eric K. Shinseki told the Department of Defense before the war that tens of thousands more troops would be needed, prompting a nearly unheard-of public rebuke by Undersecretary Wolfowitz.[51] The Bush administration and Pentagon officials still dispute the claim that troop levels were inadequate.

To provide interim order, the occupying powers set up the Coalition Provisional Authority (CPA), a military administration that managed Iraq until

June 30, 2004, and worked with Iraqi politicians and local leaders to set up a timetable and process for transition back to self-rule. The head of the CPA, administrator Paul Bremer, was faulted by many observers. Under his supervision of the reconstruction, the restoration of electricity and clean water proceeded very slowly, which embittered citizens. The CPA recruited new Iraqi police and military. Yet its rigorous policy of "de-Baathification" threw former members of the Ba'ath party out of the police, military, and civil service jobs. Because most people could not get such jobs under Saddam's rule without being a nominal member of the party, the now-purged Iraqis felt they had been treated unfairly. The brunt of the policy fell on Sunni Muslims, the ethnoreligious group that constitutes only 20 percent of Iraq's population but has been in control of Iraqi politics since 1917.

The CPA policy—and the war itself—enraged many Sunnis because their social power was now likely to decline as the power of Shiites and Kurds rose. Even before the war, this three-way sectarian division cast a shadow over the postwar stability of Iraq. Although it was not a foregone conclusion that the three groups could not live together without a dictator to hold the nation together, the challenge of crafting a political structure in which Sunnis wish to participate has been daunting. In the transitional Iraqi government that succeeded the CPA, few Sunni leaders participated. In the referendum on a new Iraqi constitution, held October 15, 2005, all but one Sunni political group boycotted the election. More positively, it seems that Sunni voters in most provinces of Iraq participated. Most Sunnis rejected the new constitution but not so thoroughly as to scuttle its adoption. Iraq's evolution to constitutional self-rule proceeds slowly and fitfully.

Hampering these efforts and overshadowing any progress has been the violent insurgency. As we have noted, former supporters of Saddam's regime, and Sunnis generally have the most reason to feel bitter about the invasion and have the most to lose by participating in the constitutional process. The insurgent movement has drawn its strength from these Iraqis. Apparently, many insurgents are coordinated by former Ba'ath regime elements. Another segment is composed of foreign jihadists who have come to Iraq under the direction of al Qaeda and other groups in order to destabilize the society. Still other insurgents act independently in very small groups. The insurgency is difficult to understand, locate, fight, and defeat. It has been responsible for one to two thousand Iraqi civilian deaths a month and almost thirty-five hundred coalition troop deaths as of March 2007. Iraqi police and military are routinely targeted, impeding efforts to turn over responsibility for security from the coalition forces to Iraqi forces. Despite the fact that many insurgents have been killed in clashes with coalition forces, their numbers seem to be steadily replenished. Attacks by insurgents and terrorists are growing in sophistication and deadliness. On top of all this, sectarian violence has been growing month by month: Sunni militants kidnap, kill, and bomb Shiites, and Shiite militants launch reprisal attacks. Political pressure has been growing in the United States for the government to set a timetable for withdrawal of American troops, but the Bush administration and many analysts fear that a quick withdrawal of forces will cause Iraq to collapse into chaos.

During the insurgency phase, coalition forces have captured hundreds of former regime leaders and thousands of suspected insurgents and terrorists. Saddam Hussein himself was captured on December 14, 2003, went on trial in Iraq in October 2005 for crimes he committed against citizens during his long reign, and was executed on December 30, 2006. Capturing criminals, however, has also been the occasion of the worst ethical violations by the United States during the entire conduct of the war. Thousands of prisoners have been held for years now without charge and without access to legal representation. (The Bush administration has even denied such rights to American citizens arrested as suspected terrorists.) Many innocent Iraqis have been caught up in the snare; many were released after several months, while others languish in prison.

In April 2004 photos came to light revealing abuse of prisoners at the American-administrated Abu Ghraib prison. The photos showed Iraqis being placed in sexually humiliating and physically strenuous positions while American guards looked on mockingly. Multiple investigative reports reveal widespread mistreatment of Muslim prisoners in Iraq and at the military base in Guantanamo Bay, Cuba, including many forms of denigration of the prisoners' religious beliefs, sleep deprivation, beatings, sexual assault, and humiliation. The soldiers charged with the Abu Ghraib abuses admitted their culpability but claimed that they were going along with an attitude that was broadly accepted in their brigade. In effect, they had simply been following orders. The incident greatly harmed the United States' moral standing with the Iraqi and Arab publics; it cast the entire military in a suspicious light, even as other soldiers who interacted with the Iraqi public were striving to be good ambassadors for their country.

How do these dire developments reflect on the morality of the war? The criterion of proportionality meant that the Bush and Blair administrations had a responsibility to strive for a beneficial outcome on matters under their control and not to proceed with war if factors outside their control would make a beneficial outcome dubious. The moral imperative was to be as minimally destructive to human life as possible and to provide a sound plan for postwar political stabilization and rebuilding. Before the war, critics doubted the Bush administration's commitment to "nation-building," a term upon which it had often heaped scorn. What was revealed in the aftermath was the administration's unwillingness to deploy sufficient troops and to plan thoroughly and properly for the postwar period. State Department planners paid excessive attention to the now-discredited expatriate politician Ahmed Chalabi and did not have good contacts with indigenous Iraqi groups. Reporter James Fallows's aptly titled article "Blind into Baghdad" reveals how the Bush administration ignored the work and the warnings of its postwar planners.[52]

For these reasons, a significant measure of fault must be attributed to President Bush and Prime Minister Blair for failing to take prudent steps to ensure postwar stability. In addition, the in bello criteria require respect for the human rights of the opposing side, both its civilians and its soldiers. The prisoner abuse scandal was a violation of these human rights, whether the detainees were guilty of something or not. Accountability for prisoner abuse must go high up the chain of command.[53] Military and civilian leaders have failed to take responsibility for ignoring early reports of abuse. No doubt the Bush administration wanted to make allowance for acts of torture. It tried to exempt itself from the Geneva Conventions against torture and resisted congressional legislation to strengthen policies against torture. The Bush administration has failed to take high-level responsibility for prisoner abuse and to repudiate torture as a tool in its war against terror. This scandalous record on torture, combined with the poor postwar planning and the faulty and deceptive weapons intelligence, negates the legitimacy of the coalition's occupation of Iraq.

DEBATING THE ISSUES

Do the just war criteria simply reveal the war was immoral, imprudent, or necessary? Was the war fundamentally unethical or could it have been redeemed if carried out differently? Does the fact that prominent just war thinkers supported the war reveal faults in just war theory itself? To explore these questions, we turn to our debate.

The Gulf War

BES The Gulf War presages the Iraq War in many ways. Although it's not accurate to say the second war is simply a continuation of the first, a number of issues carry over because we were dealing with the same aggressive, insidious regime in both cases. To the extent that there are differences, it seems to me that they lean in favor of justifying the first war. For it is undeniable that Iraq's invasion of Kuwait was a violation of international law and of the human rights of Kuwaiti citizens. So I would like to press you and the critics of the Gulf War on your reasoning. I assume that the ostensible just cause is not in dispute but that the intentions of the senior Bush administration were. I will grant straight off that, given the senior Bush's need to bring the American public along, arguments were made that called his intentions into question. But in the end, can we hold leaders to pristine standards of motivation? If we do, then no war could be just.

DLC My judgment is that the Gulf War was arguably in accordance with the just war tradition. We could debate the last resort criterion. Although it cannot properly be interpreted to require an endless delay, I believe that more could have been done diplomatically before and even after the air campaign started. The Bush administration made no diplomatic overtures toward Iraq until very late in the day and then with no intention to negotiate on any of Iraq's stated grievances. I think the chief reason for opposition to the war was not that there was no just cause in this case but that the lofty motives cited for going to war would have required intervention in many other cases that the world was happy to ignore. Most obviously, the concern for the people of Kuwait, for example, was in stark contrast to the denial of the plight of the Kurds only a few years previously. If intervention was justified for these reasons here, it was justified elsewhere, too. Why a war on Iraq at that point, then? Because of the strategic importance of oil supplies. The undeniable just cause of invasion of a sovereign state seemed to be a convenient excuse for a war actually fought for other reasons. The discussion on the morality of the war in terms of the just war tradition should, therefore, focus on the criterion of right intention. I think the criterion cannot realistically prohibit mixed motives on the part of leaders, but it does require us to assess all of their motives and to condemn them if unethical motives were the driving force behind their decision. For me, the Gulf War was a war that could be pronounced "just" according to the just war tradition but in fact was simply an example of the United States acting to strengthen its influence in the region because of its geopolitical interests in access to cheap oil. It's an example of why I don't think the just war tradition is an adequate moral framework for assessing the use of military force.

BES I strongly believe that the "no blood for oil" slogan misrepresents what the Gulf War was about. Of course, I don't associate that slogan with your careful arguments but with many secular and religious critics of the Gulf War. To be careful on the pro-war side, it is only honest to point out that the potential global-economic effect of Iraq's control of a larger oil supply was one of several concerns motivating the senior Bush administration.[54] The leading reason, and one that always provided the basis for UN resolutions, was to reverse the invasion of Kuwait. The actions of the leading powers conveyed right intention—that is, their actions were in line with the stated just case. The Bush administration's right intention was subsequently proven by its stopping the war when Iraq pulled out of Kuwait and by not taking control of Iraq. Furthermore, a criterion made so much of by critics of the Iraq War—the absence of clear international authority—can hardly be said to apply to the Gulf War. Indeed, it undermines the strength of the United Nations and the rule of international law when an unprovoked invasion is left to stand and when nations fail to act in accord with a series of Security Council resolutions.

DLC This brings us to questions about the UN. If the Security Council were a properly constituted group representing all the nations of the world in an appropriate way, with military forces under its authority, I would support its action first to work to resolve conflicts peacefully, then to deter wars with the threat of reprisals, and finally to act to punish states that violate international law. In the current context, however, the

Security Council is made up of the first countries to develop real weapons of mass destruction and who have reneged on their treaty obligations to take steps towards nuclear disarmament. Until it is reformed, it is hard to have confidence in its ability to judge equitably about wars that should be fought. We have noted the possible mixed messages Iraq was given in the run-up to the Gulf War. If Saddam Hussein had clearly known that he would be subject to immediate UN reprisals, it is unlikely that he would have invaded Kuwait.

So we agree that under just war criteria, the Gulf War could be judged just, but I am suggesting that there are questions relating to last resort and right intention. Even on its clearest applications, just war theory operates in a context that tends toward rationalizing wars rather than attempting to find alternative ways of resolving conflicts. As a pacifist, I also fault just war thinking for ignoring a wider historical and geopolitical context, attention to which would reveal that wars are encouraged by trade in arms, national strategic interests, and the neglect of measures to build for peace and prevent conflict.

Between the Wars: The UN, Weapons Inspections, and Sanctions

BES Let's take that comment as an opportunity to move forward from the Gulf War and think about the time between the two wars on Iraq. The weaknesses of international relations confront us in both wars and the times in between. It is interesting that everyone faults the United Nations, but the criticisms vary greatly given the perspective. You've just listed some pacifist concerns. Hawks toward Iraq, whether realists or just warriors, are more likely to find problems in the UN's weak posture toward Iraq. They feel that Saddam Hussein was not punished when he violated the terms of inspections regime, that European nations wanted to trade with and normalize relations with Iraq, and that some Security Council members so grudgingly went along with the pressure on Iraq that Saddam knew there were no teeth in the new round of inspections.

I find myself between the two positions. I think the United Nations has been weak toward Iraq but not at every point along the way. There was strong resolve after the invasion of Kuwait and in the early years afterward. Yet I agree with you that the powerful states—not only the United States, but Russia, China, and other military and economic powerhouses—like to bend the rules and evade the consequences when it serves their interests. Among the Western democracies, the United States too often takes an exceptionalist stance that, ironically, harms its interests in the long run. Yet it seems to me that many nations paid lip service to keeping banned weapons out of Saddam's hands but didn't want to put action behind their words. They leave it to the United States to take action but then chide it for acting unilaterally. It could be called a dysfunctional relationship. It wasn't right for other nations (with the exception of the United Kingdom) to fail to support the United States in 1998, and it contributes to the United States' mindset that it needs to go it alone, which was wrongheaded in 2003. So what kind of responsibility do you expect the UN to exercise toward regimes like Iraq?

DLC   My hope would be that the UN could become a locus of expertise of conflict resolution so that building for peace and resolving disagreements that threaten to turn violent become the heart of its work. Considering the economic cost of war—let alone the human and environmental costs—any reasonable analysis would suggest that serious investment in peacemaking would be worthwhile; if we were to spend a tenth of what is currently devoted to military expenditure on peace-building and conflict-prevention initiatives, the results would be extraordinary. However, I concede that these initiatives will not always be successful, and that the UN should retain the right to use military force to enforce international law—this is where I would recognize a legitimate analogy between the action of police forces within a nation and the use of military force in an international context. This is a very long way from individual nation-states presuming the authority to make war on other nations, which is closer to the vigilante groups that operated and still operate in some countries where there is no effective policing.

BES   Short of war and military strikes, economic sanctions are the main stick that the UN can wield. It was fairly dubious in 1990 whether sanctions would get Iraq to leave Kuwait, and it was clear through the rest of the decade that they were not an effective tool for modifying Saddam's behavior. Economic sanctions on Iraq, even with the release valve of the oil-for-food program, were hurting Iraqi citizens because of Saddam's manipulation. Many advocates of nonviolence and many churches were calling for sanctions to be lifted by the late 1990s. Do you think this was the way to go? More broadly, what methods would pacifists suggest for responding to a state like Iraq when it invades another country or refuses to comply with weapons inspections?

DLC The ideal response to breaches of international law is obviously one that punishes the perpetrator of the breach. Under national laws, we punish individuals or groups of individuals that have been shown in court to have broken the criminal law. This often has side effects for others, such as the family of a criminal who was previously the only income earner for a household. The direct effect of the punishment, however, is on the guilty party. We don't, for example, imprison the family of a criminal as a way of punishing the individual. The difficulty of translating this logic into an international context is obviously the difficulty of finding appropriately targeted measures. Economic sanctions on Iraq were, in effect, using the population as hostages in an attempt to persuade Saddam Hussein to change his policy. Given Saddam's resolve and his lack of concern for the welfare of his people, this was a policy with little potential to be effective and that inflicted grave suffering on ordinary Iraqis. It is hard to come up with quick alternatives that would have been more effective while causing less suffering. I would suggest that the impatient desire to adopt a punitive policy was problematic in itself and that the preferable alternative would have been to be prepared to engage in dialogue and diplomatic engagement with Iraq over a longer period, with other sanctions held in reserve.

BES I was likewise troubled by the effect that economic sanctions were having on Iraqi citizens. Such sanctions need to be put under a similar calculus as a decision for warfare. If they are not doing more good than harm for civilians, then the strategy needs to be rethought. The problem is, in the absence of both inspections and sanctions, Saddam Hussein could act with impunity. Collective fatigue with the whole situation took Iraq off the political radar screen for about three years, until the second Bush presidency made it a front in its war on terror. It was a problem from the outset to think of Iraq in those terms, but that was one of the consequences of the collective failure of international responsibility.

Ethical Arguments Concerning the Iraq War

DLC The failure to engage Iraq firmly and constructively in the late 1990s, which can be chalked up to many parties, doesn't justify a reckless response later on. It is my impression from the vantage point of Europe that many Americans failed to be sufficiently critical of their leadership in the run-up to the second war. Even most of the congressional Democrats voted in the fall of 2002 to give President Bush permission to launch a military attack on Iraq. On the other hand, academics, theologians, and church leaders mostly criticized preparations for war and urged nonviolent approaches. You were one of a few Christian just war thinkers who took a public stance before the war that an invasion would be just, though I know that your views have changed since.

Let's look at two obvious objections to the war being judged just under just war criteria, and perhaps you can suggest why you took this view at the time. First, it seems to me that there was no just cause because there was no imminent danger either to other nations or to citizens within Iraq. This was clear to all parties at the time, and is quite independent of the claims based on appallingly erroneous intelligence. Saddam Hussein was not threatening any attacks and did not have sufficient freedom of movement to develop weapons to become more of a danger to his neighbors. Second, even if Saddam Hussein had had this intention and was close to having the capacity to attack his neighbors—as he clearly did not—the war was clearly not a last resort because there was an ongoing and viable arms inspection process. It was a convenient time for the United States, supported by the United Kingdom, to begin a war, but the war began when peaceful alternatives were already bearing fruit. So what made you take a different view?

BES The factors that were decisive for my support at the time were those we described in this chapter as the WMD argument and the humanitarian argument. As I argued in an article in the online *Journal of Lutheran Ethics* in March 2003, I believed that together they supported the case for war.[55] In retrospect, each argument was partially flawed, and revelation of decisions made by the United States and United Kingdom also greatly undermined them as rationales for war.

Let me start with the WMD argument. It's clear that the threat of nuclear and other offensive weapons held by Iraq presented the most plausible reason under just war theory to consider a preemptive war, for imminent attack has long been an incontrovertible just cause. That's why the debate among world leaders and the actions of the UN Security Council revolved around Iraq's suspected weapons programs. I agreed with the advocates for war that Iraq's likely preparations during the period it was not being inspected (1998–2002), its poor accounting for past programs and weapons material, and its obstructions when inspectors did return constituted serious risks. We mustn't forget that before November 2002, almost everyone thought Iraq had some kind of banned weapons. Without inspections, there was no way of knowing what the threat actually was. Ironically, it was the Bush administration's threat of war in the fall of 2002 that pushed key European governments to get behind the plan and got Iraq to allow the inspectors back in.

DLC Once effective inspections were taking place, the WMD argument for war evaporated because any preparations for an attack would have been easy enough to catch. We also need to take care about the version of truth that the media portray. Hans Blix, the head of UNMOVIC, was satisfied with the cooperation shown by Saddam Hussein and very frustrated that the inspections were curtailed in favor of war. Former U.S. Marine Major Scott Ritter, who was chief weapons inspector in Iraq from 1991 to 1998, has expressed similar views at odds with those of the U.S. administration.[56] There were strong vested interests in showing Saddam Hussein to be recalcitrant, and I think the media, especially in the United States, exaggerated this. Dispensing with the "weapons of mass destruction" rhetoric is crucial here: Many thought at the time that he had chemical weapons, but these posed little immediate threat to anyone, certainly not a sufficient threat to provoke an invasion given the ongoing inspection process. American and British intelligence services had no credible evidence of nuclear weapons capability, but the WMD catch-all succeeded in suggesting a more serious threat than was suspected. As we know, even the suspicions of secret chemical and biological weapons proved completely unfounded.

BES It's here that I think my reasoning on this argument broke down. I was highly frustrated with Saddam's obstreperousness. It was not clear what Iraq possessed or didn't possess in the way of nuclear, chemical, and biological weapons programs, but it was clear that Saddam was making it very difficult for the inspectors to do their work. It seemed likely that he would dodge and evade, providing just enough information to avoid serious Security Council sanction, and wait for the will of the international community to weaken so the inspections could be further cramped without consequence. In that scenario the risk of his developing such weapons couldn't be put off indefinitely. In defense of my position at the time, I would say that it was not clear that inspections were going well. The reports from Blix through the spring of that year were very critical of Iraq for its lack of cooperation and failure to supply evidence that weapons development programs were defunct (though I do admit that Blix felt that slow progress was being made and that he requested some extra months to continue the inspections). In late February, Iraq was found to have missiles with a greater than 90-kilometer (150-mile) range, which was barred by the UN, and it resisted destroying them. Coupled with what the Bush and Blair administrations reported to the public about their intelligence on weapons programs and hidden weapons material, I accepted their argument that Saddam was hopelessly and dangerously recalcitrant.

Since the war, media investigations and studies by governmental and independent commissions present a dizzying picture of where the intelligence faults lay, but this much is clear about the Bush and Blair administrations: (a) there were crucial flaws and many ambiguities in the intelligence they received; (b) both put pressure on their intelligence agencies to paper over the ambiguities and contrary evidence and to give the findings a spin most favorable to war; (c) they presented intelligence results to the public in exaggerated terms; and (d) knowing what they knew, it was unjust to pursue a risky, ruinous invasion to disarm Iraq. Even holding aside those later developments, I have come to see waging wars to eliminate speculative risks as a weak argument. It is just not right to put human beings in harm's way in order to prevent harms that might not even be there.

DLC We're agreed, then, that preempting an imminent attack was not a legitimate just cause. As I indicated above, we need to keep separate the principled and the contingent matters. As a matter of principle, it is immoral to wage a war that does not meet strict conditions of just cause. On the contingent matter of intelligence data, we can distinguish the responsibilities of leaders and citizens. Knowing as much as they did, there is no excuse for what Bush, Blair, and their advisors and intelligence directors did. The responsibilities of citizens are different, and many may have been misled by what their leaders told them. Citizens and the media, however, are responsible for their own reasonable judgments, and there were grounds for skepticism about the reasons presented for going to war. Regarding the concern about the difficulty of keeping Saddam honest, the management of ongoing inspections and sanctions would have been difficult, but it is the burden of political leadership to manage such risks. If we suppose that it took great leadership for Bush and Blair to make the case for war and to launch an invasion, their leadership could have been exerted to keep diplomatic pressure on Iraq and to pursue other methods for transforming the political culture of the Middle East. But you said you were also influenced by humanitarian concerns?

BES Yes. The humanitarian abuses described above in the chapter speak for themselves. I thought such concerns should motivate the community of nations to do what was possible, legal, and just to change Iraq's leadership. We discussed the ambiguities and shortcomings of military intervention for humanitarian causes in chapter 3: that it is difficult to intervene in a way that is legal and just and that brings about a better situation at a tolerable human cost. I acknowledged and worried in my 2003 article that all those problems would come up in the case of Iraq. The greatest objection paralleled the WMD argument: There was no current or imminent humanitarian crisis, such as an ongoing or imminent genocide. I was not persuaded then, and I am not now, that military intervention may justly occur only when genocide is ongoing or imminent. The humanitarian argument took a broad view: Large-scale atrocities happened at certain points in the past, which deserved justice; Iraqi citizens faced ongoing low-level oppression and killing in the present; and future oppression and atrocities were all but certain to occur. The only response the world was marshalling, other than war, was a program of economic sanctions that were not changing Iraq's behavior but were taking a toll on civilians. Unlike the weapons accusation, this humanitarian problem has not been disputed. Still, the reasonable possibility of the situation getting worse rather than better should have given humanitarian advocates for war, like myself, greater pause. For me at that time, this humanitarian motive bolstered what was weak in the WMD argument, and vice versa. But now I realize that (trying to quantify roughly how strong I think the arguments were) a 40 percent case for war because of the weapons risk and an 80 percent case for war under humanitarian reasons don't add up to a 100 percent case for just war. Each of the causes proffered has to be reasonable with little doubt—more like 90 to 95 percent certain—and they can't be undermined by other just war criteria. And so, although I think a humanitarian intention for the war was ethically sound, a war on humanitarian or any other ground wouldn't be correct if the civilians of Iraq were likely to be worse off afterward.

The Troubling Aftermath, the Fragile Future

DLC The reason the bar for humanitarian intervention needs to be very high is obviously that war, especially in a modern context, brings destruction on a large scale to populations caught up in them. We calculated that at least thirty-six thousand civilians have died as a result of the conflict in the three years since it began, not counting those who have died of the war's effects on public health. Few would have endorsed war on humanitarian grounds if they had believed the casualties would be this high.

It's important to try to see a constructive way forward from this point, but the prospects don't look good. The strategy of those resisting the occupation has switched from attacks on the military of the United States and its allies to attacks on Iraqi citizens training as police or from a rival ethnic group. Despite the movement toward democracy, nothing has diminished the number or intensity of these attacks. All this is quite apart from the international threat of terrorism that is clearly related to the war. If this were an entirely unpredictable outcome, we could dismiss its relevance to the decision to go to war as based on hindsight. But it was all too predictable that war would cause this chaos and succeed as a major recruiting campaign for terrorist groups. The 2003 war has been disastrous for the Iraqi population, which we need to remember the next time someone tries to suggest waging a war for the benefit of the enemy population.

BES The aftermath has indeed been tragic in many respects. I've been driven to rethink the war because of its terrible toll on the lives of Iraqis civilians, foreign military personnel, and foreign workers, not to mention U.S. military personnel. I have three thoughts about this death toll. First, there were probably fewer than five thousand civilian deaths during the initial major combat phase of the war. Tragic though they are, they are unethical in proportionality only if the war was a mistake—which I now think it was. If they were the only human cost of liberating Iraq from Ba'athism, I think they could be accepted; I think Iraqis might have accepted that price had the liberation been the project of the people themselves with help from external nations given at their request. Second, the great bulk of all the deaths since the war began are the responsibility of the Sunni extremists, foreign jihadist terrorists, and sectarian militias. Some critics of the war have downplayed this fact; for instance, although the Iraq Body Count project has done important service by carefully cataloging deaths, their reports ascribe the responsibility for most of these deaths to the United States and the United Kingdom. But third, unlike the arch-defenders of the war, I am not saying that the United States and United Kingdom are free of responsibility for the power of the insurgency and the subsequent sectarian conflict. I do agree with you that most of the problems of the postwar period were foreseeable as probable risks. The United States in particular greatly erred in planning for the immediate aftermath of war and in allowing the insurgency to gain its initial strength, which has been very hard to squelch.

DLC It's important to recognize three different degrees of moral responsibility of the United States and the United Kingdom for deaths in Iraq. In the terminology of the Christian tradition, they are directly responsible for those they intended to kill: hopefully only Iraqi combatants fighting against them or threatening to do so. They are also responsible for the indirect killing of noncombatants as a result of their attacks. These deaths are considered permissible if the value of the military objective is sufficiently important and there is no reasonable alternative that causes fewer casualties. A third category of deaths are those caused by others: Iraqi troops and militant and terrorist groups. Obviously, the primary responsibility for these deaths belongs to those perpetrating the killings, as you suggest. However, the just war criterion of proportionality also requires those going to war to take a judgment that overall the costs of war are outweighed by the goods achieved. This means that the United States and the United Kingdom also bear responsibility for predictable outcomes of the war, whomever they are immediately caused by. In the absence of the war, Iraqi civilians would not be subject to attack by militant and terrorist groups. Those groups are morally responsible for the killings they carry out, but this does not exclude the United States and the United Kingdom from their responsibility in creating a situation that makes the civilians targets.

BES   Not every eventuality of war is the fault of those who lead it. But many errors must be ascribed to the British and American civilian leadership and to some of the American military personnel and leaders. Before the war, I worried greatly about factors that could make the war turn out badly, such as the weak commitment of the Bush administration to nation-building. My fear that the Bush administration would be unwilling to spend the necessary financial resources and would leave Iraq abruptly did not turn out to be the case; rather, the administration made an insufficient commitment to the military staffing of the war. The United States was already stretched by its commitment in Afghanistan, and it has become clear to me that it has been reckless in pursuing the military model of response to terrorism that we discussed in the chapter 5. I am stunned that the planning for occupation, security, rebuilding, and transition was so weak and misguided. The sectarian division between Sunnis, Shiites, and Kurds also concerned me, but I didn't fully appreciate how embittered the Sunni minority would be. Whether that alone could have predicted a disproportionate outcome, I don't know, but I expected State Department planners and diplomats to have a better plan than they did for managing the postwar power relations.

A final error, which I never would have expected, was the torture of prisoners by U.S. personnel at Abu Ghraib prison and the mistreatment of prisoners at other locations. We agree that these errors are significant and blameworthy. For you, these errors only confirm and extend the moral error of the decision to go to war. For me, these errors took what was a contentious but defensible case for war—one that became less and less defensible with postwar revelations—and drove a nail into its coffin. I would not have counseled starting a war under these conditions.

DLC We shouldn't conclude without speculating on the future of Iraq and suggesting what's the best way forward under the circumstances. Many of those who opposed the war are now (in January 2007) calling for American and British troops to be brought home. For some time I thought this would be a mistake; it seemed highly unlikely to bring greater stability for Iraq, and it appeared to be abandoning responsibility for the mess the war has caused. Now most Iraqis seem to want the troops out, and it seems unlikely that withdrawing troops could make things any worse. What of the longer term? I do not believe that a democratic constitution will be the panacea that many have predicted. Democracy does not solve the problem of disempowered minority ethnic groups, and the pressures for Iraq to divide into different regions based on ethnicity will remain. As we have seen in our survey of its history, Iraq was a nation that came into being through British invasion of the three Ottoman provinces of Basra, Baghdad, and Mosul, so these pressures on the current shape of the nation are not unexpected.

It may be that without a tyrannical leadership to hold the country together, the nation is unsustainable in its current form. I hope that either sufficient international support can be given to the new political authorities in Iraq to restore order quickly and bring peace or that the transition to autonomous provinces can be made smooth and orderly. However, my realistic judgment is that neither of these scenarios is likely. All the Iraq War has achieved is creating a new frontline between the United States and its allies and the extremists that oppose them. Peace in Iraq is likely to come only once progress has been made in addressing much wider issues, such as improving the relationship between Israel and Palestine and the United States taking humble steps to undo the perception of its exercising hegemonic power over weaker nations with little regard for anything but its own interests.

BES Like you, I have believed for the past three years that troops should not be pulled out precipitously. Even if the war was wrong, it would have been irresponsible of the United States and the United Kingdom to leave the nation in chaos. But I, too, have starting thinking differently, based on the endless drumbeat of death in 2006. On January 10, 2007, President Bush announced a plan for a surge in troops, but I believe that this effort is too little, too late. The United States simply does not have the personnel power, political will, or international support to engage in a large and lengthy escalation—which is the only kind of surge that could possibly make a difference for Iraq's security. I don't hear any expert opinion I trust indicating that a meager surge in troops has a good chance of quelling the violence. And the method of securing neighborhoods that Bush called for in his address is certain to be bloody. That being the case, it is irresponsible to cause more military deaths and civilian deaths for no good end in sight. It seems the United States has no responsible choice but to start removing troops in 2007. I fear the results for Iraqis; my only consolation is that a troop drawdown might incite Iraq's government to make politically difficult decisions that it has been putting off and that make a small difference (such as to disband militias, make better efforts to secure order with its own police forces, and would pursue political compromises for the sake of reconciliation among the main ethnic and religious groups).

Yet I'd like to end on a more hopeful note, even if I am not sure it is justified.[57] There is much tragedy in the aftermath but also real progress over what Iraq has known since the ascent of Saddam and over what the Kurds and Shiites have known since the nation was created by Western powers almost ninety years ago. Iraqis have voted in three significant national elections—the first free and representative Iraqi elections in decades and a rare achievement anywhere in the Middle East. Do such developments point to a better future for Iraq? We have to hope that they do. I am not talking about mere optimism, that is, wishful thinking, but a hope-filled trust in the human spirit and in God's ultimate purposes. We must dare to believe that people will not be endless enemies. The citizens of Iraq need not be enemies, and I hope that they will not be. The Sunnis are not a monolithic group. Some did participate in the elections; some will see a point in casting their lot with a constitutional Iraq rather than with nihilism. Most Shiites, although having suffered abuse under Sunni political power for decades, have not been vengeful for the most of the past three years but have engaged the political process in order to overcome the past.

America and the world need not be enemies, and I hope that they will not be. It will help greatly if the United States learns from its mistakes and takes a more humble approach in its foreign relations. There is perhaps some good that can still be done through American diplomatic outreach in the region, but we have to look for benefits more in the long term than the short term. I believe that American citizens as a whole truly desire to help others—even, implausibly, with this war—but that motive has been tarnished, and we have to work hard to restore its luster. In that effort, Christians could and should play a leading role, for they are not only a significant portion of the American population but are also part of a global church. With hope, American Christians can build better bridges between their nation and the rest of the world.

CONCLUSION

The Iraq War is the most contentious exertion of American power since the Vietnam War. American leadership of the war put it at loggerheads with the United Nations, a majority of national leaders, and a majority of the population in most other countries. It remains a bitterly divisive issue in the United Kingdom and in every other country that supported the United States diplomatically or with troops. For the United Kingdom, the war tested almost to the breaking point the Labor government of Prime Minister Tony Blair and strained the nation's relationship with the rest of Europe. The gulf between America's and Britain's current policy trend and the rest of the world bodes ill for the possibility of nations working collaboratively in the future. The rift in international relations will be slow to heal. As the sectarian violence continues in Iraq and the death toll mounts, the citizens of Iraq have every reason to grow more bitter, notwithstanding the few rays of hope offered by developments in their political process.

We can only hope that our ethical examination of, and debate about, the war encourages readers to think carefully and critically before pinning their hopes on war as a solution to terrorism, weapons proliferation, and humanitarian problems. How well have Christian pacifism and the just war tradition responded to all these issues? In the concluding chapter we will sum up and assess what we have learned from our debates.

A Christian Agenda for a Warring World

Through four chapters we have applied just war theory and pacifism to several case studies concerning contemporary problems of warfare. Now is a good time to recall a point we made in the early chapters of the book: These positions present two of three potentially acceptable Christian perspectives on war (ruling out holy war), and each position covers a range of moral and theological attitudes. We cannot speak about the just war position or the pacifist position; rather, a variety of just war perspectives and a variety of pacifist doctrines exist among Christians. There is no single, official version of these doctrines in Christianity, owing to the denominational diversity of the religion. Therefore, in the body of the chapters, we describe the range of arguments made by just war thinkers and pacifists, as well as by realists.

In the debates, each of us has applied the particular position he supports, defended its plausibility, and responded to criticisms. Brian Stiltner's version of just war theory is founded on Catholic ethical and political assumptions (such as the use of natural law, the centrality of human rights, and the notion of the common good), and his style of just war thinking might be called "mainstream" in that he tries to steer between the rule-trangressing of Christian realists and the quasi-pacifism of some recent just war thinkers. Hence, his approach has been to affirm wars—especially for humanitarian reasons or to back up the decisions of the United Nations—when they straightforwardly satisfy the just war criteria. David Clough's pacifist approach, in terms of our typology from chapter 2, has been principled (with strategic concessions to domestic policing and UN-led interventions into urgent humanitarian crises), classical (rather than absolute), politically engaged (rather than separatist), and in the middle of the communal–universal scale. Although Clough is committed to the communal pole in seeing Christian ethics first and foremost as a task for the Church, his adherence to a pacifism that is politically engaged means he has been willing to engage in political debate with Stiltner and commend approaches that could win assent in a pluralistic political forum.

As we analyzed particular issues, our aim was to work from the theological commitments we articulated in the early chapters of the book. Of course, that analysis also required us to delve into political, social, and military details. In this conclusion, we bring the ethical and theological status of the two theories into the foreground. We have three aims in this chapter: to give a summary assessment of the viability of just war and pacifism as ethical positions for contemporary Christians; to ask whether these positions can work together or, conversely, whether Christians must choose between them; and, assuming the positions have important shared goals and values, to chart out a just peacemaking agenda for Christians in the twenty-first century. The chapter is organized along these three lines.

THE BENEFITS AND SHORTCOMINGS
OF THE TWO POSITIONS

No ethical theory—no set of human ideas of any kind—is flawless. That goes even for ethical theories that base themselves upon scripture and religious tradition. Christians should expect to find weaknesses in any theory or theology that has developed out of their religious tradition. To ignore this possibility is to confuse human ways with divine purposes—one of several errors that pave the way to the holy war mentality. So we will be wise to examine how each of our ethical positions can be vulnerable to misuse or self-righteousness. The only way to recover from shortcomings is to face them frankly. At the same time, we each believe that our preferred ethical tradition embodies much wisdom from committed Christians of the past and present. The upshot is that we can find both benefits and shortcomings in each position.

Assessing Christian Just War Theory

In the introduction, we noted that the just war tradition has been the dominant method of Christian reflection on war for sixteen hundred years and asked whether it deserves to retain this privileged position today. For several reasons, just war theory could claim to be the most effective ethical approach to war for Christians and non-Christians alike. First, the tradition recognizes the reality that, in the fallen world in which we live, wars will continue to occur. The tradition engages with that reality and tries to bring some good out of a bad situation. Can we credit the just war tradition with actually ameliorating the effects of war? There are many pieces of evidence for such a claim, though one cannot so much prove the argument as offer sensible assumptions in favor of it. A long list of actions prohibited in war was developed by just war theorists over the centuries and eventually enshrined in international law. True, modern technology and methods of war have consistently outstripped the prohibitions. Although war is not necessarily safer for civilians today, it is less brutal on noncombatants than it would be with no treaties and conventions. Likewise, soldiers on both sides of conflicts have benefited from protections that are based on the traditional just war assumption of the moral equality of combatants. Furthermore, although it is hard to prove that just war reasoning ever stopped a war, it is reasonable to assume that leaders, at least in democracies, have sometimes stayed their hands from adventurous wars when they have been held to the criteria by public pressure and international law.

A second benefit of just war reasoning is that it is the only structured moral context for thinking about war as a practical matter. As we have seen, Clough often resorted to just war principles and assumptions in order to counter Stiltner's just war arguments. This strategy is perfectly reasonable and effective for pacifists, but just war thinkers would reply that pacifists must use just war language if they want to affect the shape of public affairs. During World War I, World War II, and the cold war era, just war thinkers often charged pacifists with being irrelevant at best and dangerous at worst—dangerous if their arguments were to lull the West into a passive role toward totalitarian regimes. Stiltner's just war position is more positive about the social value of pacifist witness, but he still holds that the public dialogue is best conducted within the just war framework. This framework is the best alternative to abandoning public reasoning about war to realist and nationalist rhetoric.

But why should Christians embrace these public benefits? A third strength of just war reasoning is that it honors fundamental religious beliefs and provides a path for Christians from their basic faith commitments to responsible participation in worldly affairs. The just war tradition is the attempt of Christians to come to terms with what it means to love their neighbor, protect the widow and orphan, and recognize God's providential ordering of human affairs through political authority. Seen in this way, going to war to maintain justice and defend the innocent where no other means is sufficient is not something that is morally ambivalent and, therefore, open to question by tender consciences. Rather, it is part of a fundamental Christian duty to act out of love for the neighbor. Others may stand by, but the just war tradition judges that Christians should recognize their responsibility to act.

This action is contiguous with what love and justice require in other relationships. On this view, war is not the only case where wise judgment requires decisions that are hard and costly. Just war reasoning tries to leverage the power of love, the demands of justice, and the vision of peace into political and international relations. These values cannot always be directly applied into political affairs (a point legitimately made by Christian realists), but they shape the entire practice of political justice so that it looks greatly different from what people would do under a regime of realist and nationalist values.

Yet when Christians use just war reasoning, are they really carrying God's values into the political realm, a realm that may want little to do with those values? Is there not a danger that Christians who embrace just war theory allow themselves to be duped into rationalizing nationalistic self-interests and legitimizing the killing of the innocent civilians? Undoubtedly, this is a risk, one which obliges us to note some of the shortcomings of the just war tradition. First, whether the theory has really made a difference to the practice of war can be doubted. As Clough argued in the chapter 1 debate, nations have good reason to make pragmatic agreements on the rules of war, and Christians have reason to support these pragmatic agreements without seeing them as the outworking of the natural law. To hold such treaties in too high esteem may delude us into thinking that we humans have actually redeemed the world—a violation of the humility that must accompany the doctrine of the fall. Whatever its intentions, just war theory can be seduced into providing a moral subterfuge for unjust wars so that, instead of functioning as a constraint on the resort to and conduct of warfare, it becomes merely a language for legitimizing the use of violence. Just war theorists should be wary of baptizing war in this way; they should scrutinize their own and others' appeals to the just war tradition.

Second, just war reasoning is inherently pulled in different directions: Its desire to reduce the incidence of war stands in tension with its desire to allow military action in response to evolving threats and humanitarian crises. Should the success of the just war tradition in the modern context be judged on how well it keeps nations from resorting to war? Or should it seek to encourage nations to make hard decisions to use military force when necessary to promote justice, international security, and human rights? Just war theorists differ about whether to interpret the tradition restrictively so it is close to a strategic pacifism, or to adapt it to the contemporary context of nuclear proliferation, fundamentalist terrorism, and failed states—risks that might require a resort to war even when there is no imminent threat. These two renditions of the tradition obviously serve very different geopolitical agendas. The ease with which Christian reflection on the just use of war can be shaped in either direction suggests that it is problematically indeterminate. For this strand of Christian thinking to continue to be seen as authoritative, it is important for theorists to demonstrate some consensus about the standards for justifiable war in the modern context.

Assessing Christian Pacifism

The strongest reason that Christian pacifism remains an attractive option at the beginning of the twenty-first century is the same one that made it attractive at the beginning of the second century: It points to a kind of faithful Christian discipleship that witnesses to the new ordering of the reign of God. Now, as then, many Christians experience God's call to a life that suggests there is an alternative to the continuous warring and competition among nations and subnational groups for primacy. Despite recurring hopes of a more peaceful future, war remains a significant cause of death, injury, and suffering. For instance, between 1997 and 2002, an estimated three million people were killed in war.[1] Despite recurring hopes that war itself could be made more humane and that new kinds of weapons could be more discriminating in their effects, civilians bear the brunt of war: 75 percent of those killed in this period were civilians. Christian pacifism continues to claim that the appropriate response to such devastation is not to attempt to make war more just but to abandon war as a method of solving international disputes. It claims that Christians have a particular responsibility to build peaceful relationships and find alternatives to the violent resolution of conflicts.

If the central rationale for Christian pacifism remains constant, the international context to which it relates is novel and disturbing. At least three features of the world at the beginning of the twenty-first century provide additional reasons for taking a pacifist position seriously. First, there is more potential for international initiatives to resolve conflicts peacefully. The United Nations has the potential to adjudicate between nations, to decide when international law has been breached, to deploy troops in peacekeeping roles, and to act to enforce its judgments. This suggests the possibility of an international authority with tasks and powers comparable to a nation-state's system of policing and criminal justice. Obviously, the UN would have to undergo significant development in order to assume this international role. In particular, the structure and membership of the Security Council needs revision, as it currently reflects only the balance of power between nations at the close of World War II. Furthermore, an international endorsement for the UN in this enhanced role is not close; the most powerful nations are wary of accepting constraints on their freedom of action. However, recent policy documents show willingness to reform UN structures, including the Security Council. There is reason to hope that both weaker and stronger nations will be able to recognize the advantages of a more coherent international order. [2] In such a context, war would become less common because there would be other ways of resolving grievances and breaches of international law would be consistently punished. Such a change of context would widen the area of common judgments between pacifist and just war positions because war could be identified as a last resort in fewer situations. The possibility that the UN might be required to use military force to address a breach of international law would remain, but most pacifists holding a nonabsolutist position would be prepared to accept such uses of force on the same grounds as they would accept the necessity for policing within national boundaries.

Second, one of the justifications for wars fought at the beginning of the twenty-first century is to counter terrorism. However, as our discussion has shown, war is an inappropriate tool to combat terrorism, with the possible exception of terrorism clearly sponsored by a nation-state. The Iraq War succeeded in ending whatever meager support Saddam Hussein may have given to terrorists but only at massive and dubious costs: tens of thousands killed and injured, Iraqi society thrown into sectarian conflict, and Muslims and Arabs incensed at the United States and the United Kingdom. All these results arguably have spurred recruitment to terrorist groups. The threats to modern nation-states at the beginning of the twenty-first century are simply unlike those they have previously faced, and it is becoming increasingly clear that war is not an effective way of responding to the threat of terrorism. In such a context, pacifist perspectives that offer alternative means of addressing and resolving conflicts are increasingly attractive.

Third, the destructive power of modern weaponry makes less plausible the claim that war is likely to lead to a net improvement of any given situation. Nuclear weapons are an obvious example. As we saw in chapter 4, there is widespread acknowledgment that any first use of these weapons would always be immoral, both because of the immediate devastation caused and because it would make the use of nuclear weapons by others more likely. These weapons are too destructive to be used proportionately or discriminately. It is often claimed that modern conventional weapons with smart guidance systems allow warfare to be conducted discriminately and with greater protection of civilians. Yet in Iraq, where a large proportion of the munitions used were precision guided, civilians were not well protected. Between March 19 and April 18, 2003, two-thirds of the thirty thousand munitions used by the U.S. Air Force were precision guided, but that did not prevent approximately forty-seven hundred civilians from being killed.[3] Advanced weaponry shows no sign of making war safer for noncombatants.

These three contextual changes suggest that pacifist methods of resolving conflicts could be more effective than reliance on military means. Yet for many Christian pacifists, the truth of pacifism is not based on its strategic success. For them, the central tenet remains that followers of Jesus cannot use violence, even in those cases where using violence seems to promise better results in combating evil or protecting the vulnerable. Critics of pacifism see two shortcomings in this position. First, the refusal in some versions of pacifism to take responsibility for overcoming evil through engagement in political life, including the proper use of force by political authorities, might be seen as defaulting on a Christian obligation to contribute to the earthly peace that is the basis for human flourishing. To stand back from this task suggests that pacifists value moral purity above shouldering some of the necessary burden of life. In chapter 2 we presented a critique of those pacifists who adopt a separatist position. Both authors agree that the separatist position is irresponsible and that Christians should take an interest in what structures of authority are necessary for human living. The shape of the contribution that pacifists make to society will necessarily be different from that of others; for example, pacifists will exercise rights to conscientious objection. So long as pacifists are prepared to make alternative, equally valuable—and equally costly—contributions to earthly peace, it is hard to make the charge of irresponsibility stick.

A second shortcoming critics find in Christian pacifism is that it risks abandoning one's neighbor to evildoers. This is a weighty charge against those who seek to follow the command of Jesus to love one's neighbor as oneself (Mk 12:31 and parallels). The challenge becomes stronger during an era with the potential for stronger international institutions. If a reformed UN Security Council, for example, took the view that the only way to prevent an act of genocide was to deploy troops under its authority, how could Christians oppose this act of humanitarian concern? Again, our analysis of the variation in pacifist positions makes clear that this critique would apply to some versions of pacifism more than others. For example, absolutist pacifists, who rule out even the use of force by the police, maintain that the responsibility of Christians is to be faithful to the commands of Christ; the final outcome of world events is God's responsibility rather than ours—a response unlikely to allay the concerns of critics. Classical pacifists, however, would be likely to join just war theorists in supporting the deployment of troops under these circumstances, and they would value highly the development of international institutions in order to make the use of force as similar to police action within a nation-state as possible. Clough takes this classical position, which is why he and Stiltner have been able to find consensus in such cases. The classical pacifist position would likely object to military action by an individual nation-state, especially where humanitarian motives seemed mixed with other motives, and so it might still be partially vulnerable to the criticism. However, the reluctance to support the use of force in such cases would usually be rooted in concern for innocent neighbors caught up in the devastation of war, in which case the force of the objection would be less clear.

One of the aims of this book has been to show that the terms of the debate between pacifism and the just war tradition changed at the beginning of the twenty-first century. The foregoing assessments of the merits of each position in the modern context support the case that the terms have changed. On the basis of our own weighing of the pros and cons, we reach different conclusions about which model best fits with the responsibilities of Christians both as disciples of Jesus Christ and as citizens. In short, each of us remains committed to his initial approach to war. This difference, however, masks a range of agreements and disagreements between just war and pacifism along a range of theological and political judgments. We turn now to the task of understanding the relationship between the positions.

DIVERGENCE AND CONVERGENCE BETWEEN THE POSITIONS

This section takes final stock of what is shared and not shared between these two Christian approaches to war. We will also indicate where Christian realism is located on some of these matters because that position has occasionally been featured in our debates. Agreements and disagreements can be located at three levels of reflection: the general theological doctrines that stand behind the ethical positions, the principles and theories used by the ethical positions, and practical applications of the positions.

Divergence and Convergence on Theological Doctrines

In the debates between just war and pacifism, it is easy to forget that fundamental beliefs drive all Christian ethics and underlie the family resemblances between the two positions. Christians aim to love God, neighbor, and self. They believe all humans bear the image of God. They strive to serve the neighbor as Jesus did and to live virtuously following Jesus' example. They believe that God's promises will be vindicated in the coming reign of God. They strive to bear each other's burdens in the Church. They believe that the Church should be a place of discernment—a place where believers are educated and formed in character and where they can think through ethical issues with fellow believers and decide on common actions. These basic beliefs stand in the background of the two positions on war, and their commonality has made possible the fraternal dialogue and constructive debate in this book. Although representing different positions, we are each ultimately trying to adopt an ethical position we believe is faithful to God's will as revealed in Jesus Christ. Furthermore, we are trying to discern not just a faithful personal stance but one that contributes to the communal discernment of the Church.

Yet some significant differences in theological interpretations divide the just war from the pacifist perspective. The following four points recall doctrines we discussed earlier and draw together other themes that have been running through the debate. The first is a doctrine of the human person, also known as theological anthropology. Theological anthropology offers an account of the value of human beings as created by God, their powers and moral capabilities, and their needs both as individuals and as members of communities. The doctrines of creation and the fall are significant for anthropology. All human beings are created in the image of God, and this belief can be employed as a basis for respect for human rights. The doctrine of creation supports the reality of the common good and the responsibility of political authority to protect it; it reminds us that God's goal is for the cosmos to be at peace.

However, the doctrine of the fall—symbolized by Adam and Eve's original disobedience—conveys that humans are limited and compromised by sin. Christians live in a conflicted reality between two ideal poles: the original creation and the coming reign of God. Christian positions on war appraise this tension differently. If human reason and will are not thoroughly flawed by original sin, then it is possible to develop a reasonable plan for the common good and an ethic of war in which coercive power can be restrained and directed to the common good. Yet if humans are deeply flawed by original sin, Christians might respond to sinful deeds by supporting governmental coercion and war, even if these uses of power are not restrained by ethical rules—a position associated with Augustine and Martin Luther that developed into Christian realism. Conversely, Christians impressed by the strength of human sin might refuse to contribute further to expressions of sinfulness. Such is the approach of much of the pacifist tradition. Those pacifists who believe that people cannot do God's will by relying on their own efforts and their natural powers will embrace a demanding, communal ethic that witnesses to the values of the inbreaking reign of God. Pacifists know they will often fail in this witness and even fail at being peaceful within the Church; this failure reflects the power of sin and the need to rely all the more on God's grace. Thus, even though they both accept the doctrines of creation and the fall, just war thinkers and pacifists look at the human implications of these doctrines very differently.

Eschatology—theological thinking about the significance of the end of the universe for living in the present—is a second site of difference in theological assumptions. Most Christians affirm that the reign of God has already broken into human history but is not yet fully realized. Which side of the tension is emphasized leads to different ethics of war. For pacifists, the reign of God that

Jesus proclaimed should be understood as already existing "among you" or "in the midst of you" (Lk 17:21). Therefore, Christians should live by values that accord with God's reign, including nonviolence and peace. Jesus promised "blessed are the peacemakers, for they will be called children of God" (Mt 5:9). Most Christian denominations and major Christian thinkers interpret our eschatological situation to mean that "the church will always try to transform the present reality, but at times the church will have to tolerate some evil in order to avoid greater evils."[4] If the reign of God is not yet fully realized, then Christians accept that living their lives fully governed by those values is not yet possible. Realists, guided by their strong sense of sin, emphasize the "not yet" and frankly accept the discrepancy between the ideals of the reign of God and the realities of the world. Thus, they accept war as a necessary evil to restrain sin. The just war tradition reasons similarly, but it minimizes the tension; it tries to see the ordering of society toward justice both as required under the reign of God and as a God-given task for this earthly time. Christian positions on war, therefore, vary in the stress they place on the eschatological tension. Just war thinkers might argue that pacifists do not give practical answers for dealing with evil in the real world, and pacifists charge that just warriors renounce the practices that Jesus commanded to make the reign of God more evident in our midst.

A third difference lies in doctrines of the Church, or ecclesiology. There are many variations on this doctrine, as suggested by the wide diversity of Christian denominations, each of which has a different interpretation of church organization, leadership, and functions. For our purposes, we note the general difference between a "small Church" and a "big Church" ecclesiology. If the Church (the ideal and universal Church) is supposed to be a believer's church—a gathering of Jesus' disciples who strive to follow his distinctive lifestyle—then a given church community is likely to be small and intimate. This model of the Church is often associated with pacifism. Witness to the reign of God is best accomplished in a community that is clear about its primary loyalty to God and that distances itself from some of the habits of secular society. Some pacifist church communities, such as the Amish and the Bruderhof, remove themselves from most of the common social practices. By running cooperative businesses, owning common property, and sharing all the menial tasks necessary for communal life, they try to avoid consumerism, careerism, and social climbing. They feel that these secular practices of society sow competition and aggression that can corrupt the soul of society and make it vulnerable to crime and warfare.

Many other pacifist Christians live in the midst of the secular world but may choose to belong to a church that preaches and teaches according to a vision of peace. Some participate in peacemaking activities through church committees or transchurch organizations, such as Pax Christi, Sojourners, or the Fellowship of Reconciliation. By contrast, a "big Church" ecclesiology starts with the premise that Jesus meant for his Church to incorporate a wide variety of followers, including those who currently do not live up to his demanding standards. A big Church draws in everyone to educate and shape them, giving them a chance to become better disciples. This model of the Church does not lead directly to just war or realism, but it does imply that the Church should accept its members' social roles (including those who are political leaders, military leaders, soldiers, police officers, and employees of defense equipment manufacturers) and give them guidance in living out their roles. This ecclesiology also implies that that the Church's political role is not only as a witness against society or apart from society but also as a participant in society.

This point leads to a final theological difference, which is how Christians appraise secular government and their own roles in political society. A Thomistic understanding of politics—taking its name from Thomas Aquinas—sees political authority as good in itself; it is natural and part of God's mandate for creation. Government is an institution that humans would have needed for the purpose of social coordination even if they had never fallen into original sin. The task of government is to guard and promote the common good; its basic purposes and sense of justice are indicated by natural law. Christians and non-Christians can collaborate in achieving political goals. A different perspective is provided by Augustine, especially in his later writings, who argued that human beings did not originally need political authority. Because the state is not natural and not part of God's original plan, it can hardly be called good in itself. A crucial ramification of the fall of humanity is that people now use force to control other people, all the better to satisfy their selfish desires. This "dominion," as Augustine called it, takes many forms: slavery, coercion by political leaders, and the waging of wars (even just wars). Thus, Augustine regards the state as necessary but flawed and in itself more evil than good.[5]

Although there are interpretations of the just war tradition and of pacifism that fit with both of these views of government, a just war perspective is more likely to be associated with the Thomistic position; pacifist Christians are more likely to have an Augustinian view of the state. If the state is a natural and essential part of God's original ordering of creation, then clearly Christians should play their part in directing it and fulfilling the duties it demands of citizens, including fighting for it when called upon. If the state is a necessary concession to human sinfulness, its demands may sometimes be at variance with the demands of Christian discipleship. Christians would then cooperate when appropriate but sometimes might refuse to perform duties incompatible with their faith. Although Augustine believed Christians should be prepared to fight in a just cause, others taking this view of government might consider military service to be one area in which Christians should resist the state.

Divergence and Convergence on Ethical Principles and Theories

The level of ethical principles and theories mediates between general theological doctrines and concrete moral decisions and actions. Here too, we find convergences and divergences. One stark and fundamental disagreement must be mentioned first: The just war doctrine allows a Christian to take human life, whereas absolute pacifism forbids a Christian to do so. This fundamental ethical difference is driven by a difference in ethical theory: The just war tradition factors both principles and consequences into its ethic. It enshrines principles associated with deontological ethics, notably noncombatant immunity, alongside a consequentialist commitment to bring more overall good (justice, eventual peace) out of a situation, even if some moral goods (human lives) are lost in the process. By contrast, pacifism asserts that using consequences to justify a war is wrong and deceptive. Principled pacifism holds that it is simply immoral to weigh human lives on a scale of consequences; its commitment to the principle "do not kill" overrides all else. Strategic pacifism questions just war's estimation of consequences; it maintains that nonviolent responses to conflict are far more likely to bring about positive long-term consequences.

Despite this difference, just war tradition and pacifism share certain ethical principles, and we believe that the Christian theological context makes for more ethical overlap than is often recognized. First, pacifism accepts many of the principles in the just war criteria. Indeed, pacifists urge just war advocates to hold to their criteria more rigorously, believing that if the criteria were taken seriously and stringently, just war advocates would conclude that most wars should not be approved.

Second, the positions agree that in political life the least coercion possible should be used, and when it is used by political authorities, the harm caused must be distributed fairly. The implications are that war must be minimized, policing should be humane, and all unnecessary forms of political violence should be eradicated.[6] Despite their different emphasis on the nature of government, Christians from the two traditions challenge a view of politics as (in the famous realist phrase) "war by other means." Christians have the duty to work for alternatives to war, and they should participate in political initiatives that would alleviate human misery and promote the common good; such just peacemaking initiatives would make recourse to war less likely.

Third, Christian just war tradition and Christian pacifism establish protection and care of the neighbor as a central sociopolitical principle. Jesus' reaffirmation of the Old Testament command to "love your neighbor as yourself" (Lv 18:19) in the context of the Good Samaritan parable (Lk 10:25–37) indicates that Christians must show active concern and provide assistance to any human being who happens to be in need.[7] Just war tradition moves from the principle of love to the determination to intervene on behalf of the victims of violence. Most versions of pacifism are likewise committed to intervention but with nonviolent methods. Both positions say that a commitment to the well-being of all people requires Christians to act through the Church and through political channels to make social life more just and peaceful for everyone.

Finally, we should note that some sections of each tradition will show much greater convergence than others. One clear example is classical pacifism, which accepts the need for some forms of coercive force within a nation and whose advocates may even agree with just war theorists that limited international military actions under the right authority could be justifiable.

Having charted these divergences and convergences, we must return to a question raised in chapter 2: Do the positions share a "presumption against violence" as a matter of ethical principle? Most pacifists would like just war thinkers to affirm this principle. However, this viewpoint is disputed among just war theorists. The notion that just war theory does begin with such a presumption has gained adherence among many ethicists and was endorsed by the U.S. Catholic bishops in their pastoral letter, *The Challenge of Peace,* in 1983. This view is commonsensical because just war thinkers want the incidence of war to be reduced; they want to make it hard for political leaders to rationalize war. In situations of political conflict, the most just action is typically to address systemic causes so that people and nations do not fight. Interventions to promote a more just society may be coercive but typically will not be bellicose. War is always a human tragedy and should always be a last resort. For these reasons, and given the respect that Christians should have for the teachers of nonviolence in their tradition, a presumption against violence makes sense for just war thinkers. As a just war theorist, Stiltner accepts the presumption against violence, interpreted as follows: The benefit of the doubt lies on the side of nonviolent alternatives, and any case for war has to be persuasively argued.[8] Christian just war theory and Christian pacifism should jointly affirm the methods of pursuing alternatives to war and addressing injustices systemically through just peacemaking practices.

The just war critics of the presumption against violence raise concerns about this interpretation's lack of a concept of statecraft and its twisting of just war tradition into a decision process for justifying exceptions to the presumption. We believe, however, that these problems can be avoided. Our ethical reasoning about concrete problems has hardly been unaware of the importance of statecraft. Any Christian position on war rests on a conception of government and of the political responsibilities of citizens generally and Christian citizens specifically. These conceptions must be articulated and tested for their coherence and plausibility. We have done so in this book. At times we found that we held some common notions of the state's responsibilities; often our notions of statecraft differed. Nonetheless, we share the judgment that violence is to be avoided wherever possible, only differing in our beliefs about when it can be avoided.

On the charge of twisting just war theory into exception-making, we both believe that it is not an ideal position for just war thinkers. However, the just war stance got into this position not because of the presumption-against-violence interpretation but because many Christians and non-Christians alike have lost sight of just war as a tradition. Instead, just war became a set of disembodied criteria even before the presumption-against-violence view became popular. This failure is the result of historical reasons beginning with the secularization of just war in the late Middle Ages and accelerating with the success of the just war criteria as an international common language in the twentieth century. The disembodied use of the just war criteria in our interconnected, pluralistic world is here to stay, and in a sense this is beneficial, for it allows people from many cultures to have a dialogue about the justice of war. However, just war theory does its best work when it is grounded in its historical, cultural, and religious roots. Indeed, both just war and pacifism need to be grounded, even as they also need to be able to make plausible arguments in political debates.

In this book, when we focused on a political decision (such as appropriate responses to terrorism or nuclear proliferation), both of us were able to use just war criteria and other philosophical arguments and political observations to make our arguments. When the context was Christian advocacy and action, just war criteria did not predominate; rather, we invoked more basic Christian beliefs and motivations. Again, we do not see that the presumption-against-violence interpretation has caused the disembodiment, but we think that both positions—pacifism as well as just war—have to be developed and used in the context of their traditions, especially when they are being used as tools for debate and discernment in the Christian community.

Divergence and Convergence on Practical Applications

Through our case studies, we have discovered that the two positions can arrive at common negative and positive judgments. Negatively, the two positions can agree in condemning a given war when it fails to meet just war criteria. Such was the case we presented concerning the 2003 Iraq War. A number of Christian just war thinkers agreed with Christian pacifists in standing against the war, and the witness of the Christians churches was almost uniformly condemnatory. We ourselves also find that this war was unethical, and we agree on most of the evidence and arguments leading to this conclusion. Our positions have common cause to stand firm against acceptance of preventive war.

Positively, there is substantial common ground between the two positions about how to avoid and resolve conflicts. Case by case, Christians can engage in various just peacemaking practices to help achieve these goals. Let us recall some of the common judgments at which the two of us arrived concerning the four issues. Regarding humanitarian intervention, we agree about the importance of helping victims of aggression, which reflects the two positions' shared value of Christian love that is willing to sacrifice for the good of the neighbor. On the matter of weapons, we agree that nuclear, biological, and chemical weapons are indiscriminate and that caches of these munitions need to be reduced to the point of permanent elimination. Here just war tradition and pacifism are equally motivated to protect human life created in God's image. We agree that terrorism is a wholly immoral tactic for political change because it intentionally targets civilians. Likewise, counterterrorist measures often fall into a similar error—harming civilians disproportionately—and they must be condemned when they do. This condemnation reflects again the value of human life. Neither position is willing to trade on it for a greater good. We agreed that the peacemaking initiatives derived from the overlap between our two theories would not only be the most ethical but also the most effective long-term responses.

Obviously, all the theological and ethical differences also lead to different judgments in some cases. Just war thinkers support wars that meet all their criteria or—more controversially—when good arguments can be made for many of them, whereas pacifists believe that the criteria are ripe for rationalization. Such was the case with our discussion of the Gulf War in this book. Stiltner approved it with only marginal reservations. Clough agreed that the war met the just war criteria, but he also saw the criteria much abused. The deeper problem, he feels, is that the just war criteria often only give us a way to justify war. Even if the justification is sensible, the focus on justification is a cramped approach for Christian ethics.

Just war thinkers often recommend that nations need to make use of coercion and military activity short of war to prompt political changes for justice and to ward off threats. Pacifists believe that such aggressive behavior often fuels violence more than it cures it. The chapter on terrorism provided an example of our disagreement about the value of military responses to violence. Stiltner saw some limited value in military responses combined with strong law enforcement measures. Clough would put the greatest effort into the peacemaking model because this model addresses the root causes of terrorism and does not threaten human life. Just war tradition places symbolic and practical importance on government establishing just order by preventing criminal acts and terrorism; pacifism worries precisely about the symbolism of making terrorism into a war. Different visions of social welfare and political responsibility are suggested here. The topic of nuclear deterrence suggested a similar difference. We differ in our patience with the pace of arms reductions and our acceptance of deterrence as an intermediary situation, reflecting an underlying difference in our notions of political responsibility. Finally, just war thinkers tend to be committed to humanitarian interventions both as a moral ideal and in practice, despite the limits and risks of intervention. Pacifists are critical of the selfish national interests that they find implicit in military interventions and emphasize the toll on innocent bystanders. Thus, we disagreed on the legality of the NATO attack on the Serbian army in Kosovo.

Table 7.1 summarizes the agreements and disagreements discussed above. Can any pattern be discerned? Looking over the debates in the preceding chapters, one notices that we concurred in a number of negative judgments concerning wars and acts of war. We also regularly shared an appreciation of the ethical problems that precipitate wars and that influence decisions to go to war. Neither pacifism nor just war is acceptable if it fails to help address the ethical problems that lead to war. Fortunately, we saw that both positions— perhaps especially in a Christian context—are concerned about those systemic problems and have similar ideas about addressing them. So even as advocates of the two positions will continue to disagree on a number of matters, we have reason to conclude this book with a common statement about the urgency of peacemaking.

PEACEMAKING: A CHRISTIAN VOCATION

In this book we have looked at the relationship between the pacifist and just war traditions from their roots in the Bible and Church tradition, through the theological convictions that guide them, to the judgments they provide on key problems of political life. Both in the joint analyses of each chapter and in the debates between us, we have attempted to provide a thorough and rounded account of how each tradition approaches the questions raised by the use of military force at the beginning of the twenty-first century. The diversity within each of the two traditions has become apparent in our discussion, and it will be clear to readers that we each stand in a particular place within the traditions we own. In one sense, the particularity of our positions is a weakness. There would have been greater contrast at some points between an absolutist version of pacifism and a more militant rendition of the just war tradition. Our hope is that more is gained, however, by the account we have given of an honest conversation between two persons who differ in their understandings and who continue to struggle to find the proper response of the Church to questions of war.

TABLE 7.1

Christian Pacifism and Christian Just War Tradition: A Summary of Agreements and Disagreements

Agreements	*Disagreements*
Level of Theological Doctrines	
Fundamental beliefs drive all Christian ethics and underlie the family resemblances between just war tradition and pacifism. Christians should ■ aim to love God, neighbor, and self. ■ believe all humans bear the image of God. ■ strive to serve the neighbor as Jesus did and to live virtuously following Jesus' example. ■ believe that God's promises will be vindicated in the coming Kingdom. ■ bear each others' burdens in the Church.	Diverging interpretations of at least four doctrines have divided the two ethics of war: ■ Theological anthropology: confidence in reason vs. seeing the power of sin. ■ Eschatology: accepting lesser evils in the meantime vs. being faithful to Kingdom values. ■ Ecclesiology: big Church vs. small Church style. ■ Political theory: government as positive, natural, justice-centered vs. government as lesser-evil, unnatural, pragmatic arrangement.
Level of Ethical Theories and Principles	
■ In political life, the least possible coercion should be used; any coercion must be distributed fairly. ■ Violence and war must be minimized; Christians have the duty to work for alternatives to war. ■ Both ethics establish care and protection of the neighbor as a central sociopolitical principle. ■ Pacifism supports the principle-based reasoning underlying the just war criteria and urges just war advocates to hold to their own criteria rigorously. ■ Many pacifists and just war theorists claim that their ethics share a presumption against violence. ■ The two theories join in criticizing secular realism and Christian realism on several counts.	■ Just war says a Christian may take human life; absolute pacifism says Christians may never do so. ■ Just war factors both principle and consequences into its ethic; pacifism asserts that using consequences to justify a war is deceptive and wrong. ■ Some just war theorists deny their theory shares with pacifism a presumption against violence; the continuing debate points back to differences in political theory. ■ Some just war thinkers accept key premises of Christian realism; on these grounds, they also think that pacifism is an irresponsible doctrine for political life.

TABLE 7.1 *(continued)*

Agreements	Disagreements

Level of Theological Doctrines

■ The two ethics often agree in condemning a given war when it fails to meet just war criteria. Such was the case with the Iraq War. ■ Both positions wish to see neighbors protected, justice restored, and communities healed when they are wracked by violence. Case by case, Christians can engage in various just-peacemaking practices to help achieve these goals. ■ Nonabsolute pacifists might agree on the rare necessity of military intervention into a humanitarian crisis under strict just war conditions.	■ The two ethics often disagree when it comes to a given war. Just war thinkers support wars that meet all their criteria or (more controversially) where good arguments can be made for many of them whereas pacifists believe that the criteria are ripe for rationalization. ■ Just war thinkers often recommend that nations need to make use of coercion and military activity short of war to prompt political changes for justice and to ward off threats. Pacifists believe that such aggressive behavior often only fuels violence. ■ Just war thinkers tend to be committed to humanitarian intervention, both as a moral ideal and in practice, despite its shortcomings. Pacifists are typically critical of the mixed motives behind interventions and the harm caused to innocent bystanders by fighting.

As a result of the conversation we have shared through the writing of this book, we believe it is time for Christians to step beyond the stale debate between narrow and doctrinaire versions of pacifism and just war theory, especially versions that take their cues from popular political discourse. Once allegiance is given to one of these flimsy structures, a real danger emerges that more energy is being invested in propping it up and attempting to topple its counterpart than in seeking out God's will for the Church and for the world. As a result, the Christian contribution to discussions of war and peace is too often confused and distracted instead of witnessing to the desire of God for peace among God's creatures and showing the first steps in that direction. This observation is made not to claim that there can or should be an end to Christian disagreements about war as a means of contributing to earthly peace. For the theological and practical reasons we have outlined in the previous section, there will always be differences between Christians wrestling with these questions. Those differences have been evident in our discussions, and we believe that the Church must continue to debate the issues in order to refine its collective view. Our brief common witness does not mean that the pacifist and just war traditions are saying the same thing, or close to the same thing, in different languages; we have uncovered significant differences between commitments and judgments at all levels of our debate. However, alongside these differences, Christians have an urgent responsibility to define the maximum possible area of present consensus about what should be done to establish and sustain peace between peoples. Peacemaking is too important a part of the vocation of the Church to be abandoned in favor of debating fine doctrinal differences. For this reason, we conclude this book with a brief proposal for Christians with pacifist and just war views that shows what they can do to shape the peacemaking vocation of the Church at the beginning of the twenty-first century.

Pray for peace and be a peaceful community. The first task of the Church in relation to peacemaking is to offer prayers for peace, about which there should be little difficulty in establishing consensus. A discipline of attention to the need for peace in actual and potential conflicts locally, nationally, and internationally can transform attitudes and serve as a firm foundation for action. Authentic prayer for peace will often be an uncomfortable and searching experience. One of the coauthors (Clough) remembers being brought to tears by prayers for peace during the 2003 Iraq War. He had gathered with other members of his college in Durham, England, at the beginning of the devastating bombardment of Iraq that preceded the ground invasion. The leader of the service offered prayers for peace in Iraq, but to Clough it seemed the height of pious hypocrisy to be praying for peace at the same time as his nation was launching missiles at the country. In retrospect, he thinks that praying for peace was the correct thing to do but that the prayer should have been offered in the expectation that it would challenge the gathered congregation to question their part in the current foray and to act to prevent such attacks in the future. If we have no heart for such a challenge, our prayer is empty and deceitful.

If the Church speaks of peace to others, it must go some way to show that it knows something of which it speaks. Peacemaking must begin with sisters and brothers in the local church. If we cannot be reconciled with them, what hope is there for international relationships under pressure? Of course, the visible Church is made of flawed and sinful human beings, as churchgoers know only too well. So the model of the peace of God's reign that a particular church community shows to the world will always be partial and incomplete. However, this is no excuse for resting content with factions within churches, breakdowns in communication, and hardened grudges. In order for Christians to take hope that peacemaking works, the local church, as well as the universal Church, must be where peacemaking is practiced.

Look frankly at our churches' encouragement of violence. The attacks on the United States on September 11, 2001, reignited debate about an old question: Is religion to blame for provoking or exacerbating violence? In a recent article, the atheist Richard Dawkins complains about a widespread addiction to "Gerin oil," a drug that, "if administered chronically in childhood, . . . can permanently modify the brain to produce adult disorders, including dangerous delusions that have proved very hard to treat. The four doomed flights of September 11 were, in a very real sense, Gerin oil trips: all 19 of the hijackers were high on the drug at the time."[9] Dawkins is rehearsing the Marxist critique of religion (of which "Gerin oil" is an anagram) as a drug, but he differs concerning the effects of the drug. For Marx, religion was responsible for pacifying proletarians by promising them joys in heaven if they peaceably accepted becoming tools of their capitalist masters. For Dawkins, religion instead leads to delusions with violent consequences, including wars and terrorist attacks. He gives voice to a widespread liberal view at the beginning of the twenty-first century that religion is bad for society, particularly in its potential to incite its adherents to be violent against others.

There are important reasons to be suspicious of the thesis that religion causes violence. The situation is altogether more complex. Religion has often been a reconciling force for avoiding conflict; many acts of violence, including the most destructive in the twentieth century, are inspired by atheistic world views, and even where religious affiliation seems to be a factor in a conflict, it is often one among a range of motivational factors. After these corrections have been made, however, Christians must confess that their faith has not always been an influence for peace in the world. The medieval Crusades are the most egregious example of Christians deciding that their faith required the killing of others in God's name, but they are not, unfortunately, unique.

We are troubled that Christian approval has been extended in the modern age to violence that cannot be justified according to the just war tradition, such as the Allies' use of incendiary bombs to attack civilians in Germany and Japan during World War II, the United States' use of atomic weapons in Hiroshima and Nagasaki, the protracted American engagement in Vietnam, and violations of human rights in the name of counterterrorism. At a minimum, Christian teaching on war should function to prevent the use of violence to terrorize civilians, but even in modern times, it has not always done so. Such justifications reap a bitter harvest. It may even be that recourse by the United States and the United Kingdom to indiscriminate attacks on civilians during World War II is one factor in the creation of a context in which terrorists come to believe their own targeting of civilians can be morally or religiously justified.

Given both the historical examples of the Church failing to restrain inappropriate uses of force and the new issues presented by the role of religion as a motivation for terrorism, we believe that the Church must rediscover its peacemaking heritage. It must become clearer to Christians and non-Christians alike that Christianity—like many other religions—witnesses to the will of God for peace in the world. Christians differ about when force should be used, but they should agree that building and sustaining peace and justice are a priority and that all reasonable nonviolent means of conflict resolution should be exhausted before any war can be considered legitimate. Our hope is that this consensus will soon extend to requiring the approval of a reformed and representative UN Security Council.

In response to the current discussion about whether the just war tradition should be made more permissive to allow greater scope for the kind of preemptive attack that was made on Iraq in 2003, we both believe that the established consensus of the just war tradition should stand. War should only be considered justified when used to preempt imminent threats.[10] To extend the category to threats that are not imminent would be to move in the direction of making a causal relationship between religion and violence more plausible. Among other results, such a move would allow nations identified as Christian, such as the United States and the United Kingdom, greater latitude in acting against non-Christian nations they see as threats to their security. Instead, Christians must recognize and resist any easy recourse to the use of violence, encourage all efforts towards peaceful resolution of conflicts, and support the building up of those international institutions with the potential to facilitate such resolutions.

Engage public life without illusions. Christians should accept responsibility for contributing to the earthly peace on which they depend and play a role in sustaining the common life of the societies in which they live. Christians will differ in how they understand their roles and how they should make their contributions. To contribute does not mean to assimilate uncritically the consensus of the wider population but to discern the meaning of the life to which the Church is called in the place and time in which it finds itself. All Christians will wish to celebrate some parts of the lives of the nations to which they belong and to question and refuse to participate in others. In particular, pacifist Christians will refuse to contribute to the military defense of a nation, though they should aim to shoulder a comparable burden. One part of Christian responsibility for the common life is to participate in politics by engaging in debate about decisions concerning how society should be ordered and contributing to political processes by voting and by offering themselves as candidates. Christians have a responsibility to pay attention to politics, to think carefully about the political implications of their beliefs, and to act upon their beliefs in public life. Christians should exercise this responsibility as citizens of their nations and even (properly understood) as members of the Church. Both avenues of their political participation are to be guided and limited by ethical principles. Christians primarily have to respect the ethical mandates of their faith when they participate in politics, but we do not think these mandates preclude them from being good citizens. Indeed, we believe that democratic societies benefit from the robust participation of religious citizens, and it is only in this way that the peacemaking vision of the Church will be brought into contact with the difficult day-to-day realities confronting local and national governments.

That such participation in public life be free of illusions about the nature of individuals, groups, nations, and the international order is crucial. Both pacifists and just war theorists are prone to idealistic dreams in different directions, which can render their contributions to public debate naïve and dangerously detached from their objectives. Pacifists are sometimes liable to forget that the reign of God inaugurated by the life, death, and resurrection of Christ is not yet fully realized. To hope for a time when all peoples will live in peace this side of the return of Christ is a vain hope for an impossible ideal. The truth of the Christian doctrine of original sin is that we have always to reckon with human sin, so utopian plans that depend on citizens being saints are liable to come crashing about their planners' heads. To hope that peacemaking will bear fruit in renewed relationships is essential, but those relationships must be able to withstand the stresses to which real human beings subject them.

Just war theorists can be victims of another form of self-deception: the idealization of war as a pure and honorable enterprise that efficiently and cleanly puts the world to right. Such a view cannot withstand the briefest acquaintance with the reality of warfare, which—even in short and contained occasions—is shockingly violent, frightening, and devastating to human life, social institutions, and the natural environment. In order to conduct war with any likelihood of success, soldiers need to be trained to overcome an aversion to killing, so that they may kill enemy soldiers quickly, efficiently, and without consideration. If military force is to be endorsed as a means for Christians to respond to evil, it must be done in full knowledge of the brutality of war and of its consequences for both combatants and noncombatants.

Work for peace with justice. The biblical vision of peace was set out in chapter 1, and the embracing of this peaceful vision by the early Church was described in the first part of chapter 2. We believe that this vision must be reclaimed by Christians in every age, even by Christians who favor the just war doctrine. Today, we are encouraged by the "Just Peacemaking" project, and believe it is right to identify common ground between just war theorists and pacifists in supporting the ten peacemaking practices we cited in chapter 2: supporting nonviolent action, acting to reduce threats, using cooperative conflict resolution, acknowledging responsibility for conflicts, advancing democracy and human rights, fostering just and sustainable development, working with cooperative forces in the international system, strengthening the UN and international efforts for human rights, reducing weapons and the weapons trade, and encouraging grassroots peacemaking groups.[11] These practices offer concrete ways to build up relationships that make conflicts less likely and that make it more likely that conflicts that do arise can be resolved nonviolently.

Peacemaking goes beyond these international issues. Christians must make this vision of peace their own by working out the meaning of peacemaking in every part of their lives. Peacemaking is not just about avoiding wars; it is first about sustaining peace and justice in all spheres of relationships. Just as conflict begins on a small scale, so too peacemaking begins at home—in neighborhoods, schools, places of work, churches, and local communities. Because every type of community and every aspect of human well-being matters to the Church, peacemaking becomes a task for the Christian community, a task it shares with women and men of other faiths and all people of goodwill.

The dialogue represented in this book has a place not only at those moments when a nation has to decide whether it should wage war but also, and more important, between those exceptional times when—at every level of domestic, social, ecclesial, and national life—there arise opportunities to preempt the possibility of conflict through the building of a just peace. Mindful of the Bible's counsel that a "harvest of justice is sown in peace for those who cultivate peace" (James 3:18),[12] we conclude that honoring the inseparable connection between justice and peace is the surest, most Christian, and most humane way to reduce the scourge of war.

We encourage our readers—whatever their religious affiliation and ethical stance on war—to make their own contributions to peacemaking. This encouragement is appropriate even in a scholarly book on ethics, for ethics cannot be a dispassionate activity, though it can and must be an informed, reasoned activity. We have attempted to use both head and heart throughout this book. Our goals have been to give the reader guidance in thinking about war as an ethical matter, to apply the resources of the Christian tradition to contemporary problems, and to model constructive ethical debate regarding these problems. We hope that the information, methods, and arguments we have presented in this book assist our readers in their own deliberations, discussions, and actions for ethical goals. In all the roles that each of us assumes in life—as a student of ethical issues, a participant in political life, a member of a church, a volunteer, a family member and friend—there are peacemaking tasks near at hand and opportunities to enact ethical vision in the world around us.

NOTES

NOTES TO CHAPTER 1

1. All scriptural quotations are from the *New Revised Standard Version*.

2. Thomas Aquinas, *Summa Theologica*, 5 vols., trans. Fathers of the English Dominican Province (Notre Dame, IN: Ave Maria Press, 1981), part I–II, ques. 94, art. 2.

3. Jacques Maritain, *Man and the State* (Chicago: University of Chicago Press, 1951), 88–89.

4. For balanced accounts of Christian natural law reasoning that avoid these errors, see (from among the vast literature) Jean Porter, *Natural and Divine Law* (Grand Rapids, MI: Eerdmans, 2000); and Mark Graham, *Josef Fuchs on Natural Law* (Washington, DC: Georgetown University Press, 2002). Porter places Aquinas's account of natural law in its scriptural context and shows how the right-reason use of natural law in Catholic teachings about social ethics is preferable to the biologist interpretation in Catholic teaching about sexual ethics. Graham provides a systematic account of the most productive Catholic natural law ethicist of the last fifty years. Among its other merits, Graham's account explains why natural law is not absolutist and why it cannot specify concrete moral norms. The term "port of entry" is Graham's.

5. Dietrich Bonhoeffer, *Ethics*, trans. Neville Horton Smith, ed. Eberhard Bethge (London: Collins, 1964), 17.

6. "Church" is a wide-ranging term. In some contexts it means the universal Church, that is, the organized body of all Christian believers. An understanding of the universal Church can be either actual (all the Christians constituting the early Church or all Christians in the organized Christian denominations today) or ideal (how the Church should act, teach, or be organized according to God's plan). In this book, such uses of "Church" will be capitalized. Also capitalized is the name of a particular institution, such as the Catholic Church or the Methodist Church. A lowercase usage of "church" refers to a local congregation or unspecified Christian denominations.

7. See, for example, Karl Barth, *Church Dogmatics* II/2, eds. G. W. Bromiley and T. F. Torrance (Edinburgh: T and T Clark, 1957), 509–42.

8. The canon is sixty-six books for Protestants. The Catholic version of the Bible includes seven books of the Apocrypha in its canon, for a total of seventy-three. Various Eastern Orthodox churches include the Apocryphal books and others in their canons, up to a maximum of eighty-one books for the Ethiopian Orthodox Church.

9. Richard Hays, *The Moral Vision of the New Testament* (San Francisco: HarperSanFrancisco, 1996; Edinburgh: T and T Clark, 1997), 209.

10. This interpretation goes back at least as far as Thomas Aquinas (see *Summa Theologica,* part I–II, ques. 103, art. 3).

11. See, for example, Walter Wink, *Violence and Nonviolence in South Africa: Jesus' Third Way* (Philadelphia: New Society Publishers, 1987), chap. 2.

12. For a discussion of these texts, see Stanley S. Harakas, *Wholeness of Faith and Life: Orthodox Christian Ethics* (Brookline, MA: Holy Cross Orthodox Press, 1999), chap. 6.

13. See Hays, *Moral Vision,* 329–32, for further discussion of these texts.

14. Throughout the history of Christian reflection on war, the proper power of a government that controls a military force has been a major question. Christian ethics often uses "the state" as the term for the highest political authority in a region and for government in general. The state at the time of the New Testament was the Roman Empire; today it is the nation (nation-state) of which one is a citizen. Henceforth, "the state," "government," and "political authority" will be used interchangeably when referring to this level of political power in general or in the abstract, while "nations," "states," and "nation-states" will be used interchangeably when referring to modern political entities such as the United States, the United Kingdom, and Iraq.

15. See the commentary on Exodus 20:13 in John I. Durham, *Exodus,* Word Bible Commentary, no. 3 (Dallas, TX: Word Books, 1987), 274–300.

16. See John Barton, *Understanding Old Testament Ethics: Approaches and Explorations* (Louisville, KY: Westminster/John Knox Press, 2003).

17. The theme of purity in the Old Testament is explored in Mary Douglas, *Purity and Danger: An Analysis of Concepts of Pollution and Taboo* (London: Routledge and Kegan Paul, 1966); and L. William Countryman, *Dirt, Greed and Sex: Sexual Ethics in the New Testament and Their Implications for Today* (London: SCM, 2001).

18. Gerhard von Rad, *Holy War in Ancient Israel* (Grand Rapids, MI: Eerdmans, 1991; repr., Eugene, OR: Wipf and Stock, 2000), 102. See also Ben C. Ollenburger's introduction to the text in the same volume.

19. This term is alternately translated as the "kingdom of God," and it appears many dozens of times throughout the gospels, especially those of Matthew, Mark, and Luke.

20. Several of Alasdair McIntyre's works argue that ethical discourses become incoherent if they are disconnected from the religious-philosophical traditions of reasoning that gave birth to them. See *After Virtue*, 2nd ed. (Notre Dame, IN: University of Notre Dame Press, 1984); *Whose Justice? Which Rationality?* (Notre Dame, IN: University of Notre Dame Press, 1989); and *Three Rival Versions of Moral Enquiry* (Notre Dame, IN: University of Notre Dame Press, 1991).

21. See Johannes Weiss, *Jesus' Proclamation of the Kingdom of God*, trans. R. H. Hiers and F. L. Holland (Philadelphia: Fortress, 1971); and Albert Schweitzer, *The Mystery of the Kingdom of God: The Secret of Jesus' Messiahship and Passion*, trans. Walter Lowrie (New York: Dodd, Mead, and Co., 1914).

22. Cited by Jean Bethke Elsthain, "Just War Tradition and the New War on Terrorism," A Pew Forum on Religion and Public Life Discussion (October 5, 2001), 3, http://pewforum.org/publications/reports/PFJustWar.pdf.

23. Readers lacking a background in New Testament studies will find accessible information about the social and political world of Jesus' day in Albert Nolan, *Jesus Before Christianity*, rev. ed. (Maryknoll, NY: Orbis, 2001), esp. chap. 2; Huston Smith, *The World's Religions: Our Great Wisdom Traditions*, rev. ed. (San Francisco: HarperSanFrancisco, 1991), chap. 8; and Thomas Cahill, *Desire of the Everlasting Hills: The World Before and After Jesus* (New York: Nan A. Talase/ Doubleday, 1999), chap. 1. Of the voluminous scholarly literature on the historical Jesus, a balanced and comprehensive study is John P. Meier, *A Marginal Jew: Rethinking the Historical Jesus*, 3 vols. (New York: Doubleday, 1991, 1994, and 2001).

24. On Jesus' ethic of inclusive solidarity, see Nolan, *Jesus Before Christianity*, chap. 9. Stiltner is indebted to Nolan's book for its influence on his overall thinking about the relevance of Jesus' social location for Christian ethics.

NOTES TO CHAPTER 2

1. Justin Martyr, "First Apology," chap. 39, in *The Ante-Nicene Fathers: Translations of the Writings of the Fathers Down to A.D. 325.*, eds.

A. Cleveland Coxe, James Donaldson, and Alexander Roberts. 10 vols. (Edinburgh: T and T Clark, 1997), 1: 175–76. This work is abbreviated as *ANF* in the references that follow.

2. Clement of Alexandria, "The Instructor," bk. 1, chap. 12 (*ANF* 2: 234–35).

3. Clement of Alexandria, "Who Is the Rich Man That Shall Be Saved?" chap. 34 (*ANF* 2: 601).

4. Tertullian, "On Idolatry," chap. 19 (*ANF* 3: 73).

5. Tertullian, "On the Crown," chap. 11 (*ANF* 3: 99).

6. Origen, "Against Celsus," (*ANF* 4: 558).

7. Tertullian, *Apology*, chap. 5 (*ANF* 3: 22). For other examples of Christian participation in the Roman army, see John Helgeland, Robert J. Daly, and J. Patout Burns, *Christians and the Military: The Early Experience* (London: SCM, 1987).

8. For a discussion of the evidence from the discipline manuals known as "church orders," see Cecil John Cadoux, *Early Christian Attitude to War* (New York: Seabury, 1982), 119–28; and Alan Kreider, "Military Service in the Church Orders" *Journal of Religious Ethics* 31 (2003): 415–42.

9. Tertullian, *Apology*, chap. 30 (*ANF* 3: 42); Origen, *Against Celsus*, bk. 8, chap. 73 (*ANF* 4: 668).

10. Ambrose, *Of the Christian Faith*, bk. 2, chap. 16; quoted in Roland H. Bainton, *Christian Attitudes toward War and Peace: A Historical Survey and Critical Re-evaluation* (Nashville, TN: Abingdon, 1960), 90.

11. Ronald G. Musto, *The Catholic Peace Tradition* (Maryknoll, NY: Orbis, 1986), 59.

12. Alban Butler, *Butler's Lives of the Saints*, concise ed., ed. Michael Walsh (San Francisco: Harper and Row, 1985), 371.

13. For more detail on pacifism in the monastic movement, see Musto, *Catholic Peace Tradition*, 50–61.

14. See Musto, *Catholic Peace Tradition*, 88–96.

15. See Musto, *Catholic Peace Tradition*, chap. 5–8; Bainton, *Christian Attitudes*, chap. 7.

16. John Howard Yoder, *Nevertheless: A Meditation on the Varieties and Shortcomings of Religious Pacifism* (Scottsdale, PA: Herald Press, 1992). For other typologies of pacifism, see Lisa S. Cahill, *Love Your Enemies: Discipleship, Pacifism, and Just War Theory* (Minneapolis: Fortress Press, 1994); Terry Nardin, ed., *The Ethics of War and Peace: Religious and Secular Perspectives*

(Princeton: Princeton University Press, 1996), chap. 9–10; Jenny Teichman, *Pacifism and the Just War: A Study in Applied Philosophy* (Oxford: Basil Blackwell, 1986); and Duane L. Cady, *From Warism to Pacifism: A Moral Continuum* (Philadelphia: Temple University Press, 1989). Given that these are just a few of the many authors who have offered typologies, it might well be asked why there has been such a great interest in delineating types of pacifism. For many authors, one motivation is to argue that one can embrace a moderate, not absolutist, form of pacifism.

Undoubtedly, there are historical and contemporary variations in the Christian practice of nonviolence. Yet in this book, we question the value of dispersing pacifism into camps, especially since pacifists are already so marginalized in ethical and political discourse. We present scales of motivations, goals, and practices that lead to variations that must be appreciated, but when it comes to presenting a pacifist analysis of the problems of war, we prefer to think about pacifism as a more coherent worldview that challenges the dominant discourses of just war and realism.

17. Emil Brunner, *The Divine Imperative: A Study in Christian Ethics*, trans. Olive Wyon (London: Lutterworth, 1937; original German ed., 1932), 470–71.

18. See Brian Frost, *Struggling to Forgive: Nelson Mandela and South Africa's Search for Reconciliation* (London: HarperCollins, 1998). Two short, accessible histories of the ANC are Saul Dubow, *The African National Congress* (Gloucestershire, UK: Sutton Publishing, 2000) and Heidi Holland, *The Struggle: A History of the African National Congress* (New York: G. Braziller, 1990).

19. Leo N. Tolstoy, *My Religion*, trans. Huntingdon Smith (London: Walter Scott, 1889), 38.

20. See Tolstoy, *My Religion*, especially chap. 1–4. It is difficult to ascertain exactly what nonresistance would entail for Tolstoy. For a strong criticism of Tolstoy on this score, see Lloyd Steffen, *The Demonic Turn: The Power of Religion to Inspire or Restrain Violence* (Cleveland: Pilgrim, 2003), 143–65.

21. Ernest J. Simmons, *Leo Tolstoy* (London: John Lehmann, 1949), 791–92.

22. For more information, see Robert Friedmann, *Hutterite Studies* (Goshen, IN: Mennonite Historical Society, 1961).

23. Oliver O'Donovan, *The Just War Revisited* (Cambridge: Cambridge University Press, 2003), 6.

24. O'Donovan, *Just War Revisited*, 5.

25. O'Donovan, *Just War Revisited*, 6.

26. O'Donovan, *Just War Revisited*, 6–7.

27. Paul Christopher, *The Ethics of War and Peace*, 2nd ed. (Upper Saddle River, NJ: Prentice-Hall, 1999), 23. The rest of this paragraph summarizes Christopher's account of Ambrose, at 24–26.

28. See Augustine, "The City of God against the Pagans," ed. R. W. Dyson (Cambridge: Cambridge University Press, 1998), especially bk. 19.

29. Augustine, *Reply to Faustus the Manichean*, vol. 4, bk. 22, par. 75 in *A Select Library of the Nicene and Post-Nicene Fathers of the Christian Church*, ed. Philip Schaff (Grand Rapids, MI: Eerdmans, 1979), 368, www.ccel.org/ccel/schaff/npnf104.html.

30. Augustine, "Letter 229," in *The Political Writings of St. Augustine*, ed. Henry Paolucci (Chicago: Regnery Gateway, 1962), 183.

31. Cahill, *Love Your Enemies*, 56, explaining the work of fellow Christian ethicist James Childress.

32. Augustine, "Reply to Faustus," bk. 22, par. 76, 368.

33. The primary sources for Aquinas's ethics of war are *Summa Theologica*, part II–II, question 29 ("Of Peace"), question 40 ("Of War"), and question 64 ("Of Murder"), trans. Fathers of the English Dominican Province, 4 vols. (New York: Benziger Bros., 1947); and Laurence Shapcote, trans., *The Commandments of God: Conferences on the Two Precepts of Charity and the Ten Commandments* (London: Burns, Oates and Washbourne, 1937).

34. For information on Vitoria (whose last name sometimes appears as "Victoria"), we draw on Christopher, *Ethics of War and Peace*, 53–60; and Cahill, *Love Your Enemies*, 93–94.

35. Christopher, *Ethics of War and Peace*, 60.

36. Christopher, *Ethics of War and Peace*, 98–99.

37. Hugo Grotius, *De jure belli ac pacis libri tres*, trans. Frances W. Kelsey, et al. (Washington, DC: Carnegie Institution of Washington, 1913–1925), vol. 2, bk. 1, chap. 1, par. 10.

38. For example, G. E. M. Anscombe, "War and Murder," in *War and Morality*, ed. Richard A. Wasserstrom (Belmont, CA: Wadsworth, 1970), 42–53.

39. Cited and discussed by John Courtney Murray, SJ, "Remarks on the Moral Problem of War," in *War in the Twentieth Century*, ed. Richard Miller (Louisville, KY: Westminster/John Knox, 1992), 258.

40. Second Vatican Council, "Gaudium et Spes: Pastoral Constitution on the Church in the Modern World," in *Catholic Social Thought: The Documen-*

tary Heritage, ed. David J. O'Brien and Thomas A. Shannon (Maryknoll, NY: Orbis, 1992), par. 78.

41. Richard J. Regan, *Just War: Principles and Cases* (Washington, DC: Catholic University of America Press, 1996), 48–63.

42. Regan calls this action "preventative attack," but his meaning is the same as the more standard term "preemptive attack" (*Just War*, 48–63). Walzer provides standards for distinguishing preventative war (attacking in order to reduce a future threat) from preemptive attacks (striking just before the enemy's planned strike) in *Just and Unjust Wars*, 74–85, and *Arguing about War* (New Haven, CT: Yale University Press, 2004), 143–51.

43. Yoder, *When War Is Unjust*, 150.

44. See Aquinas, *Summa Theologica*, part I–II, ques. 90, art. 4 (on law and the common good) and part II–II, ques. 42, art. 2, reply to obj. 3 (on justified revolt).

45. See Walzer, *Just and Unjust Wars*, 296–303.

46. Augustine, "Reply to Faustus," bk. 22, par. 74, 367.

47. Brian Orend, "War," *The Stanford Encyclopedia of Philosophy*, Winter 2005 edition, ed. Edward N. Zalta, http://plato.stanford.edu/archives/sum2002/entries/war/, sec 2.1.

48. Helmut David Baer and Joseph E. Capizzi argue that reconfiguring just war theory around right intention and highlighting its relationship to a theory of politics corrects shortcomings in recent applications of the tradition. See "Just War Theory and the Problem of International Politics: On the Central Role of Just Intention," *Journal of the Society of Christian Ethics* 26, no. 1 (Spring/Summer 2006): 163–75.

49. Regan links right intention to all the other just decision criteria in this manner (*Just War*, 84–86).

50. Summarizing Yoder, *When War Is Unjust*, 155.

51. An interesting set of examples from Walzer are first-person accounts by soldiers who refused to fire on unarmed and unaware enemies (*Just and Unjust Wars*, 138–43).

52. See John Ford, "The Morality of Obliteration Bombing," in *War in the Twentieth Century*, ed. Richard Miller (Louisville, KY: Westminster/John Knox, 1992), 138–77.

53. Yoder, *When War Is Unjust*, 158.

54. O'Donovan, *Just War Revisited*, 45–46.

55. Walzer, *Just and Unjust Wars*, 152–57.

56. These documents, available on various websites, are conveniently collected in Adam Roberts and Richard Guelff, eds., *Documents on the Laws of War*, 3rd ed. (Oxford: Oxford University Press, 2000).

57. Reinhold Niebuhr, "Augustine's Political Realism," in *Christian Realism and Political Problems* (New York: Scribner's, 1952), 119–46.

58. Note that double effect reasoning cannot be applied here because the requirement that the bad effect is not a means to the good result is not satisfied: the death and injury of civilians was intended as a means to influence the leaders of Japan to surrender.

59. Walzer, *Just and Unjust Wars*, 254.

60. Jean Bethke Elshtain, "Reflections on War and Political Discourse," in *Just War Theory*, ed. Jean Bethke Elshtain (Oxford: Blackwell, 1992), 268.

61. Paul Ramsey, "Is Vietnam a Just War?" in *War in the Twentieth Century*, ed. Richard B. Miller (Louisville, KY: Westminster/John Knox, 1992), 185–97.

62. George Weigel, "World Order: What Catholics Forgot," *First Things*, no. 143 (May 2004): 31–38.

63. Jean Bethke Elshtain, *Just War against Terror* (New York: Basic Books, 2003), chap. 7.

64. James Childress, "Just War Theories: The Bases, Interrelations, Priorities, and Functions of Their Criteria," *Theological Studies* 39 (1978): 427–45.

65. James Childress, "Just War Criteria," in *War or Peace? The Search for New Answers*, ed. Thomas A. Shannon (Maryknoll, NY: Orbis, 1980), 40–58.

66. Glen H. Stassen, ed. *Just Peacemaking: Ten Practices for Abolishing War*, 2nd ed. (Cleveland: Pilgrim, 2004).

67. For a short sample of this debate, see Paul J. Griffiths and George Weigel, "Who Wants War? An Exchange," *First Things*, no. 152 (April 2005): 10–11. For a fully developed argument against Childress's "presumption against violence" position, see Helmut David Baer and Joseph E. Capizzi, "Just War Theories Reconsidered: Problems with Prima Facie Duties and the Need for a Political Ethic," *Journal of Religious Ethics* 33 (Spring 2005): 119–37.

68. Resources cited by the Illinois Council Against Handgun Violence state, "A gun in the home is 4 times more likely to be involved in an unintentional shooting, 7 times more likely to be used to commit a criminal assault or homicide, and 11 times more likely to be used to attempt or commit suicide than to be used in self-defense." From www.ichv.org/Statistics.htm, accessed June 30, 2006.

69. A common good–based argument for gun control, with supporting statistics and model legislation, is Amitai Etzioni and Steven Hellend, "The Case for Domestic Disarmament," The Communitarian Network, 1992, www.gwu.edu/~ccps/pop_disarm.html.

70. See the important work of Christian ethicist and former police officer Tobias Winright. Three of his several relevant essays are "The Perpetrator as Person: Theological Reflections on the Just War Tradition and the Use of Force by Police," *Criminal Justice Ethics* 14 (1995): 37–56; "Two Rival Versions of Just War Theory and the Presumption against Harm in Policing," *Annual of the Society of Christian Ethics* 18 (1998): 221–39; and "From Police Officers to Peace Officers," in *Wisdom of the Cross,* ed. Stanley Hauerwas, et al. (Grand Rapids, MI: Eerdmans, 1999), 84–114.

71. Walzer, *Just and Unjust Wars,* 228. His analysis of problems relating to the sliding scale is found in chap. 14–18.

72. For a news report of the incident, see Steven Erlanger, "Crisis in the Balkans: Belgrade; Survivors of NATO Attack on Serb TV Headquarters: Luck, Pluck and Resolve," *New York Times,* April 24, 1999, A6. For more discussion of this and similar incidents, see the section *Pacifist Responses to the Intervention in Kosovo* in chapter 3 of this book.

73. John Howard Yoder, *The Politics of Jesus,* rev. ed. (Grand Rapids, MI: Eerdmans, 1994), chap. 12.

NOTES TO CHAPTER 3

1. Bill Clinton, "Remarks by the President to the KFOR Troops," June 22, 1999, in *Humanitarian Intervention: Crafting a Workable Doctrine. Three Options Presented as Memoranda to the President* by Alton Frye (Washington, DC: Council on Foreign Relations, 2000), 76, http://www.cfr.org/pdf/Human_Intervent_Book.pdf.

2. Kofi A. Annan, *The Question of Intervention* (New York: United Nations, 1999), 4.

3. Paul Ramsey, "Is Vietnam a Just War?" in Richard B. Miller, ed. *War in the Twentieth Century* (Louisville, KY: Westminster/John Knox, 1992), 186.

4. For an exploration of these other options—a natural or a providential way out or martyrdom—see John Howard Yoder, *What Would You Do?,* rev. ed. (Scottsdale, PA: Herald Press, 1992).

5. Paul Christopher, *The Ethics of War and Peace,* 2nd ed. (Upper Saddle River, NJ: Prentice-Hall, 1999), 193 (emphasis removed).

6. To speak of humanitarian intervention as anything other than war is controversial to some just war thinkers. This type of military action and a defensive military action are just when, among other reasons, they serve the cause of restoring just order. The political-order interpreters of just war, discussed in chapter 2, think it inappropriate to speak of the altruistic motives of humanitarian intervention in distinction to other instances of war, giving the impression that other forms of war cannot be altruistic. They think the matter is clearer when all cases of military action are analyzed in terms of just cause and right intention.

7. Nico Krisch, "Legality, Morality, and the Dilemma of Humanitarian Intervention after Kosovo," *European Journal of International Law* 13, no. 1 (2002): 323–63, www.ejil.org/journal/Vol13/No1/br1.html. See section 2 of this essay for a review of some attempts to establish legal criteria for humanitarian intervention.

8. A standard textbook in international law establishes the principle of nonintervention as a strong, prima facie duty of all states, which can be overridden only in exceptional circumstances. See Gerhard von Glahn, *Law among Nations: An Introduction to Public International Law,* 7th ed. (New York: Longman, 1995), 578–89.

9. United Nations, *Charter of the United Nations,* June 26, 1945, www.un.org/aboutun/charter/index.html.

10. To respond to this failing in international law, UN Secretary General Kofi Annan has promoted the concept of individual sovereignty, which he defines as "the human rights and fundamental freedoms of each and every individual . . . [and] the right of every individual to control his or her destiny." The principle of national sovereignty should accommodate individual sovereignty. See *Question of Intervention,* 37.

11. International Commission on Intervention and State Sovereignty, *The Responsibility to Protect* (Ottawa: International Development Research Centre, 2001), www.iciss.ca/report-en.asp.

12. For the history of the Declaration of Universal Human Rights, see Mary Ann Glendon, *A World Made New: Eleanor Roosevelt and the Universal Declaration of Human Rights* (New York: Random House, 2001). The texts of ten major human rights documents are collected in the Office of the High Commissioner for Human Rights, *Basic Human Rights Instruments,* 3rd ed.

(Geneva: Office of the High Commissioner for Human Rights, 1998). This book includes a list of countries that have ratified seven human rights covenants.

13. The Genocide Convention of 1948 is the source of the definition of genocide operative in international law; the definition includes preventing members of a group from having children or forcibly transferring their children to others. See Adam Roberts and Richard Guelff, eds., *Documents on the Laws of War*, 3rd ed. (Oxford: Oxford University Press, 2000), 179–94.

14. The Rwanda figure is from Ingvar Carlsson, Han Sung-Joo, and Rufus M. Kupolati, *Report of the Independent Inquiry into the Actions of the United Nations During the 1994 Genocide in Rwanda* (New York: United Nations, 1999), 3, http://www.un.org/Docs/journal/asp/ws.asp?m=S/1999/1257. The Coalition for International Justice, a now-defunct advocacy group, determined the Darfur figure based on statistical research, and the figure is now widely cited by humanitarian groups (for instance, www.savedarfur.org/pages/background) and by the UN.

15. *The Responsibility to Protect* report of the International Commission on Intervention and State Sovereignty, cited earlier, is one significant move in this direction.

16. In addition to the literature cited in this chapter, see the following: John B. Allcock, *Explaining Yugoslavia*, 2nd ed. (New York: Columbia University Press, 2004); Misha Glenny, *The Balkans: Nationalism, War, and the Great Powers, 1804–1999* (New York: Penguin, 2001); Tim Judah, *Kosovo: War and Revenge*, 2nd ed. (New Haven: Yale University Press, 2002); Robert D. Kaplan, *Balkan Ghosts: A Journey Through History*, reprint ed. (New York: Picador, 2005); Peter Maass, *Love Thy Neighbor: A Story of War*, reprint ed. (New York: Vintage, 1997); Laura Silber and Allan Little, *Yugoslavia: Death of a Nation* (New York: Penguin, 1997).

17. "Yugoslavia and Kosovo: A Primer" (sidebar), *New York Times*, March 28, 1999, A17.

18. Tim Judah, "A Brief History of Serbia," in *Kosovo: Contending Voices on Balkan Interventions*, ed. William Joseph Buckley (Grand Rapids, MI.: Eerdmans, 2000), 90.

19. Samantha Power, *"A Problem from Hell": America and the Age of Genocide* (New York: Perennial, 2002), 445.

20. Power, *"A Problem from Hell,"* 445.

21. Power, *"A Problem from Hell,"* 446.

22. Milosevic was not only brutal abroad, he was also corrupt at home. Serb citizens demonstrated against him as early as 1996 (Power, *"A Problem from Hell,"* 444).

23. For an analysis of Russia's role, see Zbigniew Bryzinski, "The Failed Double-Cross," in *Kosovo: Contending Voices,* 328–32.

24. Elisa Haney, "NATO in Kosovo: 1998–1999" (timeline chart), Infoplease, www.infoplease.com/spot/kosovo-timeline1.html, accessed June 30, 2006.

25. Power, *"A Problem from Hell,"* 472.

26. Developments on the war crimes tribunal can be followed at the official website for the International Criminal Tribunal for Former Yugoslavia (www.un.org/icty/) and at the Coalition for International Justice (www.cij.org), a nonprofit group that conducts advocacy and public education about war crimes trials.

27. J. Bryan Hehir, "Kosovo: A War of Values and the Values of War," in *Kosovo: Contending Voices,* 399–400.

28. Vaclav Havel, "Address to the Senate and House of Commons of the Parliament of Canada," in *Kosovo: Contending Voices,* 244–45.

29. Michael Walzer, "Kosovo" in *Kosovo: Contending Voices,* 335.

30. Walzer, "Kosovo," 335.

31. Power, *"A Problem from Hell,"* 472.

32. Alkman Granitsas, "Paradigm Slip," *New Republic,* April 11, 2005, 14–15.

33. This theory was dubbed the "wag the dog" syndrome, taken from the title of a concurrent movie in which a president starts a war (an imaginary, public-relations creation in the movie's scenario) to distract the public from his personal foibles. We take no position on whether President Clinton was so motivated. Of course, such an intention would violate just war doctrine. However, to assert it is hardly the strongest charge in the critics' portfolio.

34. Power, *"A Problem from Hell,"* 451–54.

35. See Robert S. McNamara with Brian VanDeMark, *In Retrospect: The Tragedy and Lessons of Vietnam,* reprint ed. (New York: Vintage, 1996), esp. 319–35.

36. BBC News, "NATO 'Violated Human Rights' in Kosovo," February 7, 2000, http://news.bbc.co.uk/1/hi/world/europe/633909.stm, accessed June 30, 2006.

37. Such was the charge by the organizations Amnesty International and Human Rights Watch. See BBC News, "NATO Accused of War Crimes," June 7, 2000, http://news.bbc.co.uk/1/hi/world/europe/780547.stm, accessed June 30, 2006.

38. Robert L. Phillips and Duane L. Cady, *Humanitarian Intervention: Just War vs. Pacifism* (Lanham, MD: Rowman and Littlefield, 1996), 60.

39. See Jeremy A. Rabkin, *Law without Nations? Why Constitutional Government Requires Sovereign States* (Princeton, NJ: Princeton University Press, 2005).

40. See Granitsas, "Paradigm Slip," 14–15; and Jeremy Kahn, "Final Status Quo," *New Republic*, June 26, 2006, 11–13.

41. Misha Glenny, "A Balkan Success Story: Reflections on Macedonia," *New Statesman*, September 26, 2005, www.lexis-nexis.com.

NOTES TO CHAPTER 4

1. *Encyclopædia Britannica*, 15th ed., s.v. "Amphictyony."

2. Carl von Clausewitz, *On War*, trans. Michael Howard and Peter Paret (Princeton: Princeton University Press, 1976), 75–76.

3. Michael Howard, "*Temperamenta Belli*: Can War be Controlled?" in *Just War Theory, Readings in Social and Political Theory*, ed. Jean Bethke Elshtain (Oxford: Blackwell, 1992), 27–28.

4. For more information on the Prisoner's Dilemma, see Morton D. Davis, *Game Theory: A Nontechnical Introduction*, rev. ed. (London: Dover Publications, 1997).

5. Second Lateran Council, Canon 29, in *Decrees of the Ecumenical Councils*, vol. 1, *Nicaea I to Lateran V*, ed. Norman P. Tanner (London: Sheed and Ward, 1990), 203. The canons are also available on the web at www.catholicculture.org/docs/doc_view.cfm?recnum=5333. For the Flanders ban, see Galbert de Bruges, *The Murder of Charles the Good, Count of Flanders*, rev. ed., trans. James Bruce Ross (New York: Harper and Row, 1967). For more information about archery in the medieval period, see Jim Bradbury, *The Medieval Archer* (Woodbridge, U.K.: Boydell Press, 1985).

6. James Turner Johnson, *Just War Tradition and the Restraint of War: A Moral and Historical Inquiry* (Princeton, NJ: Princeton University Press, 1981), 129.

7. For the documents of the Hague Conventions on war, together with many others, see Adam Roberts and Richard Guelff, eds., *Documents on the Laws of War*, 3rd ed. (Oxford: Oxford University Press, 2000). This quote is at 77.

8. See Julian Perry Robinson, "Chemical Weapons for NATO? A Framework for Considering Policy Options," in *Chemical Weapons and Chemical Arms Control*, Papers and Discussion From a Conference at the American Academy of Arts and Sciences, Boston, Massachusetts, January 21–22, 1977, ed. Matthew Meselson (New York: Carnegie Endowment for International Peace, 1978).

9. Wilfred Owen, "Dulce et Decorum Est," in *The Collected Poems of Wilfred Owen* (London: Chatto & Windus, 1963), 55–56. Reprinted by permission of New Directions Publishing Corp.

10. See Roberts and Guelff, *Documents on the Laws of War*, 155–67.

11. Joseph Cirincione, Jon B. Wolfsthal, and Miriam Rajkumar, *Deadly Arsenals: Nuclear, Biological and Chemical Threats,* rev. ed. (New York: Carnegie Endowment for International Peace, 2005), 13.

12. Paul Christopher, *The Ethics of War and Peace,* 2nd ed. (Upper Saddle River, NJ: Prentice-Hall, 1999), 217.

13. See Sheldon H. Harris, *Factories of Death: Japanese Biological Warfare, 1932–1945, and the American Cover-Up* (New York: Routledge, 2002).

14. Cirincione, *Deadly Arsenals*, 10–11.

15. See Gregg Easterbrook, "Term Limits," *New Republic*, October 7, 2002, 22–25.

16. "Treaty on the Non-Proliferation of Nuclear Weapons" (July 1, 1968), article 6, http://disarmament2.un.org/wmd/npt/npttext.html.

17. Geneva Graduate Institute of International Studies, *Small Arms Survey 2005* (Oxford: Oxford University Press, 2005), 256–57.

18. Stockholm International Peace Research Institute, "Financial Value of the Arms Trade," www.sipri.org/contents/armstrad/at_gov_ind_data.html. The United Kingdom figure used is Ministry of Defence data for the "Value of deliveries of defence equipment and additional aerospace equipment and services" in 2003.

19. Stockholm International Peace Research Institute, "International Arms Embargoes," www.sipri.org/contents/armstrad/embargoes.html.

20. For a survey, see Stockholm International Peace Research Institute, *SIPRI Yearbook 2004* (Oxford: Oxford University Press, 2004), 737–62.

21. International Campaign to Ban Landmines, *Landmine Monitor Report 2004* (Geneva: International Campaign to Ban Landmines, 2004).

22. Second Lateran Council, Canons 12, 14, 18, and 29, in Tanner, 199–203.

23. James Turner Johnson, *Ideology, Reason, and the Limitation of War: Religious and Secular Concepts 1200–1740* (Princeton, NJ: Princeton University Press, 1975), 179–94 (on the problems with jus ad bellum) and 195 (on the prominence of jus in bello).

24. Johnson, *Ideology*, 195.

25. Johnson, *Ideology*, 198.

26. G. E. M. Anscombe, "Mr. Truman's Degree," in *War in the Twentieth Century*, ed. Richard B. Miller (Louisville, KY: Westminster/John Knox, 1992), 240.

27. Reinhold Niebuhr, "The Atomic Bomb," in *Love and Justice: Selections from the Shorter Writings of Reinhold Niebuhr*, ed. D. B. Robertson (Louisville, KY: Westminster/John Knox, 1992), 233.

28. Reinhold Niebuhr, Letter to James B. Conant, March 12, 1946; reprinted in the appendix of James G. Hershberg, "Footnote on Hiroshima and Atomic Morality: Conant, Niebuhr, and an 'Emotional' Clergyman, 1945-46," *SHAFR Newsletter*, December 2002, www.shafr.org/newsletter/2002/dec/hiroshima.htm.

29. Niebuhr, "The Atomic Bomb," 233–34.

30. Reinhold Niebuhr, "The Bombing of Germany," in *Love and Justice*, 223.

31. Niebuhr, "The Bombing of Germany," 223.

32. Paul Ramsey, "A Political Ethics Context for Strategic Thinking," in *War in the Twentieth Century*, ed. Richard B. Miller (Louisville, KY: Westminster/John Knox, 1992), 296.

33. Ramsey, "Political Ethics Context," 302.

34. Ramsey, "Political Ethics Context," 305.

35. Pope John XXIII, "Pacem in Terris: Peace on Earth," in *Catholic Social Thought: The Documentary Heritage*, ed. David J. O'Brien and Thomas A. Shannon (Maryknoll, NY: Orbis, 1992), par. 113.

36. National Conference of Catholic Bishops, "The Challenge of Peace: God's Promise and Our Response," in *Catholic Social Thought*. See par. 147–49 on counterpopulation use, 150–56 on first use, 157–61 on limited nuclear war, and 163–99 on deterrence.

37. United Methodist Council of Bishops (U.S.A.), "In Defense of Creation: The Nuclear Crisis and a Just Peace," in *War in the Twentieth Century*, ed. Richard B. Miller (Louisville, KY: Westminster/John Knox, 1992), 428.

38. National Conference of Catholic Bishops, *Sowing Weapons of War: A Pastoral Reflection on the Arms Trade and Landmines,* June 16, 1995, par. 1, www.usccb.org/sdwp/international/armstrade.htm.

39. C. J. Chivers, "Ill-Secured Soviet Arms Depots Tempting Rebels and Terrorists," *New York Times,* July 16, 2005, A1.

40. Debate continues among historians as to whether such alternatives would have effected Japan's surrender. An influential argument that "atomic diplomacy" would have worked is found in Gar Alperovitz, et al., *The Decision to Use the Atomic Bomb and the Architecture of an American Myth* (New York: Knopf, 1995). An argument that it would not have worked and that Truman had no viable political and military option but to drop the bomb is found in Wilson D. Miscamble, *From Roosevelt to Truman: Potsdam, Hiroshima, and the Cold War* (Cambridge: Cambridge University Press, 2006), chap. 6. A survey of recent historical inquiries is found in Samuel Walker, "Recent Literature on Truman's Atomic Bomb Decision: A Search for Middle Ground," *Diplomatic History* 29 (April 2005): 311–34.

41. Stockholm International Peace Research Institute, *SIPRI Yearbook 2006* (Oxford: Oxford University Press, 2006), chap. 8.

42. Michael J. Mazarr, "Strike Out," *New Republic,* August 15, 2005, 15–17.

NOTES TO CHAPTER 5

1. National Memorial Institute for the Prevention of Terrorism, MIPT Terrorism Knowledge Database, "Glossary," s.vv. "international terrorism" and "domestic terrorism," www.tkb.org/Glossary.jsp.

2. The statistic on deaths from war is a World Health Organization estimate cited by Gregg Easterbrook, "The End of War?" *New Republic,* May 30, 2005, 19. For the statistics on deaths from terrorism, see the next note.

3. The MIPT is a nonprofit institute that receives funding from the U.S. Department of Homeland Security's Office for Domestic Preparedness. The database is managed by the Rand Corporation, DFI International, and university researchers. The database can be accessed by the public on the Internet at www.tkb.org/. The following statistics were developed using this site's Incident Analysis Wizard. The statistics are accurate through June 30, 2006.

4. The data on groups were also compiled from the MIPT Incident Analysis Wizard and are accurate through November 30, 2006.

5. The most recent list, for 2005, is found at the Department of State, Office of the Coordinator for Counterterrorism, "Fact Sheet: Foreign Terrorist Organizations (FTOs)," October 11, 2005, www.state.gov/s/ct/rls/fs/37191 .htm (accessed July 17, 2006).

6. Home Office, "Security: Proscribed Terrorist Groups," www.homeoffice .gov.uk/security/terrorism-and-the-law/terrorism-act/proscribed-groups (accessed July 17, 2006).

7. This movement is just one of several strands of a diffuse militant subculture in the United States. Some strands are motivated primarily by Christian fundamentalism, some by racism, some by pro-gun philosophy. The ideologies of all these groups, for the most part, are compatible because they see modern culture and liberal government as their common enemies. McVeigh's great passions in the movement were centered around gun ownership. For placing McVeigh in this movement, see Mark Juergensmeyer, *Terror in the Mind of God*, 3rd ed. (Berkeley: University of California Press, 2003), 30–36.

8. The following summary and quotes rely on MIPT Terrorism Knowledge Database, "Other Group Attacked Airports & Airlines Target (Dec. 21, 1988, United Kingdom)," www.tkb.org/Incident.jsp?incID=5728.

9. We use the term "jihadist" to indicate those extremists within Islam who are inspired by a holy war ideal. "Islamists" or "Muslim extremists" are among the other terms in use, but we think that these terms risk blurring the distinction between the relatively small number of adherents associated with violence and the rest of the world's 1.7 billion Muslims. "Islamism" (or "political Islam") is a term referring to the ideological movement seeking to establish strict Islamic law in historically Muslim nations and those with Muslim majorities. A good scholarly resource on these matters is Sohail H. Hashmi, ed., *Islamic Political Ethics: Civil Society, Pluralism, and Conflict* (Princeton, NJ: Princeton University Press, 2002.)

10. There is, of course, a wealth of literature on this organization and the man who plotted and inspired the airplane attacks on the World Trade Center and Pentagon. One useful, factual overview runs through *The 9/11 Commission Report* by the National Commission on Terrorist Attacks upon the United States (New York: W.W. Norton, 2004).

11. See Peter L. Bergen, *Holy War, Inc.: Inside the Secret World of Osama bin Laden* (New York: Free Press, 2001), 105–26 (on the embassy bombings), 136–38 (on the 1993 World Trade Center bombing), and 167–94 (on the USS *Cole* bombing). Bergen is a journalist for CNN who interviewed bin Laden in

Afghanistan in 1997. Bin Laden told Bergen that he was not involved in the 1995 and 1996 bombings of locations in Saudi Arabia that housed American military personnel, often attributed to al Qaeda.

12. "Group Profile: Abu Hafs al-Masri Brigade," MIPT Terrorism Knowledge Database, www.tkb.org/Group.jsp?groupID=3903 (accessed July 17, 2006).

13. Ronald Reagan, "Proclamation 4809, Afghanistan Day," March 10, 1982, The Ronald Reagan Presidential Library archive of presidential speeches, www.reagan.utexas.edu/archives/speeches/1982/31082c.htm.

14. However, the U.S. State Department denies that it gave any support to the "Afghan Arabs"; it says that it gave money only to native Afghans while Arab sources supported the ideological immigrants. In support of its position, it cites writings by al Qaeda's number two leader, Ayman al-Zawahiri. See U.S. Department of State, "Did the U.S. 'Create' Osama bin Laden?" January 14, 2005, http://usinfo.state.gov/media/Archive/2005/Jan/24-318760.html. Still, it is not clear that the United States was able to effectively sort through the complex interaction of the many groups constituting the mujahideen. Nor could it prevent its arms from flowing from native Afghans to Afghan Arab parties.

15. Caleb Carr, *The Lessons of Terror* (New York: Random House, 2002), 240.

16. Bruce Hoffman, *Inside Terrorism* (New York: Columbia University Press, 1998), 36–37. (A revised and expanded edition was issued in mid-2006, too late to be consulted in the research for this book.)

17. Hoffman, *Inside Terrorism*, 28–30.

18. Much literature on terrorism spends a lot of space working through the complexities of definition. The exercise can be useful, but it requires a book-length treatment of terrorism. For a good analysis of the factors that make terrorism difficult to define and a sensible path to a definition, see Hoffman, *Inside Terrorism*, 11–44.

19. Cynthia C. Combs, *Terrorism in the Twenty-First Century*, 3rd ed. (Upper Saddle River, NJ: Prentice-Hall, 2002), 10 (italics removed).

20. Quoted by Thomas L. Friedman, "Giving the Hatemongers No Place to Hide," *New York Times,* July 22, 2005, A19.

21. Don DeLillo, *Mao II* (New York: Viking, 1991), 157; quoted in Juergensmeyer, *Terror in the Mind of God*, 141.

22. Juergensmeyer, *Terror in the Mind of God*, 126.

23. Juergensmeyer, *Terror in the Mind of God,* 126. The IRA example that follows is our own application.

24. Hoffman, *Inside Terrorism,* 14.

25. Carr, *Lessons of Terror,* 6 (italics removed).

26. Carr, *Lessons of Terror,* 6.

27. United States Code, Title 22, Chapter 38, § 2656f. Available from various sources, including the U.S. Government, *United States Code,* www.access .gpo.gov/uscode/. A searchable version is provided by the Legal Information Institute, *U.S. Code Collection,* http://straylight.law.cornell.edu/uscode/. Hoffman notes that this is one of three official government definitions of terrorism, "each of which reflects the priorities and particular interests of the agency involved" (*Inside Terrorism,* 38).

28. These three models were suggested to us by Edward LeRoy Long Jr., *Facing Terrorism: Responding as Christians* (Louisville, KY: Westminster/John Knox, 2004), chap. 3.

29. Caleb Carr, "Terrorism as Warfare: The Lessons of Military History," *World Policy Journal* 13, no. 4 (Winter 1996/97): 1. Carr slightly rewords this statement in *Lessons of Terror,* 8–9.

30. Susan B. Glasser, "U.S. Figures Show Sharp Global Rise in Terrorism," *Washington Post,* April 27, 2005, A1, www.washingtonpost.com/wp-dyn/content/article/2005/04/26/AR2005042601623.html.

31. Mark Thompson and Bruce Crumley, "Are These Towers Safe?" *Time,* June 20, 2005, 34–42.

32. To be sure, the controversial provisions of the original Patriot Act—such as governmental powers to access library records and bookstore purchases, to place "roving wiretaps," and to search homes under loose judicial warrants—were debated in both houses of the Congress when the Act was up for extension at the end of 2005. But the Act was reauthorized by strong majorities in the U.S. Congress and signed into law by President Bush on March 9, 2006, with very few changes. The text of the U.S.A. Patriot Act of 2001 and the improvement legislation of 2005 can be found at the Library of Congress's THOMAS website, by searching http://thomas.loc.gov/bss/d107/d107laws.html for Public Law 107–56, and http://thomas.loc.gov/bss/d109/d109laws.html for Public Law 109–177. One can also search for several other bills in 2005 and 2006 that extended provisions of the original legislation that were due to expire.

NOTES TO CHAPTER 6

1. We will refer to the war to oust Iraq from Kuwait in January–March 1991 as the "(Persian) Gulf War" and the U.S./U.K.-led invasion of Iraq in March–April 2003 as the "(2003) Iraq War." President George W. Bush declared "major combat operations" to be concluded on May 1, 2003; the subsequent period of fighting against U.S. troops and other international forces is the Iraqi insurgency, which has overlapped with a growing Iraqi sectarian conflict. Both should be considered a continuation of the Iraq War.

2. It may seem too familiar or condescending to refer to the former Iraqi president as "Saddam," but it is a better representation of his proper name than "Hussein" used by itself, which is actually his father's first name. "Saddam" by itself is the name by which he was widely known in the Arab world.

3. This subsection draws on Charles Tripp, *A History of Iraq* (Cambridge: Cambridge University Press, 2000). See also Marion Farouk-Sluglett and Peter Sluglett, *Iraq Since 1958: From Revolution to Dictatorship* (London: IB Tauris, 1990); and Geoff Simons, *Iraq: From Sumer to Saddam,* 2nd ed. (Basingstoke, U.K.: Macmillan, 1996).

4. Note here Farouk-Sluglett and Sluglett's argument that the fundamental division was not religious but socioeconomic, though the two frequently coincided as most of those living in the rural south were Shiite (*Iraq Since 1958*, 190–200).

5. This dislike of Iran did not stop operatives in the Reagan administration from funneling arms to Iran in the mid-1980s in the hopes of nurturing a relationship with supposed Iranian moderates, an incident known as the "Iran-Contra Affair."

6. Estimates of casualties from the war vary widely. These figures are from Farouk-Sluglett and Sluglett, *Iraq Since 1958*, 272. Simons cites figures in the range of 105,000–300,000 for Iraqi fatalities and 262,000–580,000 for Iranian deaths (Simons, *Iraq*, 317).

7. Samantha Power, *"A Problem from Hell": America and the Age of Genocide* (New York: Perennial, 2002), 172.

8. Power, *"A Problem from Hell,"* 187.

9. Power, *"A Problem from Hell,"* 191.

10. Power, *"A Problem from Hell,"* 172–73.

11. George H. W. Bush was the forty-first U.S. president and is the father of George W. Bush, the forty-third U.S. president. We will sometimes call him "the senior Bush" to avoid confusion.

12. Lawrence Freedman and Efraim Karsh, *The Gulf Conflict 1990-1991* (London: Faber and Faber, 1993), 47–48.

13. Unofficial transcripts of the meeting indicate that Glaspie also conveyed the U.S. government's concern about Iraq's amassing of troops and public statements about Kuwait. See Micah L. Sifry and Christopher Cerf, eds., *The Gulf War Reader* (New York: Times Books, 1991), 130.

14. For more information on the history of the invasion, see Steven A. Yetiv, *The Persian Gulf Crisis* (Westport, CT: Greenwood Press, 1997), 10–11; and John Levins, *Days of Fear: The Inside Story of the Iraqi Invasion and Occupation of Kuwait* (Dubai: Motivate Publishing, 1997), 20–77.

15. United Nations, "Security Council Resolutions—1990," s.v. Resolution 660 and Resolution 661, www.un.org/Docs/scres/1990/scres90.htm.

16. The meeting is described in Freedman and Karsh, *The Gulf Conflict*, 253–60.

17. The casualty figures in the table are discussed in Jack Kelly, "Estimates of Deaths in First War Still in Dispute," *Pittsburgh Post-Gazette*, February 16, 2003, www.post-gazette.com/nation/20030216casualty0216p5.asp. The number of civilian deaths caused by coalition forces and crossfire is not as widely disputed or as hard to estimate as the number of Iraqi soldier deaths.

18. One American colonel described what he told his soldiers: "It's not just a retreating army. These guys are rapists, killers, murderers. And coincidentally, a Scud [missile] had just hit Dahran airport and killed 60 Americans. And I convinced them, and I'm sure that I did, that they needed to put some hate in their heart and go out and stop the son of a bitches from getting out of Kuwait." Col. David Baker interviewed on the PBS show "Frontline," February 4, 1997, "Transcript: part 2," www.pbs.org/wgbh/pages/frontline/gulf/script_b.html.

19. U.S. General Barry R. McCaffrey was criticized for allowing these actions to occur on his command. He was cleared by an Army investigation shortly after the war, even though a full picture of the massacre didn't come to light until much later. The argument that McCaffrey was responsible for war crimes was first made by Seymour Hersh, "Overwhelming Force: What Happened in the Final Days of the Gulf War?" *New Yorker*, May 22, 2000, 49–82. McCaffrey responded in print in "The *New Yorker's* Revisionist History," *Wall Street Journal*, May 22, 2000, A38. He was further defended by journalist Georgie Anne Geyer, "Seymour Hersh's Gulf War Misconceptions," *Chicago Tribune*, May 19, 2000, 23.

20. Frank J. Gaffney Jr., and James A. Baker, "Pro/Con: Should the Gulf War Coalition Have Pursued the War into Iraq in 1991?" *The Retired Officer Magazine* 57, no. 2 (February 2001): 32–38.

21. See Hans Blix, *Disarming Iraq* (New York: Pantheon Books, 2004), 20–40.

22. Anthony H. Cordesman, *Iraq and the War of Sanctions: Conventional Threats and Weapons of Mass Destruction* (London: Praeger, 1999), 128–29.

23. Richard Garfield, "Morbidity and Mortality in Iraq, 1990–1998," Occasional Paper, Fourth Freedom Forum, Indiana, July 1999, www.casi.org.uk/info/garfield/dr-garfield.html. For a broader assessment of the impact of sanctions on Iraq, see Sarah Graham-Brown, *Sanctioning Saddam: The Politics of Intervention in Iraq* (London: IB Tauris, 1999), 153–72.

24. A final problem was revealed at the end of this sorry episode: After the second war on Iraq, it was revealed that some UN officials administering the oil-for-food program were themselves abusing the program for their own benefit. These officials included the son of UN Secretary General Kofi Annan. In short, almost every player involved in the sanctions had dirty hands. See the Independent Inquiry Committee into the United Nations Oil-for-Food Programme, "Report on the Management of the Oil-for-Food Programme," September 7, 2005, www.iic-offp.org/documents/Sept05/WG_Impact.pdf and related documents at www.iic-offp.org/documents.htm.

25. The term is from Christopher J. Insole, *The Politics of Human Frailty: A Theological Defence of Political Liberalism* (London: SCM Press, 2004), chap. 3. Insole finds the language in Bush's post–September 11 speeches. The theological roots of this eschatology, according to Insole, are the doctrines of John Calvin and of the Protestant denominations that followed him. The historical roots of this eschatology in America are the Puritans. Their Calvinist faith inspired a sense of grand mission in the New World, not simply to practice their faith freely but to become the modern-day versions of the biblical "city on a hill" and "light to the nations."

26. Both advocates and critics have presented creative interpretations of the reasons for war or attempted to discern the real underlying motives of the American and British administrations. There is a vast literature of print journalism, internet sites, and mass-market books about these issues. We bypass these discussions not because they are not worth considering, but to keep our discussion manageable. As it is, most of the additional pro and con arguments can be allied to the four that we discuss.

27. The use of the terms in the run-up to the war could lead to confusion, since the term "preventive war" had not been systematically used before 2002 and many popular media accounts after 2002 used the two terms interchangeably. The Bush administration employed the term "preemption" but applied it in a way that we consider preventive. The criteria we are about to cite from Walzer are essential to keeping the arguments clear.

28. Michael Walzer, *Just and Unjust Wars*, 3rd ed. (New York: Basic Books, 2000), 81.

29. For instance, Christopher Hitchens wrote, "Totalitarian regimes are innately and inherently aggressive and unstable. . . . If there is to be a war with them, as there must needs be, then it is ill-advised to let them choose the time or the place of engagement." *A Long Short War: The Postponed Liberation of Iraq* (New York: Plume, 2003), 4.

30. "German bishops warn Iraq war would violate international law," *Agence France Presse*, January 21, 2003, www.lexis-nexis.com.

31. For the transcript of his presentation, see the White House, "U.S. Secretary of State Colin Powell Addresses the U.N. Security Council," February 5, 2003, www.whitehouse.gov/news/releases/2003/02/20030205-1.html. Powell later stated his regret for making this presentation, although he said that did not change his mind about the rightness of the war ("Powell regrets UN speech on Iraq WMDs," ABC News Online, September 9, 2005, www.abc.net.au/news/newsitems/200509/s1456650.htm).

32. Foreword by Tony Blair to the U.K. Government Report, "Iraq's Weapons of Mass Destruction: The Assessment of the British Government," September 24, 2002, www.number-10.gov.uk/output/Page271.asp.

33. United Nations, "Security Council Resolutions 2002," s.v. Resolution 1441, November 8, 2002, www.un.org/Docs/scres/2002/sc2002.htm.

34. See the relevant briefs and reports at United Nations Monitoring, Verification, and Inspection Commission, "Selected Security Council Briefings," www.un.org/Depts/unmovic/new/pages/security_council_briefings.asp.

35. Reported by Sam Tanenhaus, "Bush's Brain Trust," *Vanity Fair*, July 2003, 114–19, www.lexis-nexis.com.

36. "The Secret Downing Street Memo," *The Sunday Times* (London), May 1, 2005, www.timesonline.co.uk/article/0,,2087-1593607,00.html (emphasis added). For a wider range of British documents and commentary, see the independent website *The Downing Street Memo(s)*, www.downing streetmemo.com.

37. Peter W. Galbraith, "How to Get Out of Iraq," *New York Review of Books*, May 13, 2004; quoted in *A Matter of Principle: Humanitarian Arguments for War in Iraq*, ed. Thomas Cushman (Berkeley: University of California Press, 2005), 200.

38. Norman Gervas, "Pages from a Daily Journal of Argument," in *A Matter of Principle*, 201. The "if it was" qualification in this sentence seems to reveal a residual hesitation on behalf of Gervas, and some others who made this argument for war, as to whether the case was really strong enough.

39. Paul Savoy, "The Moral Case against the Iraq War," *Nation*, May 31, 2004, 18.

40. Savoy, "Moral Case," 20.

41. "Disarm Iraq without War: A Statement from Religious Leaders in the United States and United Kingdom," November 26, 2002, www.sojo.net/index.cfm?action=action.US-UK_statement.

42. One well-known, but hardly convincing, example is Stephen Hayes, *The Connection: How al Qaeda's Collaboration with Saddam Hussein Has Endangered America* (New York: HarperCollins, 2004).

43. The National Commission on Terrorist Attacks upon the United States, *The 9/11 Commission Report* (New York: W. W. Norton, 2004), 66. On a specific point that the Bush administration had alleged, the Commission found no evidence that a meeting occurred between lead 9/11-hijacker Mohammed Atta and an Iraqi intelligence official (Staff Statement No. 16, "Outline of the 9/11 Plot," June 16, 2004, 8, www.9-11commission.gov/staff_statements/ staff_statement_16.pdf).

44. Pew Research Center for People and the Press, "Post-Blix: Public Favors Force in Iraq but . . . U.S. Needs More International Backing," February 20, 2003, 3, http://people-press.org/reports/display.php3?ReportID=173.

45. Andrew Sullivan, "The War You've Got," *The Stranger* (Seattle, WA), July 7–13, 2005, www.thestranger.com/seattle/Content?oid=22095.

46. Sullivan, "The War You've Got."

47. Fareed Zakaria, *The Future of Freedom: Illiberal Democracy at Home and Abroad* (New York: W. W. Norton, 2003).

48. Fareed Zakaria, "Invade Iraq, but Bring Friends," *Newsweek*, August 5, 2002, www.fareedzakaria.com/articles/newsweek/080502.html.

49. Figures for Iraqi civilian deaths are taken from The Iraq Body Count Project, www.iraqbodycount.net. Founded in January 2003, the project involves about twenty independent researchers culling media reports; its data can be

viewed in many kinds of breakdowns. The website provides a minimum and maximum range only of reported deaths. Coalition, Iraqi police/military, and reconstruction figures come from the Iraq Coalition Casualty Count website, http://icasualties.org/oif/. This website is also run by a small group of independent researchers compiling media reports. The U.S. Department of Defense does not maintain a public listing of soldiers killed, but several websites compile a list and obituaries, including CNN, "Forces: U.S. and Coalition/Casualties," www.cnn.com/SPECIALS/2003/iraq/forces/casualties/index.html. The U.K. Ministry of Defence maintains an official list and obituaries of British soldiers killed, "Operations in Iraq: British Fatalities," www.mod.uk/DefenceInternet/FactSheets/OperationsInIraqBritishFatalities.htm. (These sources last accessed July 5, 2006.)

50. Les Roberts and others, "Mortality Before and After the 2003 Invasion of Iraq: Cluster Sample Survey," *Lancet* 364 (October 30, 2004): 1857–64. The authors say that this increased risk adds up to one hundred thousand or more excess deaths. If accurate, that figure, subtracting the deaths caused by military action, would suggest forty thousand or more deaths from war-related health effects.

51. Eric Schmitt, "Threats and Responses: Military Spending; Pentagon Contradicts General on Iraq Occupation Force's Size," *New York Times*, February 28, 2003, A1.

52. James Fallows, "Blind into Baghdad," *Atlantic Monthly*, January/February 2004, 52–74.

53. In support of this position, see the work of one of the journalists who first delved into the Abu Ghraib story: Seymour Hersh, *Chain of Command: The Road from 9/11 to Abu Ghraib* (New York: HarperCollins, 2004).

54. Bush cited as his rationales for action: the inherent injustice of the invasion, the regional instability caused by a puppet regime, the defense of Saudi Arabia, and the economic and political effects of Iraq's increased control of oil. George Bush, "In Defense of Saudi Arabia (Speech of August 8, 1990)," in *The Gulf War Reader*, ed. Micah L. Sifry and Christopher Cerf (New York: Times Books, 1991), 197–99.

55. Brian Stiltner, "The Justice of War in Iraq," *The Journal of Lutheran Ethics* 3, no. 3, March 21, 2003, www.elca.org/jle/article.asp?k=9.

56. See Blix, *Disarming Iraq*; and William Rivers Pitt and Scott Ritter, *War on Iraq: What Team Bush Doesn't Want You to Know* (New York: Context Books, 2002).

57. I owe a debt for the framing of the positive developments stated in this paragraph (particularly the significance of elections, that Sunnis are not a monolithic group, and that Shiites have not been not vengeful) to the editorial "A Constitution" in the *New Republic*, October 31, 2005, 7.

NOTES TO CONCLUSION

1. Dan Smith, *The Penguin Atlas of War and Peace*, rev. ed. (New York: Penguin, 2003), 38–40.

2. See, for example, General Assembly Working Group, *Report of the Open-Ended Working Group on the Question of Equitable Representation on and Increase in the Membership of the Security Council and Other Matters Related to the Security Council* (New York: United Nations, 2004), www.global policy.org/security/reform/2004/gawkgrrep2004.pdf. This and other reports from the *Working Group* dating back to 1994 are available at the Global Policy Forum website, www.globalpolicy.org/security/reform/reports.htm. For a balanced assessment of the past, present, and future of the United Nations, see Paul Kennedy, *The Parliament of Man: The Past, Present, and Future of the United Nations* (New York: Random House, 2006). Kennedy is a political scientist who cochaired an early-1990s UN commission to study proposals for UN reform.

3. U.S. Air Force munitions statistics are from Michael Moseley, *Operation Freedom—By the Numbers*, U.S. Central Command Air Forces, April 30, 2003, 11, www.globalsecurity.org/military/library/report/2003/uscentaf_oif_report_30apr2003.pdf. The report is discussed in Fred Kaplan, "Bombing by Numbers: The Iraqi Air War Wasn't as Modern as it Looked," *Slate*, May 29, 2003, www.slate.com/id/2083605. The estimate of civilian casualties in this period is compiled from the Iraq Body Count database, www.iraqbodycount.net.

4. Charles E. Curran, "Roman Catholic Teaching on Peace and War within a Broader Theological Context," *Journal of Religious Ethics* 12, no. 1 (Spring 1984): 73.

5. A helpful analysis of these two basic strands of Christian political theory is R. A. Markus, "Two Conceptions of Political Authority: Augustine's *DCD* XIX, 14–15 and Some Thirteenth-Century Interpretations," *Journal of Theological Studies* 16, no. 1 (1965): 68–100.

6. Whether the death penalty is a form of unnecessary political violence is a matter of debate among Christians, especially in the United States. Certainly many Christians accept war and capital punishment as potentially legitimate actions of the government. However, major Christian bodies, Church leaders, and theological ethicists have been joining a chorus of opposition to the death penalty. As for the coauthors, our respective interpretations of pacifism and just war lead us to affirm that the death penalty is inhumane and unnecessary, and therefore un-Christian. For representative pro and con analyses from the Christian tradition, see Glen H. Stassen, ed., *Capital Punishment: A Reader*, Pilgrim Library of Ethics (Cleveland: Pilgrim, 1998).

7. For an account of Christian agape love as active concern and equal regard for all persons, see Gene Outka, *Agape: An Ethical Analysis* (New Haven, CT: Yale University Press, 1972).

8. The debate over the "presumption against violence" appears to be resolving itself by distinguishing different meanings of presumption. Although this will not satisfy all the disputants in the debate, it seems to us that just war theory can affirm both an argumentative presumption against violence and a political presumption in favor of justice. We appreciate conversation with Jeffrey Stout for helping us think about this issue, as well as a paper by William Werpehowski, "A Tale of Two Presumptions: The Development of Roman Catholic Just War Theory," presented at the Catholic Theological Ethicists in the World Church conference, Padua, Italy, July 9, 2006. A somewhat different approach to arguing in favor of the presumption is John Hymers, "Regrounding the Just War's 'Presumption Against Violence' in Light of George Weigel," *Ethical Perspectives* 11, no. 2–3 (June–September 2004): 111–21.

9. Richard Dawkins, "Opiate of the Masses," *Prospect* 115 (October 2005), www.prospectmagazine.co.uk/article_details.php?id=7036.

10. Some Christian authors who have argued in the direction of preventive war are George Weigel, "Moral Clarity in a Time of War," *First Things*, no. 129 (January 2003): 20–27; Jean Bethke Elshtain, *Just War against Terror* (New York: Basic Books, 2003). These and similar authors remain imprecise about how flexible they are willing to be with the criteria for preventive war. For a careful discussion of the question, rooted in Augustine's writings, see J. Warren Smith, "Augustine and the Limits of Preemptive and Preventive War," *Journal of Religious Ethics*, 35 (2007): 141–70.

11. Glen H. Stassen, ed. *Just Peacemaking: Ten Practices for Abolishing War*, 2nd ed. (Cleveland: Pilgrim, 2004), iii–iv.

12. This translation of the verse is made by the National Conference of Catholic Bishops of the United States as the epigraph of a document issued on the tenth anniversary of their famous 1983 pastoral letter on war and peace. The anniversary document is *The Harvest of Justice Is Sown in Peace*, November 17, 1993, www.usccb.org/sdwp/harvest.htm.

Bibliography

Allcock, John B. *Explaining Yugoslavia*. 2nd ed. New York: Columbia University Press, 2004.

Alperovitz, Gar. *The Decision to Use the Atomic Bomb and the Architecture of an American Myth*. New York: Knopf, 1995.

Annan, Kofi A. *The Question of Intervention*. New York: United Nations, 1999.

Anscombe, G. E. M. "Mr. Truman's Degree." In *War in the Twentieth Century*, edited by Richard B. Miller, 237–46. Louisville, KY: Westminster/John Knox, 1992.

———. "War and Murder." In *War and Morality*, edited by Richard A. Wasserstrom, 42–53. Belmont, CA: Wadsworth, 1970.

Aquinas, Thomas. *The Commandments of God: Conferences on the Two Precepts of Charity and the Ten Commandments*. Translated by Laurence Shapcote. London: Burns, Oates and Washbourne, 1937.

———. *Summa Theologica*. 5 vols. Translated by Fathers of the English Dominican Province. Notre Dame, IN: Ave Maria Press, 1981.

Augustine. *The City of God against the Pagans*. Edited by R. W. Dyson. Cambridge: Cambridge University Press, 1998.

———. *The Political Writings of St. Augustine*. Edited by Henry Paolucci. Chicago: Regnery Gateway, 1962.

———. "Reply to Faustus the Manichaean." In *A Select Library of the Nicene and Post-Nicene Fathers of the Christian Church*. Vol. 4, *St. Augustine: Writings against the Manichaeans and against the Donatists*, edited by Philip Schaff, 171–427. Grand Rapids, MI: Eerdmans, 1979. www.ccel.org/ccel/schaff/npnf104.html.

Baer, Helmut David, and Joseph E. Capizzi. "Just War Theories Reconsidered: Problems with Prima Facie Duties and the Need for a Political Ethic." *Journal of Religious Ethics* 33, no. 1 (Spring 2005): 119–37.

———. "Just War Theory and the Problem of International Politics: On the Central Role of Just Intention." *Journal of the Society of Christian Ethics* 26, no. 1 (Spring/Summer 2006): 163–75.

Bainton, Roland H. *Christian Attitudes toward War and Peace: A Historical Survey and Critical Re-evaluation*. Nashville, TN: Abingdon, 1960.

Bandow, Doug. "The Myth of Iraq's Oil Stranglehold." In *The Gulf War Reader*, edited by Micah L. Sifry and Christopher Cerf, 216–18. New York: Times Books, 1991.

Barth, Karl. *Church Dogmatics*. Vol. II/2. Edited by G. W. Bromiley and T. F. Torrance. Edinburgh: T and T Clark, 1957.

Barton, John. *Understanding Old Testament Ethics: Approaches and Explorations*. Louisville, KY: Westminster/John Knox, 2003.

Bergen, Peter L. *Holy War, Inc.: Inside the Secret World of Osama bin Laden*. New York: Free Press, 2001.

Blix, Hans. *Disarming Iraq*. New York: Pantheon Books, 2004.

Bonhoeffer, Dietrich. *Ethics*. Translated by Neville Horton Smith. Edited by Eberhard Bethge. London: Collins, 1964.

Bradbury, Jim. *The Medieval Archer*. Woodbridge: Boydell Press, 1985.

Brunner, Emil. *The Divine Imperative: A Study in Christian Ethics*. Translated by Olive Wyon. London: Lutterworth, 1937.

Bryzinski, Zbigniew. "The Failed Double-Cross." In *Kosovo: Contending Voices*, edited by William Joseph Buckley, 328–32. Grand Rapids, MI: Eerdmans, 2000.

Buckley, William Joseph, ed. *Kosovo: Contending Voices on Balkan Interventions*. Grand Rapids, MI: Eerdmans, 2000.

Bush, George. "In Defense of Saudi Arabia (Speech of August 8, 1990)." In *The Gulf War Reader*, edited by Micah L. Sifry and Christopher Cerf, 197–99. New York: Times Books, 1991.

Butler, Alban. *Butler's Lives of the Saints*. Concise ed. Edited by Michael Walsh. San Francisco: Harper and Row, 1985.

Cadoux, Cecil John. *Early Christian Attitude to War*. New York: Seabury, 1982.

Cady, Duane L. *From Warism to Pacifism: A Moral Continuum*. Philadelphia: Temple University Press, 1989.

Cahill, Lisa S. *Love Your Enemies: Discipleship, Pacifism, and Just War Theory*. Minneapolis: Fortress Press, 1994.

Cahill, Thomas. *Desire of the Everlasting Hills: The World Before and After Jesus*. New York: Nan A. Talase/ Doubleday, 1999.

Carlsson, Ingvar, Han Sung-Joo, and Rufus M. Kupolati. *Report of the Independent Inquiry into the Actions of the United Nations During the 1994 Genocide in Rwanda*. New York: United Nations, 1999. www.un.org/Docs/journal/asp/ws.asp?m=S/1999/1257.

Carr, Caleb. *The Lessons of Terror*. New York: Random House, 2002.

———. "Terrorism as Warfare: The Lessons of Military History." *World Policy Journal* 13, no. 4 (Winter 1996/97): 1–12.

Childress, James. "Just War Criteria." In *War or Peace? The Search for New Answers*, edited by Thomas A. Shannon, 40–58. Maryknoll, NY: Orbis, 1980.

———. "Just-War Theories: The Bases, Interrelations, Priorities, and Functions of Their Criteria." *Theological Studies* 39 (1978): 427–45.

Chivers, C. J. "Ill-Secured Soviet Arms Depots Tempting Rebels and Terrorists." *New York Times*, July 16, 2005, A1.

Christopher, Paul. *The Ethics of War and Peace*. 2nd ed. Upper Saddle River, NJ: Prentice-Hall, 1999.

Cirincione, Joseph, Jon B. Wolfsthal, and Miriam Rajkumar. *Deadly Arsenals: Nuclear, Biological and Chemical Threats*. Rev. ed. New York: Carnegie Endowment for International Peace, 2005.

Clausewitz, Carl. *On War*. Translated by Michael Howard and Peter Paret. Princeton, NJ: Princeton University Press, 1976.

Clement of Alexandria. "The Instructor." In *The Ante-Nicene Fathers*, edited by A. Cleveland Coxe, James Donaldson, and Alexander Roberts. Vol. 2, 209–96. Edinburgh: T and T Clark, 1997.

———. "Who Is the Rich Man That Shall Be Saved?" In *The Ante-Nicene Fathers*, edited by A. Cleveland Coxe, James Donaldson, and Alexander Roberts. Vol. 2, 591–604. Edinburgh: T and T Clark, 1997.

Clinton, Bill. "Remarks by the President to the KFOR Troops," June 22, 1999. In *Humanitarian Intervention: Crafting a Workable Doctrine. Three Options Presented as Memoranda to the President* by Alton Frye, Appendix A. Washington, DC: Council on Foreign Relations, 2000. www.cfr.org/pdf/Human_Intervent_Book.pdf.

Combs, Cynthia C. *Terrorism in the Twenty-First Century*. 3rd ed. Upper Saddle River, NJ: Prentice-Hall, 2002.

Cordesman, Anthony H. *Iraq and the War of Sanctions: Conventional Threats and Weapons of Mass Destruction*. Westport, CT: Praeger, 1999.

Countryman, L. William. *Dirt, Greed and Sex: Sexual Ethics in the New Testament and Their Implications for Today*. London: SCM, 2001.

Coxe, A. Cleveland, James Donaldson, and Alexander Roberts, eds. *The Ante-Nicene Fathers: Translations of the Writings of the Fathers Down to A.D. 325*, 10 vols. Edinburgh: T and T Clark, 1997.

Curran, Charles E. "Roman Catholic Teaching on Peace and War within a Broader Theological Context." *Journal of Religious Ethics* 12, no. 1 (Spring 1984): 61–81.

Cushman, Thomas, ed. *A Matter of Principle: Humanitarian Arguments for War in Iraq*. Berkeley: University of California Press, 2005.

Davis, Morton D. *Game Theory: A Nontechnical Introduction*. Rev. ed. London: Dover Publications, 1997.

Dawkins, Richard. "Opiate of the Masses." *Prospect* 115 (October 2005), www.prospectmagazine.co.uk/article_details.php?id=7036.

De Bruges, Galbert. *The Murder of Charles the Good, Count of Flanders*. Rev. ed. Translated by James Bruce Ross. New York: Harper and Row, 1967.

"Disarm Iraq without War: A Statement from Religious Leaders in the United States and United Kingdom." November 26, 2002. www.sojo.net/index.cfm?action=action.US-UK_statement.

Douglas, Mary. *Purity and Danger: An Analysis of Concepts of Pollution and Taboo.* London: Routledge and Kegan Paul, 1966.

Dubow, Saul. *The African National Congress.* Gloucestershire, U.K.: Sutton Publishing, 2000.

Durham, John I. *Exodus.* Word Bible Commentary. no. 3. Dallas: Word Books, 1987.

Easterbrook, Gregg. "The End of War?" *New Republic,* May 30, 2005, 18–21.

———. "Term Limits." *New Republic,* October 7, 2002, 22–25.

Elshtain, Jean Bethke. *Just War against Terror.* New York: Basic Books, 2003.

———, ed. *Just War Theory.* Readings in Social and Political Theory. Oxford: Blackwell, 1992.

———. "Reflections on War and Political Discourse." In *Just War Theory,* edited by Jean Bethke Elshtain, 260–79. Oxford: Blackwell, 1992.

Erlanger, Steven. "Crisis in the Balkans: Belgrade; Survivors of NATO Attack on Serb TV Headquarters: Luck, Pluck and Resolve." *New York Times,* April 24, 1999, A6.

Etzioni, Amitai, and Steven Hellend. "The Case for Domestic Disarmament." The Communitarian Network, 1992. www.gwu.edu/~ccps/pop_disarm.html.

Fallows, James. "Blind into Baghdad." *Atlantic Monthly,* January/February 2004, 52–74.

Farouk-Sluglett, Marion, and Peter Sluglett. *Iraq Since 1958: From Revolution to Dictatorship.* London: IB Tauris, 1990.

Ford, John. "The Morality of Obliteration Bombing." In *War in the Twentieth Century,* edited by Richard B. Miller, 138–80. Louisville, KY: Westminster/John Knox, 1992.

Freedman, Lawrence, and Efraim Karsh. *The Gulf Conflict, 1990–1991.* London: Faber and Faber, 1993.

Friedman, Thomas L. "Giving the Hatemongers No Place to Hide." *New York Times,* July 22, 2005, A19.

Friedmann, Robert. *Hutterite Studies.* Goshen, IN: Mennonite Historical Society, 1961.

Frost, Brian. *Struggling to Forgive: Nelson Mandela and South Africa's Search for Reconciliation.* London: HarperCollins, 1998.

Gaffney Frank J. Jr., and James A. Baker. "Pro/Con: Should the Gulf War Coalition Have Pursued the War into Iraq in 1991?" *The Retired Officer Magazine* 57, no. 2 (February 2001): 32–38.

Garfield, Richard. "Morbidity and Mortality in Iraq, 1990–1998." Occasional Paper, Fourth Freedom Forum, Indiana. July 1999. www.casi.org.uk/info/garfield/dr-garfield.html.

General Assembly Working Group. *Report of the Open-Ended Working Group on the Question of Equitable Representation on and Increase in the Membership of the Security Council and Other Matters Related to the Security Council.* New York: United Nations, 2004. www.globalpolicy.org/security/reform/2004/gawkgrrep2004.pdf.

Geneva Graduate Institute of International Studies. *Small Arms Survey 2005.* Oxford: Oxford University Press, 2005.

Gervas, Norman. "Pages from a Daily Journal of Argument." In *A Matter of Principle,* edited by Thomas Cushman, 197–206. Berkeley: University of California Press, 2005.

Geyer, Georgie Anne. "Seymour Hersch's Gulf War Misconceptions," *Chicago Tribune,* May 19, 2000, A23.

Glasser, Susan B. "U.S. Figures Show Sharp Global Rise in Terrorism." *Washington Post,* April 27, 2005, A1. www.washingtonpost.com/wp-dyn/content/article/2005/04/26/AR2005042601623.html.

Glendon, Mary Ann. *A World Made New: Eleanor Roosevelt and the Universal Declaration of Human Rights.* New York: Random House, 2001.

Glenny, Misha. "A Balkan Success Story: Reflections on Macedonia." *New Statesman,* September 26, 2005. www.lexis-nexis.com.

———. *The Balkans: Nationalism, War, and the Great Powers, 1804–1999.* New York: Penguin, 2001.

Graham, Mark. *Josef Fuchs on Natural Law.* Washington, DC: Georgetown University Press, 2002.

Graham-Brown, Sarah. *Sanctioning Saddam: The Politics of Intervention in Iraq.* London: IB Tauris, 1999.

Granitsas, Alkman. "Paradigm Slip." *New Republic,* April 11, 2005, 14–15.

Griffiths, Paul J., and George Weigel. "Who Wants War? An Exchange." *First Things,* no. 152 (April 2005): 10–11.

Grotius, Hugo. *De jure belli ac pacis libri tres.* 2 vols. Translated by Frances W. Kelsey, et al. Classics of International Law, no. 3. Washington, DC: Carnegie Institution of Washington, 1913–1925.

Harakas, Stanley S. *Wholeness of Faith and Life: Orthodox Christian Ethics.* Brookline, MA: Holy Cross Orthodox Press, 1999.

Harris, Sheldon H. *Factories of Death: Japanese Biological Warfare, 1932–1945, and the American Cover-Up.* New York: Routledge, 2002.

Hashmi, Sohail H., ed., *Islamic Political Ethics: Civil Society, Pluralism, and Conflict.* Princeton, NJ: Princeton University Press, 2002.

Havel, Vaclav. "Address to the Senate and House of Commons of the Parliament of Canada." In *Kosovo: Contending Voices*, edited by William Joseph Buckley, 240–45. Grand Rapids, MI: Eerdmans, 2000.

Hayes, Stephen. *The Connection: How al Qaeda's Collaboration with Saddam Hussein Has Endangered America*. New York: HarperCollins, 2004.

Hays, Richard. *The Moral Vision of the New Testament*. San Francisco: HarperSanFrancisco, 1996; Edinburgh: T and T Clark, 1997.

Hehir, J. Bryan. "Kosovo: A War of Values and the Values of War." In *Kosovo: Contending Voices*, edited by William Joseph Buckley, 399–405. Grand Rapids, MI: Eerdmans, 2000.

Helgeland, John, Robert J. Daly, and J. Patout Burns. *Christians and the Military: The Early Experience*. London: SCM, 1987.

Hersh, Seymour. *Chain of Command: The Road from 9/11 to Abu Ghraib*. New York: HarperCollins, 2004.

———. "Overwhelming Force: What Happened in the Final Days of the Gulf War?" *New Yorker*, May 22, 2000, 49–82.

Hitchens, Christopher. *A Long Short War: The Postponed Liberation of Iraq*. New York: Plume, 2003.

Hoffman, Bruce. *Inside Terrorism*. New York: Columbia University Press, 1998; rev. ed., 2006.

Holland, Heidi. *The Struggle: A History of the African National Congress*. New York: G. Braziller, 1990.

Howard, Michael. "*Temperamenta Belli*: Can War Be Controlled?" In *Just War Theory*, edited by Jean Bethke Elshtain, 23–35. Oxford: Blackwell, 1992.

Hymers, John. "Regrounding the Just War's 'Presumption against Violence' in Light of George Weigel." *Ethical Perspectives* 11, no. 2–3 (June–September 2004): 111–21.

Independent Inquiry Committee. "Report on the Management of the Oil-for-Food Programme." September 7, 2005. www.iicoffp.org/documents.htm.

Insole, Christopher J. *The Politics of Human Frailty: A Theological Defence of Political Liberalism*. London: SCM, 2004.

International Campaign to Ban Landmines. *Landmine Monitor Report 2004*. Geneva: International Campaign to Ban Landmines, 2004.

International Commission on Intervention and State Sovereignty. *The Responsibility to Protect*. Ottawa: International Development Research Centre, 2001. www.iciss.ca/report-en.asp.

John XXIII. "Pacem in Terris: Peace on Earth." In *Catholic Social Thought: The Documentary Heritage*, edited by David J. O'Brien and Thomas A. Shannon, 129–62. Maryknoll, NY: Orbis, 1992.

Johnson, James Turner. *Ideology, Reason, and the Limitation of War: Religious and Secular Concepts 1200–1740*. Princeton, NJ: Princeton University Press, 1975.

———. *Just War Tradition and the Restraint of War: A Moral and Historical Inquiry*. Princeton, NJ: Princeton University Press, 1981.

Judah, Tim. "A Brief History of Serbia." In *Kosovo: Contending Voices*, edited by William Joseph Buckley, 89–96. Grand Rapids, MI: Eerdmans, 2000.

———. *Kosovo: War and Revenge*. 2nd ed. New Haven, CT: Yale University Press, 2002.

Juergensmeyer, Mark. *Terror in the Mind of God*. 3rd ed. Berkeley: University of California Press, 2003.

Kahn, Jeremy. "Final Status Quo." *New Republic*, June 26, 2006, 11–13.

Kaplan, Fred. "Bombing by Numbers: The Iraqi Air War Wasn't as Modern as it Looked." *Slate*, May 29, 2003. www.slate.com/id/2083605.

Kaplan, Robert D. *Balkan Ghosts: A Journey through History*. Reprint ed. New York: Picador, 2005.

Kelly, Jack. "Estimates of Deaths in the First War Still in Dispute." *Pittsburgh Post-Gazette*, February 16, 2003. www.post-gazette.com/nation/20030216 casualty0216p5.asp.

Kennedy, Paul. *The Parliament of Man: The Past, Present, and Future of the United Nations*. New York: Random House, 2006.

Kreider, Alan. "Military Service in the Church Orders." *Journal of Religious Ethics* 31, no. 3 (2003): 415–42.

Krisch, Nico. "Legality, Morality, and the Dilemma of Humanitarian Intervention after Kosovo." *European Journal of International Law* 13, no 1 (2002): 323–63. www.ejil.org/journal/Vol13/No1/br1.html.

Levins, John. *Days of Fear: The Inside Story of the Iraqi Invasion and Occupation of Kuwait*. Dubai: Motivate Publishing, 1997.

Long, Edward LeRoy, Jr. *Facing Terrorism: Responding as Christians*. Louisville, KY: Westminster/John Knox, 2004.

Maass, Peter. *Love Thy Neighbor: A Story of War*. Reprint ed. New York: Vintage, 1997.

Maritain, Jacques. *Man and the State*. Chicago: University of Chicago Press, 1951.

Markus, R. A. "Two Conceptions of Political Authority: Augustine's *DCD* XIX, 14–15 and Some Thirteenth-Century Interpretations." *Journal of Theological Studies* 16, no. 1 (1965): 68–100.

Martyr, Justin. "First Apology." In *The Ante-Nicene Fathers*, edited by A. Cleveland Coxe, James Donaldson, and Alexander Roberts. Vol. 1, 163–87. Edinburgh: T and T Clark, 1997.

Mazarr, Michael J. "Strike Out." *New Republic*, August 15, 2005, 15–17.

McCaffrey, Barry R. "The *New Yorker*'s Revisionist History." *Wall Street Journal*, May 22, 2000, A38.

McIntyre, Alasdair. *After Virtue*. 2nd ed. Notre Dame, IN: University of Notre Dame Press, 1984.

———. *Three Rival Versions of Moral Enquiry*. Notre Dame, IN: University of Notre Dame Press, 1991.

———. *Whose Justice? Which Rationality?* Notre Dame, IN: University of Notre Dame Press, 1989.

McNamara, Robert S., and Brian VanDeMark. *In Retrospect: The Tragedy and Lessons of Vietnam*. Reprint ed. New York: Vintage, 1996.

Meier, John P. *A Marginal Jew: Rethinking the Historical Jesus*. 3 vols. New York: Doubleday, 1991, 1994, and 2001.

Miller, Richard B., ed. *War in the Twentieth Century: Sources in Theological Ethics*. Louisville, KY: Westminster/John Knox, 1992.

Miscamble, Wilson D. *From Roosevelt to Truman: Potsdam, Hiroshima, and the Cold War*. Cambridge: Cambridge University Press, 2006.

Moseley, Michael. *Operation Freedom—By the Numbers*. U.S. Central Command Air Forces, April 30, 2003. www.globalsecurity.org/military/library/report/2003/uscentaf_oif_re port_30apr2003.pdf.

Murray, John Courtney. "Remarks on the Moral Problem of War." In *War in the Twentieth Century*, edited by Richard B. Miller, 247–71. Louisville, KY: Westminster/John Knox, 1992.

Musto, Ronald G. *The Catholic Peace Tradition*. Maryknoll, NY: Orbis, 1986.

Nardin, Terry, ed. *The Ethics of War and Peace: Religious and Secular Perspectives*. Princeton, NJ: Princeton University Press, 1996.

National Commission on Terrorist Attacks upon the United States. *The 9/11 Commission Report*. New York: W.W. Norton, 2004.

———. "Outline of the 9/11 Plot." Staff Statement No. 16. June 16, 2004. www.9-11commission.gov/staff_statements/staff_statement_16.pdf.

National Conference of Catholic Bishops. "The Challenge of Peace: God's Promise and Our Response." In *Catholic Social Thought: The Documentary Heritage*, edited by David J. O'Brien and Thomas A. Shannon, 492–571. Maryknoll, NY: Orbis, 1992.

———. *The Harvest of Justice Is Sown in Peace*. November 17, 1993. www.usccb.org/sdwp/harvest.htm.

———. *Sowing Weapons of War: A Pastoral Reflection on the Arms Trade and Landmines*. June 16, 1995. www.usccb.org/sdwp/international/arms trade.htm.

New Republic. "A Constitution." October 31, 2005, 7.

Niebuhr, Reinhold. "The Atomic Bomb." In *Love and Justice: Selections from the Shorter Writings of Reinhold Niebuhr*, edited by D. B. Robertson, 232–35. Louisville, KY: Westminster/John Knox, 1992.

———. "The Bombing of Germany." In *Love and Justice: Selections from the Shorter Writings of Reinhold Niebuhr*, edited by D. B. Robertson, 222–23. Louisville, KY: Westminster/John Knox, 1992.

———. *Christian Realism and Political Problems*. New York: Scribner's, 1952.

———. Letter to James B. Conant, March 12, 1946. In "Footnote on Hiroshima and Atomic Morality: Conant, Niebuhr, and an 'Emotional' Clergyman, 1945–46" by James G. Hershberg. *SHAFR Newsletter*, December 2002. www.shafr.org/newsletter/2002/dec/hiroshima.htm.

Nolan, Albert. *Jesus before Christianity*. Rev. ed. Maryknoll, NY: Orbis, 2001.

O'Brien, David J., and Thomas A. Shannon, eds. *Catholic Social Thought: The Documentary Heritage*. Maryknoll, NY: Orbis, 1992.

O'Donovan, Oliver. *The Just War Revisited*. Cambridge: Cambridge University Press, 2003.

Office of the High Commissioner for Human Rights. *Basic Human Rights Instruments*. 3rd ed. Geneva: Office of the High Commissioner for Human Rights, 1998.

Orend, Brian. "War." *The Stanford Encyclopedia of Philosophy*. Winter 2005 ed. Edited by Edward N. Zalta. http://plato.stanford.edu/archives/sum2002/entries/war/.

Origen. "Against Celsus." In *The Ante-Nicene Fathers*, edited by A. Cleveland Coxe, James Donaldson, and Alexander Roberts. Vol. 4, 395–669. Edinburgh: T and T Clark, 1997.

Outka, Gene. *Agape: An Ethical Analysis*. New Haven, CT: Yale University Press, 1972.

Owen, Wilfred. "Dulce et Decorum Est." In *The Collected Poems of Wilfred Owen*, 55–56. London: Chatto and Windus, 1963.

Pew Forum on Religion and Public Life. "Just War Tradition and the New War on Terrorism." October 5, 2001. http://pewforum.org/publications/reports/PFJustWar.pdf.

Pew Research Center for People and the Press. "Post-Blix: Public Favors Force in Iraq but . . . U.S. Needs More International Backing." Washington, DC: Pew Center, February 20, 2003.

Phillips, Robert L., and Duane L. Cady. *Humanitarian Intervention: Just War vs. Pacifism*. Lanham, MD: Rowman and Littlefield, 1996.

Pitt, William Rivers, and Scott Ritter. *War on Iraq: What Team Bush Doesn't Want You to Know*. New York: Context Books, 2002.

Porter, Jean. *Natural and Divine Law*. Grand Rapids, MI: Eerdmans, 2000.

Power, Samantha. *"A Problem from Hell": America and the Age of Genocide*. New York: Perennial, 2002.

Rabkin, Jeremy A. *Law without Nations? Why Constitutional Government Requires Sovereign States*. Princeton, NJ: Princeton University Press, 2005.

Ramsey, Paul. "Is Vietnam a Just War?" In *War in the Twentieth Century*, edited by Richard B. Miller, 185–97. Louisville, KY: Westminster/ John Knox, 1992.

———. "A Political Ethics Context for Strategic Thinking." In *War in the Twentieth Century*, edited by Richard B. Miller, 290–310. Louisville, KY: Westminster/John Knox, 1992.

Reagan, Ronald. "Proclamation 4809, Afghanistan Day," March 10, 1982. The Ronald Reagan Presidential Library archive of presidential speeches. www.reagan.utexas.edu/archives/speeches/1982/31082c.htm.

Regan, Richard J. *Just War: Principles and Cases*. Washington, DC: Catholic University of America Press, 1996.

Roberts, Adam, and Richard Guelff, eds. *Documents on the Laws of War*. 3rd ed. Oxford: Oxford University Press, 2000.

Roberts, Les, Riyadh Lafta, Richard Garfield, Jamal Khudhairi, and Gilbert Burnham. "Mortality Before and After the 2003 Invasion of Iraq: Cluster Sample Survey." *Lancet* 364 (October 30, 2004): 1857–64.

Robinson, Julian Perry. "Chemical Weapons for NATO? A Framework for Considering Policy Options." In *Chemical Weapons and Chemical Arms Control*. Papers and Discussion from a Conference at the American Academy of Arts and Sciences, Boston, MA, January 21–22, 1977. Edited by Matthew Meselson. New York: Carnegie Endowment for International Peace, 1978.

Savoy, Paul. "The Moral Case against the Iraq War." *Nation*, May 31, 2004, 16–20.

Schmitt, Eric. "Threats and Responses: Military Spending; Pentagon Contradicts General on Iraq Occupation Force's Size." *New York Times*, February 28, 2003, A1.

Schweitzer, Albert. *The Mystery of the Kingdom of God: The Secret of Jesus' Messiahship and Passion*. Translated by Walter Lowrie. New York: Dodd, Mead, and Co., 1914.

Second Vatican Council. "Gaudium et Spes: Pastoral Constitution on the Church in the Modern World." In *Catholic Social Thought: The Documentary Heritage*, edited by David J. O'Brien and Thomas A. Shannon, 164–237. Maryknoll, NY: Orbis, 1992.

Sifry, Micah L., and Christopher Cerf, eds. *The Gulf War Reader*. New York: Times Books, 1991.

Silber, Laura, and Allan Little. *Yugoslavia: Death of a Nation*. New York: Penguin, 1997.

Simmons, Ernest J. *Leo Tolstoy.* London: John Lehmann, 1949.

Simons, Geoff. *Iraq: From Sumer to Saddam.* 2nd ed. Basingstoke, U.K.: Macmillan, 1996.

Smith, Dan. *The Penguin Atlas of War and Peace.* Rev. ed. New York: Penguin, 2003.

Smith, Huston. *The World's Religions: Our Great Wisdom Traditions.* Rev. ed. San Francisco: HarperSanFrancisco, 1991.

Smith, J. Warren. "Augustine and the Limits of Preemptive War." *Journal of Religious Ethics,* 35 (2007): 141–70.

Stassen, Glen H., ed. *Capital Punishment: A Reader.* Pilgrim Library of Ethics. Cleveland: Pilgrim, 1998.

———, ed. *Just Peacemaking: Ten Practices for Abolishing War.* 2nd ed. Cleveland: Pilgrim Press, 2004.

Steffen, Lloyd. *The Demonic Turn: The Power of Religion to Inspire or Restrain Violence.* Cleveland: Pilgrim, 2003.

Stiltner, Brian. "The Justice of War in Iraq." *The Journal of Lutheran Ethics* 3, no. 3, March 21, 2003. www.elca.org/jle/articles.asp?K-9.

Stockholm International Peace Research Institute. "Financial Value of the Arms Trade." www.sipri.org/contents/armstrad/at_gov_ind_data.html.

———. "International Arms Embargoes." www.sipri.org/contents/armstrad/embargoes.html.

———. *SIPRI Yearbook 2004.* Oxford: Oxford University Press, 2004.

———. *SIPRI Yearbook 2006.* Oxford: Oxford University Press, 2006.

Sullivan, Andrew. "The War You've Got." *The Stranger* (Seattle, WA), July 7–13, 2005. www.thestranger.com/seattle/Content?oid=22095.

Tanenhaus, Sam. "Bush's Brain Trust." *Vanity Fair,* July 2003, 114–19.

Tanner, Norman P., ed. *Decrees of the Ecumenical Councils.* Vol. 1, *Nicaea I to Lateran V.* London: Sheed & Ward, 1990.

Teichman, Jenny. *Pacifism and the Just War: A Study in Applied Philosophy.* Oxford: Basil Blackwell, 1986.

Tertullian. "Apology." In *The Ante-Nicene Fathers,* edited by A. Cleveland Coxe, James Donaldson, and Alexander Roberts. Vol. 3, 17–55. Edinburgh: T and T Clark, 1997.

———. "On Idolatry." In *The Ante-Nicene Fathers,* edited by A. Cleveland Coxe, James Donaldson, and Alexander Roberts. Vol. 3, 61–76. Edinburgh: T and T Clark, 1997.

———. "On the Crown." In *The Ante-Nicene Fathers,* edited by A. Cleveland Coxe, James Donaldson, and Alexander Roberts. Vol. 3, 93–103. Edinburgh: T and T Clark, 1997.

Thompson, Mark, and Bruce Crumley. "Are These Towers Safe?" *Time,* June 20, 2005, 34–42.

Tolstoy, Leo N. *My Religion*. Translated by Huntingdon Smith. London: Walter Scott, 1889.

"Treaty on the Non-Proliferation of Nuclear Weapons." July 1, 1968. http://disarmament2.un.org/wmd/npt/npttext.html.

Tripp, Charles. *A History of Iraq*. Cambridge: Cambridge University Press, 2000.

United Kingdom Government. "Iraq's Weapons of Mass Destruction: The Assessment of the British Government." September 24, 2002. www.number-10.gov.uk/output/Page271.asp.

United Methodist Council of Bishops (U.S.A.). "In Defense of Creation: The Nuclear Crisis and a Just Peace." In *War in the Twentieth Century*, edited by Richard B. Miller, 417–38. Louisville, KY: Westminster/John Knox, 1992.

United Nations. *Charter of the United Nations*. June 26, 1945. www.un.org/aboutun/charter/index.html.

———. "Security Council Resolutions—1990." www.un.org/Docs/scres/1990/scres90.htm.

———. "Security Council Resolutions—2002." www.un.org/Docs/scres/2002/sc2002.htm.

United Nations Monitoring, Verification, and Inspection Commission. "Selected Security Council Briefings." www.un.org/Depts/unmovic/new/pages/security_council_briefings.asp.

United States Congress. USA PATRIOT Act of 2001. Library of Congress. http://thomas.loc.gov/bss/d107/d107laws.html, s.v. "Public Law 107–56."

———. USA PATRIOT Improvement and Reauthorization Act of 2001. Library of Congress. http://thomas.loc.gov/bss/d109/d109laws.html, s.v. "Public Law 109–177."

United States Department of State. "Did the U.S. 'Create' Osama bin Laden?" January 14, 2005. http://usinfo.state.gov/media/Archive/2005/Jan/24-318760.html.

Von Glahn, Gerhard. *Law among Nations: An Introduction to Public International Law*. 7th ed. New York: Longman, 1995.

Von Rad, Gerhard. *Holy War in Ancient Israel*. Grand Rapids, MI: Eerdmans, 1991. Reprint ed., Eugene, OR: Wipf and Stock, 2000.

Walker, Samuel. "Recent Literature on Truman's Atomic Bomb Decision: A Search for Middle Ground." *Diplomatic History* 29 (April 2005): 311–34.

Walzer, Michael. *Arguing about War*. New Haven, CT: Yale University Press, 2004.

———. *Just and Unjust Wars: A Moral Argument with Historical Illustrations*. 3rd ed. New York: Basic Books, 2000.

———. "Kosovo." In *Kosovo: Contending Voices*, edited by William Joseph Buckley, 333–35. Grand Rapids, MI: Eerdmans, 2000.

Weigel, George. "Moral Clarity in a Time of War." *First Things*, no. 129 (January 2003): 20–27.

———. "World Order: What Catholics Forgot." *First Things*, no. 143 (May 2004): 31–38.

Weiss, Johannes. *Jesus' Proclamation of the Kingdom of God*. Translated by R. H. Hiers and F. L. Holland. Philadelphia: Fortress, 1971.

Werpehowski, William. "A Tale of Two Presumptions: The Development of Roman Catholic Just War Theory." Paper presented at the Catholic Theological Ethicists in the World Church Conference, Padua, Italy, July 9, 2006.

White House. "U.S. Secretary of State Colin Powell Addresses the U.N. Security Council." February 5, 2003. www.whitehouse.gov/news/releases/2003/02/20030205-1.html.

Wink, Walter. *Violence and Nonviolence in South Africa: Jesus' Third Way*. Philadelphia: New Society Publishers, 1987.

Winright, Tobias. "From Police Officers to Peace Officers." In *Wisdom of the Cross*, edited by Stanley Hauerwas, Harry Heubner, and Chris Heubner, 84–114. Grand Rapids: Eerdmans, 1999.

———. "The Perpetrator as Person: Theological Reflections on the Just War Tradition and the Use of Force by Police." *Criminal Justice Ethics* 14 (1995): 37–56.

———. "Two Rival Versions of Just War Theory and the Presumption against Harm in Policing." *Annual of the Society of Christian Ethics* 18 (1998): 221–39.

Yetiv, Steven A. *The Persian Gulf Crisis*. Westport, CT: Greenwood Press, 1997.

Yoder, John Howard. *Nevertheless: A Meditation on the Varieties and Shortcomings of Religious Pacifism*. Scottsdale, PA: Herald Press, 1992.

———. *The Politics of Jesus*. Rev. ed. Grand Rapids, MI: Eerdmans, 1994.

———. *What Would You Do?* Rev. ed. Scottsdale, PA: Herald Press, 1992.

———. *When War Is Unjust: Being Honest in Just War Thinking*, 2nd ed. Maryknoll, NY: Orbis, 1996.

Zakaria, Fareed. *The Future of Freedom: Illiberal Democracy at Home and Abroad*. New York: W. W. Norton, 2003.

———. "Invade Iraq, but Bring Friends," *Newsweek*, August 5, 2002. www.fareedzakaria.com/articles/newsweek/080502.html

Index